A FISHABLE FEAST

A FISHABLE FEAST

FLY FISHING & EATING YOUR WAY AROUND THE WORLD

KIRK DEETER & MATTHEW SUPINSKI

FOREWORD BY TOM ROSENBAUER

Contents

Foreword

Tom Rosenbauer

People who just fish with me probably think I don't like to eat. During a twelve-hour day of fishing, I might eat a few handfuls of cashews and pistachios, a piece of chocolate, and drink nothing but lukewarm water, preferably lapping it from the river like a Labrador if I think it's safe. Nothing annoys me more than a guide who prepares a shore lunch, which can take an hour out of a day, and it seems always to be at the same time the PMDs are hatching (although one exception would be John Herzer's lunch I had on the Bitterroot once when he set up a table, grilled elk sausage, and served it along with a tray of smoked salmon, nuts, various cheeses, and fresh fruit).

But after fishing, the same people might wonder why I don't weigh north of three hundred pounds. In Magic Waters in Chile often the best part of the day is dinner, where I'll have several pisco sours, an intemperate dose of Carmenere wine, will hover over the sushi appetizers, eat everything on my plate, and then maybe eat two desserts of dulce de leche if I can scrounge a second one from the person next to me who is either on a no-carb diet or does not have a sweet tooth. And of course, yeah I almost forgot . . . another time I don't mind eating during a fishing day is when the cheerful gaucho Alfredo grills a lamb over an open fire on the banks of the river. But I willingly rise to lamb whenever someone casts it my way.

I do confess to foraging while I'm fishing, snacking on wild blueberries or watercress on the run. And once, on Grand Bahama, I found myself walking (carefully) over a huge bed of urchins. I pulled one from the rocks and asked the guide if he had a knife. He was not sure what I was up to, but when I smashed open the urchin and began slurping the uni right out of the shell, he forcefully slapped my hand away from my mouth, telling me "That stuff is poison!" Maybe I picked the wrong species of urchin but it tasted fine and my intestinal tract was later 100 percent. Maybe he just never saw anyone eating uni.

Two of my favorite people have written a book that combines two of my favorite passions: eating and fly fishing. I've known these two characters for many decades and have had the pleasure of eating and fishing with both. Kirk and I have fished together on the Delaware, in Colorado, in the Bahamas, and in Chile over the years and have enjoyed some fine meals at lodges as well as my miserly lunches. On a trip to the Catskills, while showing me a secret river he'd fallen for, Matt once brought me a Polish Hunter's Sandwich that he made that morning: Polish garlic sausage kielbasa lightly smoked, with a Bigos-style topping that included sweet sauerkraut, caramelized wild mushrooms and onions, plus applewood smoked bacon, homemade dill pickles, and horseradish Dijon mustard. Al on a fresh poppyseed kaiser roll. I can't cook like this formally trained chef, but I do tease him with texted photos of the chanterelles I have foraged and then Matt will get back to me with exactly how to cook them and what to serve them with.

Kirk and Matt are pros in everything they do and this book is no exception. They've fished in many more locations than I have, and in the process have brought recipes back from the far corners of the world to share with us, as well as juicy stories of exotic places many of us will never see. They are superb at telling

Rocky Mountain reservoirs collect snowmelt and feed some of the world's most famous trout rivers, like the Yampa in northern Colorado. **FOLLOWING PAGES:** Fall in the Austrian Alps is as close to paradise as one will get. Wolfgang Ladin probes the waters of the Gmundner Traun.

stories, sharing what it's like to fish for trout in New Zealand or salmon in Scotland. If we'll never get there, at least we can create the meals from these regions, as none of the recipes in here are overly complex. Just great meals with simple, local ingredients. We may not be able to cook like the Poles, but we can whip up a decent wild mushroom borscht with a little foraging at the local farmers market.

It's a fishable feast, indeed, on many levels. You can get a sense of what angling is like on the serene chalk streams of Hampshire, delight in some glorious images, and then afterward move to your kitchen to extend the pleasure by creating an authentic English country meal of watercress soup, fish and chips, mushy peas, and Eton mess. I think I would pass on the mushy peas but I'm in on the rest of the menu. And true to style, I might have a second helping of dessert.

Introduction

Kirk Deeter
Colorado

"If you are lucky enough to have lived in Paris as a young man, then wherever you go for the rest of your life, it stays with you, for Paris is a moveable feast."

—ERNEST HEMINGWAY

The more you fly fish, the more you realize that the sport isn't really much at all about pulling on fish; rather, it's about the miles you roll, the people you meet along the way, and the amazing natural places you are lucky enough to experience.

If you do it *just right*, you might also savor some distinctly local flavors along the way.

I've been lucky indeed, in that I've carved a career out of going to places all over the world to write stories about fly fishing. Someone had to do it, so I took one for the team (I say with a wink). And everywhere I've been has followed me home.

It's all been a moveable, *fish*able feast.

For example, when I reminisce about fishing in Argentina, I surely envision massive brown trout inhaling dry flies. But I also remember encounters with gauchos, and watching guanacos graze the hillsides as condors soared above. Perhaps what lingers most vividly in my mind is the smoky aroma of wood-fired asado, chimichurri slathered on meat, and the empanadas I ate on the riverbank as night fell and the Southern Cross illuminated the sky.

I fondly recall stalking bonefish on vast flats in the Out Islands of the Bahamas, but even more than that, I remember ice-cold Kalik beers and cracked conch. In Cuba, it was casting to willing permit, but even better, the uncanny refreshment of an authentic mojito and pickle-laden ham sandwiches. In Ireland, I recall casting for bright salmon in the Ridge Pool on the River Moy, but also the pints of Guinness (in waders) at Doherty's Ridge Pool Bar and hearty shepherd's pies. I sometimes still hear echoes of the Bolivian jungle as I sleep, and when I do, I remember banana-leaf-wrapped surubí catfish cooked over an open campfire with my friends, "the jungle anglers."

Now, when I want to remember those places, or share the stories and experiences with other friends and family as best I can, that often starts in the kitchen, recreating some of the authentic feasts of fly fishing that have moved with me over the years.

If you fish long enough, you'll come to realize that some of the greatest adventures carve a path that ultimately leads right back home where you started in the first place. And so, that's also how things turned out with this project.

I learned to fly fish purely to impress a girl I was dating—or, more accurately, her father and grandfather, who were dyed-in-the-wool trout anglers. I simply wasn't going to make the cut had I not at least shown an interest in fly fishing. So, I accepted an invitation to fish at their family cabin on the Baldwin River in Michigan—interestingly, where the first brown trout was planted in the United States, in 1884. I immediately took a shine to fly fishing for trout, and the Baldwin became my proving grounds and home water. (Things also worked out with the girl, since we've been married now for thirty-six years.)

As writing stories and editing magazines about fly fishing became a career focus, it seemed ironic that many of the adventures and story angles that took me to far points on the globe involved chasing that same dang fish—the brown trout—that got me hooked in Michigan in the first place. Indeed, the sun never sets on the empire of the brown trout.

I was once so fired up about all of this that I wanted to write a book that would be the ultimate homage to the über-trout, but just as I was ramping up, I got a review copy of *The Brown Trout-Atlantic Salmon Nexus* written by some writer/guide from right down the road . . .

Matt Supinski.

Because Matt had done such a thorough, thoughtful job with that book (leaving me little new hay to cut) I had no other option but to write a glowing review in *TROUT* magazine and become his friend.

So that's what I did. In doing so, I learned that Matt had an impressive "real-world" background in food, as a trained chef, restaurateur, manager, and consultant, and he had racked up accolades like Michelin stars and developed his own foodie following along the way. It just so happened I had another book idea that had been kicking around in my head for a number of years . . .

Now, if I've learned anything as an angler, it's that you don't throw nymphs when the trout are feeding off the surface, and it's always best to trade casts and share the water with someone else who really knows what they're doing. That's how you learn.

Thus, what you're about to bite into here is a labor of love, shared by two kindred spirits, who joined forces with the belief that fly fishing is about a heckuva lot more than matching hatches, making roll casts, and tugging on fish.

We hope cooking some of these dishes will help you fondly remember fishing adventures of your own—or dream up plans to chase new ones. By design, we focused on "gourmet comfort food"—dishes that are accessible, not terribly complicated, and easy to improvise around your own personal tastes. With all due apologies to the Bahamas, for example, which undeniably has some of the deepest roots and finest flavors in fly fishing, it isn't so easy to find conch to make fritters in Kalamazoo.

But it has never been easier to dream, wherever you are, about the places you've been or those you yearn to discover.

PREVIOUS: Lake casting in Rocky Mountain National Park, Colorado. **OPPOSITE:** "The Magic Hour," eleven p.m., waiting and watching for signs of sea-run brown trout along the banks of the Rio Grande in Argentina.

ORVIS
HELIOS

The Power of Comfort Food and Fond Fishing Memories

Matthew Supinski
Michigan

"Many go fishing all their lives without knowing that it is not fish they are after."

—HENRY DAVID THOREAU

Any sporting angler, no matter if they fly fish, use fancy gear, or simply dangle a worm on a hook, becomes deeply connected and embraces the natural world every time they wet a line. It is often the soothing solitude they experience, as water has the power to transport us to a place of tranquility that can be attained few other ways. The thrill is the "tug is the drug." It's that excitement where the bite, the fight, and the capture bring out a refreshingly primal, Neanderthal-like savageness to capture and possess something wild, even if only briefly. The catch brings out an ancient emotion of the basic need of gathering food. The look of pure joy and elation in an angler's eyes—whether young or old—when they catch their first fish is priceless.

I had an intense and anxiety-filled career as a food and beverage director in a series of large hotels, in Washington, D.C., and beyond. In that insane industry, I lived in a daily state of trench warfare, where you are only as good as your last meal served. Patrons see, taste, and smell a world of gastronomic beauty on the plate, along with the mood and ambience each establishment creates. But back in the kitchens, there are battles raging. Chefs screaming, servers crying, plates being thrown—everyone in some state of panic. That is just the daily normal. Add to it stoves catching fire, people quitting on the spot, managers playing mind games, food deliveries missing because "someone" didn't pay the bill. This all adds up to professional mayhem—a true hell's kitchen. Year after year, I had a saving grace: an annual vacation to fly fish from dawn to dusk in Montana. It restored my sanity. Hence it was to that true Big Sky paradise, and *the* one and only Paradise Valley by the magnificent Yellowstone River, where I would escape to restore and refuel. The Montana of old, which I write about later in the book, still exists today, if you look for it. Those days, before cell phones, were a sheer blessing to any trout bum. Today it seems as though texts and calls always pop up when you are waist deep in your favorite pool right during a mayfly hatch.

In the Big Sky I could go totally rogue, take off my watch, and not worry about time. To dance with trout every day on the stream, and later share my accomplishments or misadventures with other passionate trout bums over a few bourbons by the firepit, was a ritual I never wanted to end. That feeling of complete peace eventually led me to leave the food and beverage industry and become a fly-fishing guide—not only to save my own physical and mental health, but also to provide that often elusive sense of peace to others.

One of the most beautifully colored and perfect in-form brown trout I ever caught and photographed. Keeping it wet and happy.

Smells and aromas of foods, along with scents and sounds in nature, often become associated with fond, emotional memories. They can take our thoughts to happy places. Those unforgettable, delectable scents can come from a family kitchen or neighborhood restaurant, an open-air charcuterie market grilling sausages, or a food truck and backyard smoker. In this book, they often come from those epic fishing trips where I caught my personal best on a fly I tied myself and where I had the most memorable lodge meal afterward. Or perhaps on that fishing excursion where I explored local cuisine and time-honored, traditional customs with my family. Together they trigger those powerful emotions associated with the joys of gourmet comfort food we forever strive to replicate.

Yet it's uncanny how my lifetime taste template slowly evolved from when I was young. Like the classic urge for steak and potatoes as I recall those juicy, tender New York strip steaks my dad made when we fished on our camping trips. After a long day of wading a beautiful little stream, we rested on a big rock and were mesmerized as we watched wild trout eat mayflies off the surface right at dusk on a delightful May evening. It was my first lesson in matching the hatch as I caught my biggest brown ever on a Cahill fly I tied and perfected.

Later at the campfire and super hungry from the long day, I watched the steaks sear on a hot rock stove dad built by the stream. He smothered the steaks with fresh wild mushrooms he picked at his secret spot. It's amazing how just salt, pepper, and butter made everything taste good. As the potatoes roasted in the coals, before being smothered with the wild chives we picked, we sang songs and gazed at the Milky Way. Afterward, as the marshmallows roasted, we indulged in the chocolate and graham cracker decadence of s'mores, then we had the best sleep ever. Those fond, youthful associations with food psychologically formed my sophisticated adult palate.

Fresh air, flowing rivers, and nature always spark happy food-related memories. They come to mind when I forage for watercress and other edible greens or for wildflowers emanating from a damp, fern-laden glen alongside a spring creek. These are the secret little places where we can always escape the world as we fish a little gem of a stream few know about—and what saves and nurtures many an angler's soul.

It is always amazing to me how the change of seasons plays such a key role in food memories. Spring is by far the most precious and sends my nose and taste buds into overdrive after a long, dormant winter. I recall picking thick, purple-tipped asparagus ready to grill and splash with balsamic vinegar, olive oil, and sea salt. It's when the earthy, thyme-like scent of thawing soil warms in the sun on a hillside glen, as wild morel mushrooms pop up after April showers and become the Holy Grail you hunt for. There is also something powerfully liberating and soothing about a drive in the country to hike through the meadows, as spring's emerging greenery is everywhere. The scents of freshly plowed farm fields and herbaceous cow dung always sting the nostrils: It's a pungent, savory scent I have grown to love.

On those early spring outings with my dad, we were on the lookout for fiddleheads and ramps to throw in the wicker creel with fresh-caught trout for my mom's kitchen. My Austrian-Polish mother would frown if we did not bring home *forellen* (brown trout in Austrian), since it was an old-world delicacy. She wrapped the trout in smoked bacon and pan-sautéed them in a thyme-dill butter with white wine. She then added the picked fiddleheads and ramps, along with springtime red new potatoes. Dried chanterelle mushrooms, sent to us by my aunt in the old country,

The sunsets along the sandy dunes of Lake Michigan's shoreline have been celebrated from generation to generation.

added an earthy smokiness. The dish was amazingly delicious.

Today, more than ever, those pleasurable memories release soothing endorphins—ones so badly needed in our stress-filled world. That is what we hope to achieve with this book. The joys of fishing and spending time in nature keep us grounded to terra firma. When combined with the soulful, heartwarming beauty and taste of delicious foods prepared with love and passion, they unleash a spiritual power one can never forget.

HSA 287

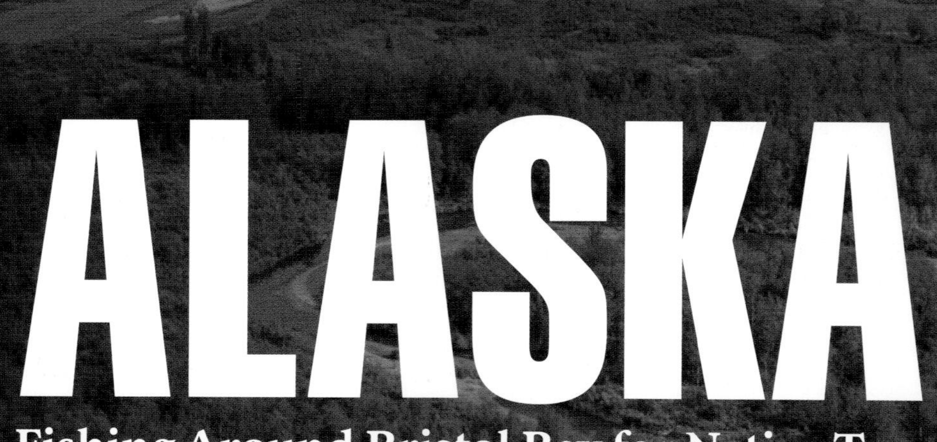

ALASKA

Fishing Around Bristol Bay for Native Trout and Salmon

KIRK DEETER

“Alaska is a great,
solemn poem,
set to music by glaciers
and volcanoes, with an
accompaniment of forests
and Aurora Borealis.”

—JOHN BURROUGHS

If you want to believe in fly-fishing miracles, you should go fishing in Alaska. The options are limitless. You just need to decide when and where you want to go.

After all, Alaska is about the size of one-fifth of the entire Lower 48. And, as such, pinning down a single fishing adventure is like throwing darts at a board. The Panhandle and its islands are jagged and wet, with snowpack, frequent rains, and receding glaciers feeding myriad small streams, which, depending on the month, see various runs of salmon as well as trout. The vast Tongass National Forest is called the salmon forest because the old-growth trees and waterways make for an ideal habitat for anadromous fish. And the waters in the fjords are primed with bright, staging salmon, black cod, and halibut. (I would learn on one Alaskan adventure that halibut could even be caught with a fly rod.)

On the Water

Kodiak Island is loaded with massive brown bears, enough that you need to keep eyes peeled and ears open wherever you hike, and even as you fish. But it's worth the nerves, especially on the Karluk River, where early October runs of steelhead trout are so thick you can catch and release several or more by swinging flies on an average-to-good day. True steelhead aficionados—tolerant souls with twisted minds, who are often willing to shell out big bucks to visit a lodge in British Columbia or stand in miserable sideways rainstorms for days on Washington's Olympic Peninsula with the hope of landing a few fish in a *season*—will appreciate this.

PREVIOUS: A typical shoreline in Bristoi Bay, Alaska, where the rivers meet the sea. **OPPOSITE:** Renowned artist and guide Bob White makes a cast. **TOP:** The dorsal of an Arctic grayling. **BOTTOM:** A native Alaskan leopard rainbow trout.

TOP: Arctic char are among the most beautifully colored fish an angler can behold. **BOTTOM:** Sometimes the salmon in Alaska run so thick it seems as if you could almost walk across the river on their backs.

Interior Alaska has plenty of rivers, small streams, and lakes with trout and grayling, which, with sail-like dorsal fins and intricate, colorful scales, are really like living jewels. The larger rivers like the Yukon are laden with northern pike, and in some places you can even catch sheefish—a type of large whitefish that's called the tarpon of the tundra.

I have gravitated to the Bristol Bay region most often. This pocket of coastline, just above where the Aleutian chain juts into the Pacific Ocean and the complex array of interconnected waterways feed into it, produces 50 percent of the world's sockeye salmon. It's also home to native leopard rainbow trout (so nicknamed for their vividly spotted backs and ruby-red flanks) and Arctic char, Dolly Varden, grayling, and other salmon species that, as smolt, run out of the rivers where they were born and return after a few years at sea as adults. Many will cover thousands of miles in the open ocean and swim back to within yards of the very spot where they were hatched to spawn, die, and close one of the most mysterious life cycles and feats of nature. It really is nothing short of a miracle.

Seasons of Salmon

The salmon run in their own distinct seasons. First to arrive—usually in June—are the Chinook (king) salmon. They're the big ones, usually ranging from ten to thirty pounds, but the world record king nearly broke one hundred. In a culinary sense, Chinook salmon are considered a delicacy because they have a milder, more buttery taste thanks to a higher natural fat content in their big bodies. Recent runs of Chinook have been concerningly light in some places, so you have to think carefully about where to go if you want to play with just them.

After the Chinooks come the sockeye. The sockeyes are the foundation of commercial

LEFT: Wade fishing in Bristol Bay; low, clear water in August. **BELOW:** A rainbow trout is promptly released after having been caught. While we may eagerly eat some fresh-from-the-sea salmon . . . we usually let the resident rainbows go.

salmon fishing. They're the ones that turn from silver to bright red with green jaws when they migrate from the ocean to spawn. At times, and in certain rivers, the water literally appears deep red with all the salmon packed together and pushing upstream—another phenomenon that seems like a miracle when you see it.

Following the sockeyes, chum salmon and pink salmon spawn in certain areas in alternating years. These salmon typically aren't favored as table fare—chums are often called dog salmon—but they're fun to catch at a time in the season when the days are still long, the bears are getting fat and happy, and the bugs aren't quite as thick.

Late August to early September is typically when the coho (silver) salmon run in many places. These fish are fine eating, but they're not often that big, usually averaging between eight to twelve pounds. But the silvers are often sporting anglers' favorites, because they fight well above their weight class, often making acrobatic leaps, and they eat flies—sometimes even pink "wog" flies—off the river surface. Skating wogs with a two-handed rod and watching silvers crush dry flies in a brawling river is truly an art form when done by anglers who really know what they're doing.

Although salmon make the Alaskan fishing world go around—from commercial gill netters to fly-fishing lodges with float planes, jet boat "sleds," and otherwise, I've always found the native rainbow trout to be extra special because you can catch them in different ways—mayflies, mouse flies, running beads, swinging streamers, and more.

Is my net too big? *Nah* . . . not for Alaska.

Tractors in the Sky

I remember my first trip to the Last Frontier as if it were yesterday. Flying into Anchorage on a plane from Denver, looking wide-eyed and slack-jawed out the window at the alpenglow as we made our descent, and realizing it was nearing midnight local time, blew my mind. The next morning, I was on another flight to King Salmon where I was met by Tyler Palmerton, who would be my guide (and remains a close friend). Not long after getting off one plane we were in full wading gear in another one—a De Havilland Beaver headed off for a short float plane ride to fish somewhere around Brooks Falls (the place made famous by photos of brown bear grabbing salmon out of the air as they jump the flume) in Katmai National Park.

The De Havilland Beaver isn't very fast, and doesn't climb all that high. It's more like a tractor in the sky. Even though this plane hasn't been commercially produced in over half a century, there still exists a niche industry of refurbishing and maintaining them, and there are many in routine operation throughout Alaska and the Pacific Northwest. That's because nobody's thought up a more efficient workhorse machine that can shuttle people around the Alaskan Bush, landing and taking off on water that's sometimes only waist-deep. The distinctive grumble-to-purr sounds of a Beaver idling on the lake and then throttling up is something Alaskans can recognize with their eyes closed. In many places, the Beaver remains as much a part of Alaskan sporting culture as the dogsled is in wintertime. A mechanical miracle of sorts.

Tyler and I hopped out of the plane, grabbed our gear, then watched the Beaver take off from the lake before marching into the alders along a feeder creek.

"Popcorn, peanuts, cold beer!" Tyler shouted like a stadium vendor at the top of his lungs.

Trent Kososki scanning the sky for the ride back to the lodge on Kodiak Island. **OPPOSITE:** the De Havilland Beaver swoops in for a supply drop.

ABOVE: Bristol Bay Lodge's De Havilland Beavers are iconic bush planes. They haul supplies and take anglers to pristine waters that are nearly impossible to reach otherwise. **RIGHT:** Cruising over the Bristol Bay region by float plane, where you're skimming just above the peaks and can often see bears, caribou, and other animals. It is one of the most photogenic places in the world.

He turned around and noticed the curious look on my face, and simply said, "Bears." I understood.

We found a pod of fish sipping on the surface and tied on a Root Beer Baetis dry fly, and immediately connected. Tyler decided to up the ante and tied on a mouse pattern (I believe it was a Mercer's Lemming). And let me tell you, right when you get to thinking that rainbow trout are timid creatures that only sip bugs on or below the river or lake surface, a wild Alaskan leopard bow that has to make its living in a short summer season will rock your world when it torpedoes from behind a log jam into the middle of the river to explode on a mouse.

Halibut . . . On a *Fly*?

The irony of this trip was that I was there to do a story about fishing for "everything *but* the salmon." The local outfitters and lodges wanted to play up the fact that there was plenty of fishing to be had outside the salmon seasons, so I showed up in June when the trout season opened and ended up focusing on the "smolt bust," when the big rainbows (some thirty inches or longer) run out of Naknek Lake and into the river to feed on the hapless little salmon smolt drifting toward the sea. That's a lot like chasing striped bass off Montauk or Nantucket: You look for flocks of diving birds and motor toward the choppy water, then fire casts with big white streamers or crease fly poppers, and the trout shred them up in a veritable feeding frenzy.

Once we had knocked that story angle out of the way (not that we grew bored with pulling on two-foot-plus rainbow trout), we decided to go *way* off script and try to catch a halibut on a fly. So, we talked Luke the pilot into flying us over the Valley of Ten Thousand Smokes—the ash-coated terrain that still looks like a moonscape over a century after the Novarupta volcano eruption—to Geographic Harbor. As usual, this area was thick with bears, but they weren't nearly as interested in us as they were in digging clams off the beach at low tide.

Fishing just offshore from one of the plane's pontoons, we first dropped a mushroom anchor and clacked the weight on the rocks on the sea floor, maybe fifty to sixty feet down. Apparently, that's like ringing the dinner bell for halibut—a flat-bodied fish that feeds along the bottom like a super flounder—and they came running. We dropped a large, heavily weighted Clouser Fly tied on a 2/0 hook down to the bottom with a fast-sinking fly line, then started gently jigging the fly up and down. Sure enough, within minutes it got bit, and after a brief but difficult fight (trying to pull a halibut up from the depths can feel like trying to lift your car's transmission off the ocean floor by pulling on a string), we landed a thirty-pounder!

The whole fishing part of the adventure took maybe thirty minutes. Then we threw the fish in a hatch in one of the pontoons, took off down the coast, circled a couple times above a pair of fin whales, then poked back over the peninsula via Becharof Lake to land the plane on the Naknek River.

We cut that fresh halibut into steaks, grilled them that evening over an open fire, and glazed the fish with a mixture of fresh berries—which is how roasted halibut with a berry glaze became my favorite dish from Alaska, and how I best remember times fishing there. I think we ate so much that by nine p.m. we were all sated enough that we didn't even go out to fish anymore . . . even though we could have gotten in another few hours if we really wanted to.

On the Table

When I think of Alaskan food, a couple things come to mind. First, I think of Indigenous communities that have literally subsisted for many generations by catching the various species of salmon, hunting moose and caribou, and harvesting wild berries and plants. The First Nation people are among the most resourceful in the world—hunting and gathering what they can during short seasons, and making it last throughout the whole year. The salmon salad here is a variation of a sandwich spread made with "three-day smoked" sockeyes Chief Luki Akelkok fed me when I first landed in the village of Ekwok to teach at the Bristol Bay Fly Fishing and Guide Academy. The program keeps Indigenous youth connected to their villages by teaching them to become fly-fishing guides. Today, graduates manage some of the finest fishing lodges in Alaska.

The other thoughts that come to mind when I remember Alaskan cuisine are of hearty meals like stews and loaves of sourdough bread, biscuits, and preserves—stuff I imagine being staples in the camps during the Gold Rush.

Whatever your tastes or inspiration, we encourage you to buy wild-caught Alaskan seafood. There are numerous companies that catch it, clean it, pack it, freeze it, and ship it directly to your door. You can tell a wild sockeye salmon fillet by its rich color and firm texture—things some farmed salmon that need coloring up with dye just don't have. And buying wild Alaskan seafood supports the conservation of these irreplaceable wild places. By supporting and working together with the commercial fishing industry and Indigenous communities, sporting fly anglers are making sure the runs of salmon, migrations of caribou, and other natural phenomena that make Alaska special will be sustained well into the future.

"Shore lunch" in Alaska is often hearty and usually involves some sort of fish. **OPPOSITE:** Fried halibut with jalapeño mayo. **RIGHT:** Chargrilled Arctic char.

Baked Halibut with Blueberry Glaze

The beauty of halibut is that its meat is mild and relatively firm, so it can be cooked in many ways (grilled, baked, poached . . .) and it will absorb whatever flavors you want to surround it with. Given how wild berries are such staples of Alaskan fare, I think a hearty slice of halibut steak drizzled with berry glaze is sea-meets-land quintessential Last Frontier. In addition to pairing with the halibut steaks, this sauce is also delicious with grilled meats and chicken, pancakes and waffles, and ice cream. It is *especially* good on grilled caribou or elk tenderloin, see page 153.

Serves 4

- 1 (1-pound) halibut steak, cut into 4 equal pieces
- 3 cloves garlic, minced
- 2 tablespoons extra-virgin olive oil
- 2 teaspoons lemon zest
- Coarse sea salt and freshly ground black pepper
- Blueberry Glaze (recipe follows)

Preheat the oven to 425°F and line a baking sheet with parchment paper.

Use paper towels to blot the halibut dry and place the fish on the baking sheet.

In a small bowl, combine the garlic, olive oil, and lemon zest and season with salt and pepper.

Brush the tops and sides of the halibut with this garlic and oil mixture.

Bake until flaky, 12 to 15 minutes.

Place each portion of halibut on individual plates. Spoon some of the blueberry glaze over each fish steak and serve any remaining glaze on the side. Delicious with rosemary-roasted new potatoes (page 321) and beet salad (page 155).

Blueberry Glaze

- ½ teaspoon lemon zest
- 2 tablespoons lemon juice
- 2 tablespoons maple syrup
- 2 teaspoons cornstarch
- 1 cup blueberries

In a small saucepan, whisk together the lemon zest and juice, maple syrup, and cornstarch. Stir in the blueberries.

Over medium-high heat, bring the blueberry sauce to a boil, then reduce the heat to low and simmer, stirring frequently, until the sauce thickens, about 5 minutes. Turn off the burner and set aside (for up to 20 minutes).

Wild Salmon Salad

When the salmon run, the work begins to harvest, smoke, and store this staple for year-round subsistence. This salad resembles the "three-day smoked" sockeye salmon salad we'd slather on crackers at the end of a day on the water, or stuff into sourdough bread to make sandwiches to take to the river.

Serves 12 as an appetizer with crackers, or 4 in sandwiches

2 (6-ounce) wild-caught salmon steaks

⅓ cup mayonnaise

⅓ cup finely chopped red onion

⅓ cup finely diced celery

3 teaspoons Dijon mustard

½ teaspoon lemon zest

3 teaspoons freshly squeezed lemon juice

½ teaspoon dried dill

Salt and freshly ground black pepper

Crackers or 8 slices toasted sourdough bread for serving

Provolone, lettuce, and sliced tomato, if making sandwiches

Smoke the salmon over low heat in a wood (alder) smoker for 2 to 3 hours, grill over medium heat for 10 to 15 minutes, or bake in an oven at 325°F for 15 to 20 minutes. After the salmon is cooked, let cool to room temperature.

Flake the salmon into a medium bowl, discarding any bones. Gently mix with the mayonnaise, onion, celery, mustard, lemon zest and juice, and dill. Taste and season with salt and pepper. Chill, covered, in the refrigerator for at least 1 hour or up to 24 hours for the flavors to meld.

Serve as an appetizer with crackers or make sandwiches by mounding the salad on 4 slices of bread and topping with provolone, lettuce, tomato, and the other 4 slices of bread.

Mixed Berry Cobbler

When you fish in the land of the midnight sun, there are no rules regarding timing when it comes to a traditional dessert dish. A good berry cobbler is just as fair game for breakfast with a bit of syrup as it is as an after-dinner course, or a midnight snack with ice cream.

Serves 8

- 4 tablespoons unsalted butter, melted, plus more for the baking dish
- 1 cup all-purpose flour
- 1 cup granulated sugar
- 1½ tablespoons baking powder
- ½ teaspoon salt
- Zest of 1 lemon
- ¾ cup whole milk
- 1 cup blackberries
- 1 cup blueberries
- 1 cup raspberries
- Confectioners' sugar for sprinkling (optional)
- Vanilla ice cream for serving (optional)

Preheat the oven to 350°F. Butter a 9-inch round or square baking dish.

In a medium bowl, whisk the flour, all but 2 tablespoons of the granulated sugar, the baking powder, salt, and lemon zest.

Add the milk and melted butter and whisk to create a batter. Pour into the prepared baking dish.

Spread the berries evenly over the top of the batter. Sprinkle the berries with the reserved 2 tablespoons sugar.

Bake until the cobbler is golden brown and you can poke the center with a toothpick and it comes out clean, 50 to 60 minutes. Let cool for 20 minutes, then sprinkle with confectioners' sugar, if using.

Spoon the cobbler into bowls and add a scoop of vanilla ice cream to each serving, if desired.

ARGENTINA

Fishing for Trout in Patagonia

KIRK DEETER

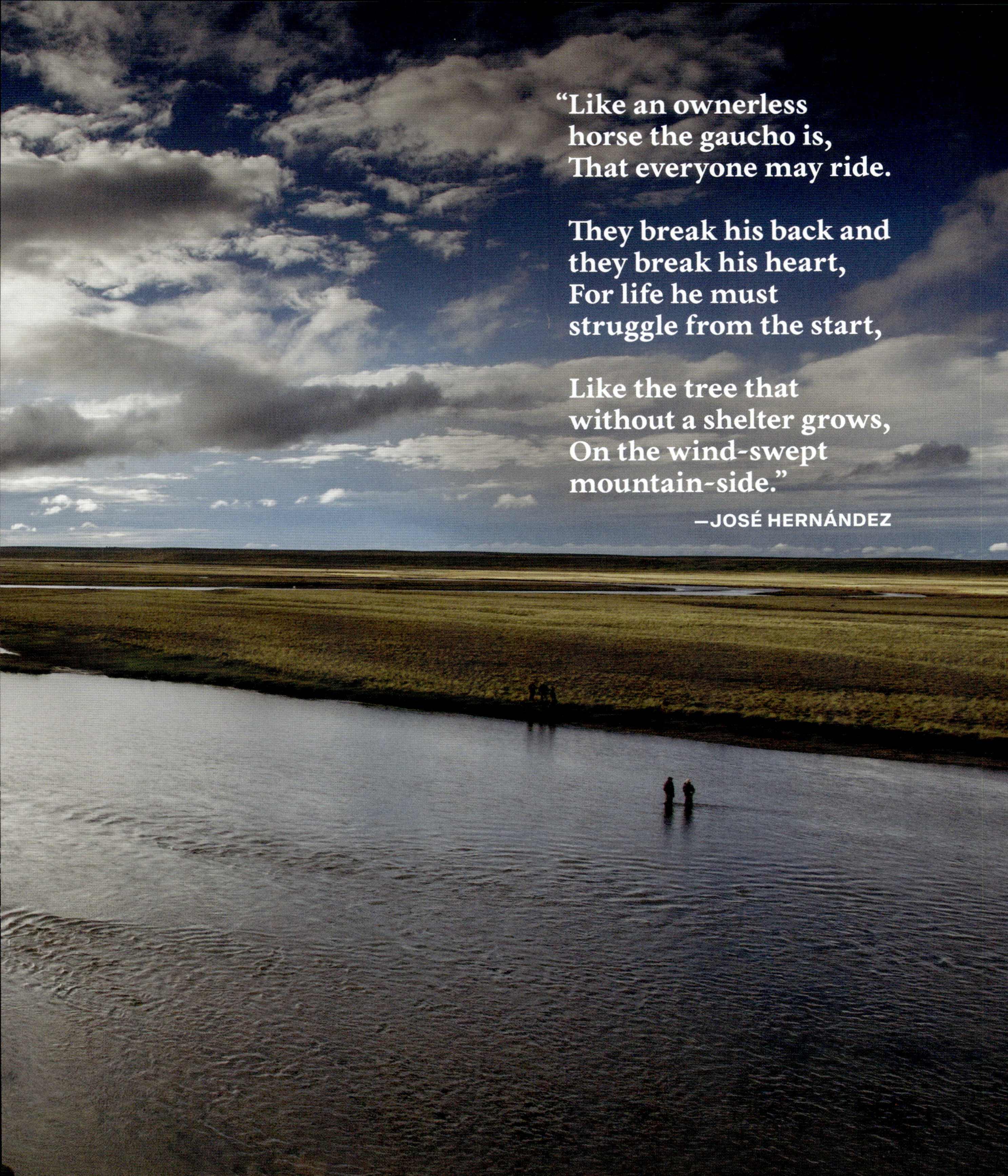
"Like an ownerless
horse the gaucho is,
That everyone may ride.

They break his back and
they break his heart,
For life he must
struggle from the start,

Like the tree that
without a shelter grows,
On the wind-swept
mountain-side."

—JOSÉ HERNÁNDEZ

PREVIOUS: The vast, windswept Rio Grande in Tierra del Fuego is now arguably the greatest sea-run brown trout fishery in the world. **ABOVE:** Brown trout were introduced into Argentina in the early twentieth century, because ships that carried wool from the sheep estancias to mills in England would return with trout ova that were hatched and planted in rivers. **OPPOSITE:** Monkey trees and a trout river in northern Patagonia.

You don't go fishing in Argentina to catch fish you cannot catch anywhere else. You visit Argentina to go back in time.

Back to a place without billboards and telephone lines. Where you might spend hours on dirt roads to reach the water. Where trout willingly eat dry flies, because they still haven't seen that many artificial patterns.

Throw in a layover in Buenos Aires—the Paris of South America—maybe a fine Malbec and some tango, and you'll immediately fall in love. Vast . . . complex . . . complicated . . . alluring . . . sometimes austere . . . often stunningly beautiful. Fly fishing in Argentina is much like the landscape and the country itself. There are distinctly different "theaters" of fly fishing here, each with its own appeal. They're all wonderful, and all worth a dedicated visit.

On the Water

The far north of the country, around Corrientes on the Paraná River (the second-longest in South America after the Amazon), is home to vast marshes that hold abundant populations of golden dorado. Brightly gilded with black spots and a ferocious reputation, dorados are often referred to as piscatorial "jewels" because they are indeed elusive and treasured as quarry. Dorado fishing is a hot, flats-style game that's closer in character to saltwater fishing than river fishing for trout, but it's a unique enough experience to cultivate its own following of angling aficionados.

The trout fishing starts in Northern Patagonia, around the Rio Aluminé (the "golden cauldron") area south of the Mendoza wine region and

PREVIOUS: Fly fishing for sea-run browns involves casting two-handed rods in a windy, austral landscape. **THESE PAGES:** Fishing Tierra del Fuego will challenge your skills and endurance, but the rewards are extraordinary. If you can figure this game out, you can catch trout anywhere on the planet.

west of the vast Pampas. The areas closest to the town Neuquen are warm and dry, and the fishing feels akin to fly fishing in southern Colorado or New Mexico. This part of the region is a bit less traveled, and therefore less publicized, but it's home to some stunning spring creeks that run crystal clear and hold scads of fat brown and rainbow trout.

The Rio Chimehuin flows through this area as does the Rio Malleo (the double *l* in the Argentine dialect is pronounced more like a *j* thus, Rio Ma-je-o or pojo al a parrija . . .). The Malleo runs into the Aluminé and consistently produces some of the best dry-fly action I've ever enjoyed because trout hammer big, gaudy terrestrial patterns off the surface.

Extending even farther south (but still in "northern" Patagonia) you get into the heart of the trout region around the towns of San Martín de los Andes and San Carlos de Bariloche (locally just called San Martín and Bariloche). San Martín is the smaller, quainter of the two, but they are essentially the Vail and Aspen of Argentina. Long a favorite vacation destination for Argentines, this area has a distinctly Alpine-European flair. Here, the seasons are more pronounced, and the vistas are stunningly beautiful with many lakes and rivers, including now-famous trout icons like the Traful, the Limay, and Collón Curá. This area was "discovered" and really took off as a destination for venturing American and European anglers in the 1970s and 1980s. It's still home to many of the most famous fishing lodges, and it's an excellent place to bring a non-angling companion who likes to hike, bike, sail, swim, paddle, shop, eat, or just chill in beautiful places.

Central Patagonia, around the town of Esquel, is loaded with parks, lakes, and rivers, and the fishing here is a little quieter, a bit cooler, and a lot more diverse. Depending on which direction you turn, you might be chasing rainbows in a lake with streamer flies, brook trout in small creeks, or brown trout on brawling rivers.

Continuing south, you encounter the "heart" of Patagonia, which has the most dramatic Andean peaks, such as Mount Fitz Roy, the mountain depicted on the Patagonia (the adventure apparel maker) logo. The fishing here is simply odd—some might call it supernatural, others consider it grossly unnatural.

Fantasyland

Lago Strobel, a.k.a. Jurassic Lake, is where anglers from around the world will fly to Calafate, then drive several hours to reach for a shot at catching a rainbow trout that tips the scales at twenty pounds or more. I did this once to visit a nameless lake in the region. After the bumpy flight from Buenos Aires to Calafate, we drove seven hours on mostly dirt roads to a thirty-thousand-acre sheep estancia (which was wonderful), where I learned that the rainbow trout were originally planted in the lake so they could be farmed and turned into cat food. The fish farm went belly-up, leaving the trout in cold, clear water with no natural predators and an abundance of freshwater shrimp ("scuds"). So, what did they do? Eat. And grow. And eat. And grow. And now the Swedes and English, Americans, and Canadians flock down in hordes to catch these mutant fish, if only to take photos to hang on their office walls. Not my flavor, but it is what it is.

In truth, there's nothing natural at all about trout fishing in Argentina, for all trout species were introduced in one way or another. It started in the early twentieth century when the ships that carried wool sheared off of sheep from the massive Argentine estancias to mills in England returned with brown trout eggs that were planted in the rivers. Then came the rainbows, then the *fontinalis* brook trout, then Pacific salmon and steelhead trout, which now make the Rio Gallegos a sought-after angling destination in its own right. Go figure.

Sea-Run Brown Trout

Sometimes *I* feel like the real native species—wondering if the guanacos (like smaller versions of llamas) and the condors soaring overhead are looking and laughing at the gringo anglers flailing away in a largely artificial playground.

That said, the brown trout took so well that Tierra del Fuego (the fourth "theater") is now widely considered the de facto home of sea-run brown trout fishing worldwide, because they thrive here like no place else, including the European rivers from whence their ancestors came.

This brand of Argentine fishing may very well be my favorite because it's harsh, challenging, and also rewarding. You typically fly to the town of Rio Grande, then stay in one of a handful of massive estancias that line the river itself. Wake up and fish a few hours. Eat a hearty midday meal. Siesta until six p.m. or later, then head back to the river to swing articulated streamers with two-handed rods until it gets dark, around midnight.

When the giant brown trout come in from the sea and up the river, they don't eat. You just want to agitate them by dangling a black fly in front of them. They usually bite during the eleventh hour (literally), and I can tell you that wrestling a twenty-pound brown at nightfall is an experience like no other.

As is battling the near-constant winds in this treeless, austral landscape. I once watched a newbie guide fresh from the States make the mistake of parking a truck along the riverbank in the wrong, downwind direction. When he opened the door of the vehicle, it blew clean off into the river. He was put on a plane home the next morning.

ABOVE: Steve Roberts with a sea-run brown caught just before nightfall, which is after eleven p.m. during the South American summer. **LEFT:** Long casts, long drifts . . . swinging articulated black streamer flies just below the river surface is what it takes to coax an eat from a sea-run brown.

On the Table

Argentina is a foodie paradise, with fresh produce, bountiful catches from the sea, and more. But the star attraction, wherever you fish in Patagonia, is the traditional asado, where the gauchos build a wood fire and slowly roast lamb and/or beef on a traditional cast-iron-cross grill for hours. The smell alone will make your mouth water. And when the meat is chopped and served with homemade chimichurri, a side of roasted *papas* (potatoes), and a leafy salad, along with fine red wines and fresh spring water, you'll want to return immediately whether you fish or not.

Another staple in Argentina, as in many other Latin American countries, is the empanada—a pillow of dough with any variety of fillings, from eggs and cheese to beef and onions. Let your empanada imagination run wild. I like ground lamb empanadas most of all. They're best served warm with chimichurri, salsa, or even ranch dressing. But I found them to be the perfect river breakfast, lunch, or evening snack when I wrapped them up and stuffed them in my pockets. Even cold, they burst with flavor and offer the energy boost to keep you casting for hours.

In Argentina, the midday meal is often the biggest production and usually involves firing up the *parilla*. After lunch . . . a hard-earned siesta, then fish again until sundown.

Ground Lamb Empanadas

Makes 12 empanadas

DOUGH

4 cups all-purpose flour, plus more for dusting

14 tablespoons cold unsalted butter, cut into small cubes

½ teaspoon sea salt

1 large egg, beaten

½ cup warm water, plus more as needed

FILLING

2 tablespoons extra-virgin olive oil

½ large yellow or white onion

4 cloves garlic, minced

1 pound ground lamb

1 teaspoon dried oregano

1 teaspoon ground cumin

½ teaspoon salt

¼ teaspoon freshly ground black pepper

½ red pepper, diced, or 1 seeded jalapeño pepper for a spicier filling

1 tablespoon tomato paste

Crushed red pepper and/or chili powder to taste

8 pitted, chopped green olives

1 hard-boiled egg, coarsely chopped

2 tablespoons finely chopped flat-leaf parsley

2 large eggs, beaten

Make the dough: Place the flour in a large bowl. Use a fork to cut the butter into the flour until you have small crumbles. (Alternatively, use your hands to work the flour and butter together.)

Add the salt and mix by hand, then add the egg and mix with a fork. Add the warm water and incorporate with a fork.

Transfer this dough to a stand mixer with a dough hook and slowly knead on low speed until the dough is smooth with no lumps, about 5 minutes. If the dough seems too dry, you can add up to another ⅓ cup warm water.

Shape the dough into a ball, wrap in plastic wrap, and refrigerate for 1 hour.

Make the filling: Warm the olive oil in a large skillet over medium heat. Sauté the onion and garlic until the onion is translucent, about 5 minutes.

Add the lamb and mix into the onion and garlic. Add the oregano, cumin, salt, and black pepper. As the lamb begins to brown, add the diced pepper and tomato paste, stirring often. Transfer to a bowl. Season with crushed red pepper. Once cool, stir in the olives, egg, and parsley. Set aside.

To assemble, preheat the oven to 375°F and line a baking sheet with parchment paper.

Lightly dust a work surface with flour, then roll the dough to a ¼-inch thickness (or slightly thinner). Using a large plate with a 5- or 6-inch diameter as a guide, cut the dough into 12 circles.

Brush the egg wash on the dough circles. Scoop ¼ to ⅓ cup of the lamb filling into the center of each circle. Holding the dough up like a taco, squeeze the edges closed. Repeat until you've filled all the dough rounds.

Place the empanadas on the prepared baking sheet. Lightly press down to spread the filling throughout each pocket. Crimp the edges with a fork and brush egg wash over the top.

Bake until the pastry turns golden brown, 25 to 30 minutes. Let the empanadas cool slightly, then serve.

Store extras frozen for up to 6 months or in a refrigerator for up to a week. They're easily reheated in a microwave oven, or in a conventional oven at 325°F for 30 minutes.

Our ancient and biodiverse vines
thrive in the high-altitude peaks of the
cared for by the Catena family for over a
SINCE
1902

Beef Asado

The traditional Patagonian asado usually involves lamb roasted on a cast-iron cross over a wood fire, often in the hearth. Beef is also an option in many places in gaucho country.

To closely resemble the beef asado, I grill over charcoal with some wood chips added for flavor. Lightly coat the steaks (ribeye, filet) in olive oil, and season with salt and pepper. Then sear the meat on high heat for 2 minutes per side. Move to a cooler spot on the grill and cover to cook for another 5 to 10 minutes. An internal temperature of 125°F is perfect medium-rare.

Chimichurri

Hand-chopping the parsley, garlic, and oregano enables the flavors and texture to evolve with every bite. Each bite should be slightly different from the last.

1 cup flat-leaf parsley

5 cloves garlic

2 tablespoons fresh oregano

½ cup extra-virgin olive oil

2 tablespoons red wine vinegar

Dash balsamic vinegar

1 teaspoon sea salt

½ teaspoon freshly ground black pepper

½ teaspoon red pepper flakes

Hand-chop the parsley, garlic, and oregano and transfer to a small bowl with the olive oil. Stir in the vinegars, salt, black pepper, and red pepper flakes. You can serve immediately, but it's best if you let it sit in the refrigerator, in an airtight container, for a few days. When I'm planning an asado dinner, I make my chimichurri a few days ahead.

AUSTRIA

Fishing the Salzach and Traun Rivers for Brown Trout and Grayling

MATTHEW SUPINSKI

"Cooking is like painting or writing a song. Just as there are only so many notes or colors, there are only so many flavors—it is how you combine them that sets you apart."

—WOLFGANG PUCK

PREVIOUS: Albert Pesendorfer captures the ethereal beauty of fly fishing Alpine rivers. **ABOVE:** Fishing the Salzach and Traun Alpine Rivers, surrounded by the stunning, breathtaking Alps and its foothills, is amazing. Along with the bigger rivers, smaller brooks like the Felber and others invite you to hike up them. The German Black Forest and Alpine rivers have the same stunning beauty and brown trout. **LEFT:** The European Grayling, the “Lady of the Stream,” is an indigenous fish that is a unique catch. Its fins are precious, and contrary to popular belief these fish can be as stubborn as any snooty brownie when taking small dry flies.

We always envision the land of Mozart as a joyous place. His invigorating music creates surreal scenes of what this paradise is like. Listening to his Jupiter Symphony—one of the greatest classical works of all time—inspires our thoughts to hover high above his homeland and its Alpine-surrounded pastures. Here we imagine fresh mountain air permeating the jagged, snow-capped peaks. In the valley below, purple harebells and white edelweiss wildflowers adorn the hilltop chalets. There, a glacial mountain stream runs through it. And swimming in its icy, chalky-blue waters, which seduce and beckon an angler to cast their fly, is the "Lady of the Stream," the European grayling. In addition, in the rocky stream shadows lurks the coy and finicky indigenous *forellen* (brown trout)—a fish so capricious and beautiful that Schubert wrote a string quartet in honor of this piscatorial jewel. No Alpine setting could be more perfect.

I can't describe Austria without using anything but superlatives, and this is true for the cuisine too. The aromas intoxicate in this fairy-tale land of superb scenic views and food. The comforting scents can come from a family's kitchen, with Wiener schnitzel and spaetzle on the stove. Or on Saturdays, the smells that permeate a whole town square, where street vendors sell wieners, weisswurst, sauerkraut, and potato pancakes before the local team's soccer match. A backyard smoker hut on a farm hillside curing hams and *bündnerfleisch* (Alpine air-dried beef), can disperse its aromas through a whole valley. All are part of the comforting charm I know as Austria.

I have had very fond thoughts of Austria since visiting my cousins there as a young man. I always appreciate the Austrians and their richness of culture and cuisine, like their strudels—both the sweet apple version topped with rich whipped cream or French vanilla ice cream or the hearty savory versions stuffed with wild mushrooms and Gruyère. I flashback to the days of my European train travels that seemed to always take me through Austria. I can still envision the Trans-Alpine train car crawling, clanking, and making steel-sheering, grinding sounds on the tracks as it climbed a steep mountain cliff-side. It is almost impossible to fathom how a train can climb such narrow tracks and perch on a cliff at the top of a mountain. From that height, the Austrian towns and villages below looked like the view from an airplane. It's a testament to human ingenuity. Those were daring and adventurous days indeed—I mostly slept on trains in sleeping bags to avoid having to pay for lodging, since I was on a very tight post-college budget. Life was free of constraints back then, a time I dearly miss today. In Austria, empires and civilizations were built. Its music, its food and beers, its joyous and friendly people, and, above all, its beautiful mountain trout streams, will live forever in my soul.

On the Water

I have been to Austria many times since but the beauty of Europe is that nothing changes. Trout fishing in the Alps is a surreal experience still privatized and very expensive. In Europe, the rivers and streams belong to the landowners, and that is the king's law carried down through the centuries.

Fly fishing for trout and grayling in Austria is like coming to pay homage to the pioneering holy waters and work of the great fly-fishing legend Roman Moser. His amazing photographer, Albert Pesendorfer, accompanied him everywhere he fished. Moser is the Lee Wulff or Tom Rosenbauer of Europe. His fly designs and study of Alpine trout behavior are second to none. Pesendorfer's photographic art captures that on his shutters. No discussion of European fly fishing would be justified without paying tribute to them.

Steinfliegen Stone Flies and Hungry Trout

Putting aside the frightening heights it traveled, the Trans-Alpine train ride took me past the iconic snowcapped Matterhorn, through green valleys of grazing sheep and cattle, and over countless cascading blue-green rivers that teemed with trout and grayling. It also connected me with family I had only heard stories of from my mother. It was my cousin Katrina who greeted me at the bus station in Bicheln, a charming mountain town where she lived. We hopped in her Volkswagen station wagon and cruised the winding mountain road dotted with charming Alpine chalets. After enjoying her great dinner of local sausages, sauerkraut, and spaetzle, I indulged in a large stein of Märzen beer, with shots of powerful schnapps. Feeling no pain from my libations and exhausting travel, I naïvely asked where I could fish for trout. She informed me that the rivers in Austria are private, owned by country inns, and very expensive—too expensive for me to fish.

She then told me she knew a family who had a sheep farm along the Salzach and Felber Rivers near Mittersill, not far away. Several of their sons were *fliegen fischer* (fly fishers). After a few phone calls, they invited me to stay on their farm estate. There, I met Stefan and Jurgen, who were in their mid-thirties.

They were passionate anglers who tied their own flies and had French-made Pezon et Michel cane rods and some good German reels. They said they guided tourists from France, Switzerland, and Vienna during the summer. I told them I was a poor American with a ravenous appetite for big brown trout, beer, sausages, and schnapps. I said I could only repay the favor by sitting at their vise and tying some fancy Kaufmann-style American stone fly nymphs for them. I also offered

TOP: A thick-bodied Alpine brown that is on the hunt for larger carnivorous food forms will relish the meaty big stone fly/*Isoperla*. Here, a rubber-legged Bunyon Bug (the fly used by Brad Pitt in *A River Runs Through It*) includes foam and rubber legs for more movement. **ABOVE, LEFT:** J:son Golden Stone Fly. **ABOVE, RIGHT:** A mountain river's moveable feast of stone fly nymphs, caddis larvae, and large mayfly nymphs—a trout smorgasbord.

ABOVE: The world-famous European master Roman Moser casts to a rising brown during the larger *Ephemera-Epeorus-Maccaffertium* mayfly and stone fly hatches these Alpine rivers get. Due to the often amazing clarity, the angler must stalk a trout from below. **LEFT:** The scenery is idyllic, like that in *The Sound of Music*. The fresh mountain breezes and grazing sheep and cattle, and wildflowers as far as the eye can see, intoxicate the senses. The architecture is a mix of Western and Eastern Tyrolean design.

to take them steelhead fishing on my home waters of the Great Lakes if they ever came to America. They loved big rainbow trout, since Austria was introduced to our American trout. We had a deal.

They told me I could not have timed my arrival better: The *steinfliegen* (stone flies) were on the water. They said the trout and grayling were sucking them up fast, but that they could be really fickle. Ernest Schwiebert's *Nymphs* was my bible in high school, along with *Selective Trout*. I was familiar with *Pteronarcys*, *Isoperla*, and *Acroneuria* stone flies. I had a good selection of them in the one fly box I brought with me, the ones I used on my Southern Tier New York State trout streams back home. When I woke up the first of two mornings, I scoured the rocks and boulders along the shoreline of the river by my farm bunkhouse. Giant yellow brown and black stone fly shucks were everywhere: it was like finding Alpine gold! The brothers lent me a hand-me-down bamboo rod reserved for guests, for which I was much obliged, along with some French Tortue tippet material and a few of their crude stone fly imitations. "No thanks on the flies . . . I have a few of my own," I said, and proceeded to open my fly box. Their eyes popped wide open, and they started grabbing a few. No worries, I thought, I have plenty! Most of my patterns were Kaufmann- and Brooks-style Western Madison River patterns, along with some sofa-pillow dries.

The first thing that caught my attention on the beautiful mountain freestone river with its bluish-green tint was how fascinating it was that the browns and grayling hunted the rocks along the shoreline areas for stone flies, migrating there in order to pounce on the hatching nymphs. It was a dark, rainy day, and sporadic stone fly emergence was consistent. Now I know why Czech-Polish nymphing is so effective in these tight, boulder-laden waters. In that technique you are, in effect, dredging the bottom, often close to shore and rocky pocket situations—perfect hangouts for stone flies and caddis larvae in the fast-flowing mountainous waters. In the original Polish-style Euro-nymphing you lead the fly slightly with a very tight line, allowing the nymphs to slide up and down the rocks and boulders just like a natural crawling stone fly. The graylings were much more cooperative. They were the easy catch, with some pretty fat specimens taken. But the wild browns were a different matter. The giant golden *Acroneuria* stone fly nymphs had a peculiar crawling and tumbling behavior that these freestone trout keyed in on in a selective-reflective fashion. Due to the extreme clarity of the water, I could sit on a giant boulder on shore and watch them feed. When I fished my weighted nymphs, I dead drifted as I got them in the pockets quickly, then twitched them and drifted them again. So even with very swift waters, the trout were particular to stone fly movement, and that made the art of stone fly nymphing a challenge and delight to fish.

Dances with Stone Flies

Charles Brooks, in his great book, *Nymph Fishing for Larger Trout*, described the "potshot" method of nymphing the boulder-strewn Madison in Montana, which was similar to what I developed on those Austrian waters. My first good-size brown trout, a beautifully colored sixteen-inch specimen, smashed the nymph pattern very hard—I could see the golden-orange belly in the deep rocky pocket of swiftly moving water. But for every take I had, there were many "flash" refusals. They either missed the fly due to the shear flow of the water, or rejected it at the last second. Most of the fish were beautiful wild browns in the eleven- to fourteen-inch range, and had magnificent red dots with white circles—brown trout genetics perfected over hundreds of thousands of years.

At the end of the day, I reflected by writing notes on my expedition in my diary.

TOP: The most perfect Bachforellen brown trout, with its red spots and white circles, with an artistic styling that reflects the author's interest in *Salmo trutta* "bling." **BOTTOM:** A classic Peerless reel, time- honored bamboo rod, and gray drake. This is a Hemingway Mayfly, foam-style abdomen spinner pattern. The *Siphlonurus* genus exists throughout Europe.

While enjoying a beer on a bench alongside the river, I managed to see one very large twenty-plus-inch brown over the two days of living the Austrian dream stream. The big brown wanted nothing to do with me and gave me two major refusals—even to big, meaty stone flies. Über-selectivity and fussiness were at work with these wild and wary fish. Here, the key factor for success was the behavior of the natural, and moving the stone fly the way it did as it gyrated, crawled, and bumped along the swift Alpine river's floor. In an afterthought, I believe the flashes by the trout, which I assumed were refusals, were actually "takers," where I set the hook too early or too late and pulled the nymphs out of the fish's mouth. The moral of this story is let the fish take your fly in swift current waters—the flow will set the hook for you. Don't blow the hook-set!

Late in the day, when the sun finally appeared and warmed everything up, the first brown mayflies of March began to hatch, and also began their waxing and waning spinner flights high above the water in the evening sunset. Warblers and swallows snatched up as many as they could. A good trout started to feed above the bridge as I prepared to depart. I knew the call of the river and these beautiful Alpine waters would whisper in my ears and haunt me until I returned.

On the Table

Austrian Cuisine: More Than Strudels and Wiener Schnitzel

If there ever was a modern-day chef who embodies everything we love about food—comfort, creativity, formality, and sumptuousness—it is Wolfgang Puck. He started his apprenticeship and schooling at the finest French restaurants of the time, such as Maxim's in Paris and the Hotel de Paris in Monaco. He arrived in Los Angles and worked at Ma Maison, the dining hub for the Hollywood elite. Then he opened Spago and Chinois, the foundations for modern American bistro food today. There, he incorporated a fusion of French, Italian, and Asian cuisine, always sprinkling in his Austrian roots, and fueled the modern American desire for comfort food.

But it is those Austrian ski chalets, gasthaus country inns, rathskellers hofbraus, and traditional German-fare restaurants, with

old names like Aplenhof and Edelweiss, that have been breeding grounds for Michelin-star restaurants of today, such as Amador and Steirereck. This is where traditional contemporary Austrian cuisine is being forged by modern Austrian chefs who are imparting variations to traditional Viennese dishes. Today, on the Salzach River where I fished, stands the wonderful four-star Hotel Bräurup, the only fishing lodge in Austria. It has private fly-fishing waters, guides, and a fly shop. Their house brewery offers specialty lagers and ales, and you can dine on excellent cuisine with house specialties like Wiener schnitzel or fresh-caught trout from the Salzach.

We stereotype traditional European fare with certain signature dishes of the motherland, but the new contemporary beat of cuisine is the forager and hunter. Culinary fusion means wild game like elk and deer, duck and wild boar, grouse and pheasant, rabbit and other hunter's fare. This has always been the food of the country that practices nose-to-tail butchering. The sausages, meat pies, pâtés, and charcuterie boards featured in their gasthaus eateries embody that ideal. The pastries and beer are literally the icing on the cake, where the traditional meets the modern-day comfort gourmet.

PREVIOUS AND ABOVE: When fishing an Alpine river, you never know what will come parading through: cattle, a European stag or deer, mountain goats, wild boar—the wildlife is part of the experience. Not to mention the clanging of herding bells and an occasional Alpine horn (alphorn). Also, the clear, cold waters harbor a stone fly heaven, along with burrowing mayflies and caddis larvae that all Euro nymphers try to imitate.

Weissenkirch
Riesling
Federspiel 202
Wachau | Austria

Alpine Strudel
with Wild Mushroom Duxelles, Asparagus & Gruyère

This dish just sums up the whole amazing Alpine comfort food experience.

Serves 4 to 6

- 1½ pounds mixed mushrooms, coarsely chopped
- 1 shallot, coarsely chopped
- Leaves from 3 thyme sprigs, plus more for garnish
- 2 tablespoons unsalted butter
- Coarse sea salt and freshly ground black pepper
- 6 green or white asparagus spears, cooked and chopped
- 2 (14-ounce) sheets Dufour puff pastry, thawed
- 1 cup shredded Gruyère
- 1 large egg, beaten
- Flaky salt for sprinkling

In a food processor, pulse the mushrooms, shallot, and thyme until finely chopped.

Melt the butter in a medium skillet over medium heat. Add the mushroom mixture and cook until the liquid has evaporated, about 25 minutes. Season with salt and pepper. Gently mix in the asparagus.

Preheat the oven to 425°F.

Unfold one sheet of pastry, flatten out the creases by pressing lightly with damp fingers, and roll to even out. Repeat with the second sheet.

Place the rectangle on a parchment-lined baking sheet. Spread the duxelle mixture over the puff pastry in a mounded shape; don't spread to the edges of the puff pastry. Sprinkle with the cheese. Top with another sheet of puff pastry and pinch the edges all the way around to seal the pastry, forming a log shape.

Make a few slits in the top of the pastry dough with a sharp knife. Brush with egg wash and sprinkle with flaky salt.

Bake until the pastry is cooked through and golden, about 10 minutes. Let rest 10 minutes before slicing and serving.

Tyrolian Choucroute Garni
with Red Cabbage

Pork schnitzel, various weiss, brat and knackwurst, and wieners—coupled with my mother's sinfully delicious red cabbage, which I served on my guide trips with onions and applewood bacon, is simply pure comfort, Austrian style. Accompany with potato pancakes and you have died and gone to Alpine heaven! (Photo of dishes on following pages.)

Serves 4

RED CABBAGE

1 medium head red cabbage, thinly sliced

6 to 8 slices bacon

1½ cups apple cider vinegar

¾ cup sugar

¼ to ½ cup freshly ground black pepper

1 medium red onion, chopped

PORK CHOPS

4 (1-inch-thick) bone-in pork loin chops

Coarse sea salt and freshly ground black pepper

1 large egg

½ cup all-purpose flour

1 cup Italian-style seasoned breadcrumbs

4 teaspoons unsalted butter

SAUSAGE

2 (12-ounce) cans ale or lager

2 pounds sausage (any combo of Austrian wieners, wurstel, bratwurst, knackwurst, weisswurst, or Polish kielbasa)

Make the cabbage: Bring a large pot of water to a boil over high heat.

Add the cabbage and cook until softened but not completely limp, about 10 minutes. Drain in a colander and transfer the cabbage to a large bowl.

Cook the bacon in a large skillet over medium-low heat until crispy, 8 to 10 minutes. Transfer the bacon to a plate lined with paper towels. Discard half of the bacon grease. Stir the vinegar into the bacon fat left in the pan, then add the sugar and stir until dissolved. Stir the pepper. The mixture should be syrupy and have a sweet and sour taste with a peppery kick.

Pour this mixture over the cabbage. Add the onion and toss to combine. Set aside at room temperature until ready to serve. Crumble the bacon over the top just before serving.

Make the pork: Season the pork chops on all sides with salt and pepper.

Beat the egg in a shallow bowl. Put the flour and breadcrumbs in separate shallow bowls. Dredge the pork in flour, shaking off excess. Then turn the chops in the egg and coat thoroughly with breadcrumbs.

In a large skillet, melt the butter over medium heat. Place the breaded pork in the skillet and cook until browned and cooked through, 2 to 3 minutes per side. Set aside.

Make the sausages: Preheat the oven to 400°F or a grill on medium-high to 400°F.

In a large pot, bring the beer to a boil over high heat.

Boil the sausages in the beer until parcooked, 10 minutes. Transfer the sausages to a baking sheet and bake in the oven until browned and clear liquid seeps out, about 8 minutes for thick sausages and 6 minutes for thinner sausages. Or, if grilling, transfer the sausages to a platter, place them on the grill, and grill until clear liquid seeps out, about 8 minutes for thick sausages and 6 minutes for thinner. Set aside until ready to serve.

When ready to serve, transfer the cabbage to a large platter and top with the pork chops and sausage.

Potato Pancakes

Makes 16 pancakes

- 2 large eggs
- 2 tablespoons all-purpose flour
- Coarse sea salt and freshly ground black pepper
- 2½ pounds (about 4 medium) russet potatoes, peeled
- 1 medium yellow onion
- ½ cup extra-virgin olive oil
- Sour cream for serving
- Chopped chives for garnish

In a large bowl, whisk the eggs and flour with some salt and pepper.

Using the large holes of a box grater, grate the potatoes and onion, draining as much liquid as you can. Add the potatoes and onion to the egg mixture and mix gently with your hands.

In a large skillet over medium-high heat, warm the olive oil. Use a ¼ cup measuring cup to scoop mounds of the potato mixture into the skillet and flatten slightly. Add as many scoopfuls as will fit without overcrowding the pan (you will need to work in batches).

Fry until golden brown on both sides, 2 to 3 minutes per side. Transfer to a plate lined with paper towels to drain. Serve hot with a dollop of sour cream and a sprinkle of chives.

THE
WOLFGANG PU
COOKBOO
Recipes from Spago, Chinois and Points East and West
cilantro sauce
fried spinach

BAJA

Fishing the Sea of Cortez for Pez Gallo

KIRK DEETER

“The sea, once it casts its spell, holds one in its net of wonder forever.”

—JACQUES-YVES COUSTEAU

PREVIOUS: Scanning for shadows in search of roosterfish. **ABOVE:** The roosterfish, "pez gallo," is the prize for fly anglers in the Sea of Cortez. **OPPOSITE, TOP:** Sometimes you can chase them from the beach (you may have to wade into the water to reach them, like Jeff Rogers does here). **OPPOSITE, BOTTOM:** But the grandes are usually caught from a panga, casting back toward the shoreline.

The Sea of Cortez, also commonly known as the Gulf of California, is a roughly 750-mile-long section of the Pacific Ocean between Mexico's Baja California peninsula and the Mexican mainland. It was dubbed "the aquarium of the world" by none other than Jacques-Yves Cousteau, due to its amazing biodiversity. Nearly nine hundred species of fish can be found here, as well as 39 percent of the world's marine mammals.

For the sporting angler, there is no greater proving ground. From cabrilla (leopard grouper) that can be caught from the beach in the northern stretches of the Sea of Cortez in and around Gonzaga Bay, to the tip of Baja where the world-famous Bisbee's billfish tournament is based in Cabo San Lucas, there really might not be a more abundant and rewarding place for saltwater anglers to fish anywhere on the planet.

On the Water

For most fly anglers, the action is rightfully concentrated in an area known as the East Cape, starting northeast of Cabo San Lucas near Cabo Pulmo (where the only true coral reef on the Mexican Pacific coast is found) and extending north along the gulf toward the city of La Paz and beyond.

Here, depending on the season, an angler might encounter any number of fish species that can be caught on a fly pattern—from yellowfin tuna and yellowtail to dorado (called dolphin or mahi-mahi in other places), giant crevalle jacks the locals simply call *toros* because they fight like bulls, several different species of marlin, sailfish, snapper, grouper,

and the king of them all, the vaunted pez gallo (roosterfish).

The beautiful thing about fishing this region is that the seafloor drops dramatically within a short distance from the beach (the San Andreas Fault runs straight down the middle of the Sea of Cortez) so you can literally catch dorado or skipjacks and many other species in the pretty blue water within a few strokes off the beach on a stand-up paddleboard.

But the star of the show, the roosterfish, can be caught *from* the beach, as well as from a panga boat you might hire a local captain to run. Made famous by the short film *Running Down the Man*, pez gallo (anywhere from three to one-hundred-plus pounds) occupies its own sacred niche in the fly-fishing world. These fish cruise the drop-offs in search of baitfish, and when they lock in on a target near the surface, they charge like rockets. A rooster's distinctive combed dorsal fin slices above the waterline as the fish accelerates with primal velocity. You have to strip the line as fast as you can (sometimes with both hands, having tucked the rod under your arm). And when you see that distinctive comb and know the fish is chasing *your* fly—that'll make the knees of even the most seasoned angler buckle.

Roosters are not the fastest, maybe not the fiercest, fish. It's the combination of those things that sets them apart. If they were football players, they'd be linebackers. They are arguably the most uniquely beautiful fish—exotic and sleek, with fins that seem as much decorative as functional—to be caught anywhere in the world on the fly. Ask any die-hard tarpon angler, trout master, or bonefish guru what their bucket-list fish is, and the

When you see that comb stand up and start chasing your fly, there's nothing else in the fly world quite as exciting. Expert roosterfish guide Jeff DeBrown of The Reel Baja releases a sporty rooster.

The Drake

ABOVE: The desert meets the ocean in Baja. It's a hot, unforgiving landscape that's uniquely alluring. **LEFT:** The famous rock formation "El Arco" marks land's end at the tip of the Baja peninsula at Cabo San Lucas. This natural arch is seen by many as the gateway to the greatest sport fishery in the world.

roosterfish is sure to be at or near the top of the list, with very good reason.

As such, in my humble opinion, no saltwater fly angler's life is complete without at least having a go at pez gallo.

But be careful what you wish for, and know the deal going in. Fishing the Sea of Cortez from the beach, or a boat, is extremely physical. It's hot (the fishing season is typically the less windy months between late April and early October, half of which is also hurricane season). The fish themselves take no prisoners—even a little skipjack will turn you into a sweaty mess, and any sizable roosterfish means at least a thirty-minute fight.

Fishing here demands long casts with heavy rods and lines. You need backups . . . rods shatter regularly. You strip line until your fingers bleed, and you literally wilt under the tropical sun (you're almost directly on the Tropic of Cancer in most places).

An Angler's Rite of Passage

My best roosterfish memory happened with my friend, Gary Bulla, a Californian turned Baja roosterfish guru, who has organized trips here for decades. While riding along the shoreline of Isla Cerralvo, we spied a pair of bruiser roosterfish in an ocean swell. They were booking down the beach, obviously on the hunt. I somehow managed to cast a silver and white baitfish imitation right where both fish could see it. One literally bumped the other out of the way and charged the fly. I'll never forget watching that giant rooster open its maw, wider than a dinner plate. It sucked that fly down like it was eating a peanut M&M.

"He's on it! He's got it!" Gary belted.

I knew darn well that fish had it. From the time the fly hit the water to the "eat," with all the shouting in between, might have really taken two seconds. But it seemed like much longer. I gave that fly line three sharp tugs to set the hook, and once I knew I was buttoned on, I let go of the line. We just listened to the reel purr as that fish ripped line toward the horizon.

So, as is often the case with fly fishing, during the fight it's easy to think that making the cast in the first place only "seemed like a good idea at the time." That rooster surely brought the notion home. But after some bloody knuckles, a lot of sweat, and a little bit of mumbled prayer, we brought it to the boat, unhooked it, snapped a couple photos, and that was that. My life goal of catching a fat rooster on a fly was accomplished. It stands as one of my favorite fishing feats—ever, anywhere.

The roosters tend to show up in numbers around the East Cape in Baja around April and last into the middle of summer. In late summer and early fall, when the water is warmest, the focus of the fly fishing shifts to dorados. This is when you can find the big "bulls" around weed mats, mooring buoys, and other structures. There's something special about seeing a neon-colored dorado all lit up, slashing at your fly. The take is often violent, and the subsequent jumps are spectacular.

Dorado are also among the fastest-growing (and best-tasting) fish in the ocean. So, taking a few home to turn into ceviche or fish tacos isn't much of a strain on the resource.

Winter months tend to be windy, and the beach resorts are taken over by kite surfers who'd just as soon yield the hot, less breezy months to anglers. It's a good symbiosis that keeps the East Cape beach towns in business and, for the most part, safe.

To borrow from Sinatra, if you can make it as an angler in Baja, you can make it anywhere, and there isn't a bonefish or tarpon flat, striper blitz, or even giant trevally spot in the world that might intimidate you on any level after you've proven yourself on the Sea of Cortez.

On the Table

As for the fly-fishing food scene, Baja is among the most eclectic in the world. That certainly begins with traditional Mexican food—tortillas, rajas, beans, and the like—but given how Baja has been a magnet for Californians looking to fish, surf, or just chill, there's now also a hefty influence of Cali culture, and much of that is also Asian influenced. Add to that the fact that Baja juts into the world's most prolific natural aquarium, and the fare is understandably dominated by riches from the sea.

Put all of that together and you'll find a diverse, savory array of options, ranging from staples like fish tacos and wahoo ceviche, to sushi cakes, yellowtail or yellowfin tuna sashimi, barbecued snapper and grouper (*a la parilla*), octopus salad, and more.

It's worth noting that certain drinks stand out as Baja favorites as well. Given how hot it can be—and with any luck, how strenuous the fishing action often can be—you will find no more welcome refreshment on a fishing boat than a glass bottle of Mexican Coca-Cola (made with real sugar), dug from the bottom of an ice-packed cooler . . . or an equally chilled bottle of cerveza, perhaps with a pinch of salt and wedge of lime dropped down the bottleneck before your first sip (watch that bubbling backsplash if you add the salt!). Margaritas are best saved for happy hour, and since you've likely been up fishing since five a.m. limited to one, otherwise you might zonk out before sunset.

But that's okay. Tomorrow's almost always another sunny day in Baja.

Days end on the East Cape in Baja usually signals an abrupt shift from piscatorial pursuit to epicurean adventure. From sweet, salty margaritas to spicy fish tacos . . . *todo bien*.

SALADITAS

Fish Tacos

The type of fish you use to make fish tacos, and how you choose to cook it, is totally up to you. In Baja, dorado (mahi-mahi) is a common option. But that often depends on the catch of the day—could be wahoo, grouper, snapper, or any number of species. If you were to order fish tacos at many food trucks or restaurants in Baja, there's a good chance the fish will be deep-fried. A simple batter of flour, baking powder, garlic powder, paprika, salt, and pepper mixed with beer or water to make a pasty consistency is usually fine. See the batter recipe for English fish and chips on page 174 for a good starting point . . . just know the batter will be on a different type of fish.

If you're not into frying (or air-frying), baking the fish in an oven at 425°F for 12 minutes will work just fine.

The real lesson I've learned when it comes to fish tacos is that *less is more.* Focus on fewer ingredients. Do them well, and combine them in a way that matters, rather than packing so many flavors into a tortilla it will only confuse your taste buds. And you don't do lettuce with fish tacos . . . you do cabbage.

Serves 6

The best way to serve fish tacos is to make a "build your own" taco bar and let everyone choose their own toppings. Here's what you will need:

Flour or corn tortillas, lightly toasted to the point of crispiness (I lean toward flour)

1 to 2 pounds fresh fish, fried, baked, or blackened on a hot skillet, preferably dorado, halibut, grouper, wahoo, or snapper

3 cups shredded red cabbage

2 medium to large red onions, finely chopped

2 cups picked cilantro leaves

1 to 2 (15.5-ounce) cans black beans, warmed, for serving

4 cups cooked white rice for serving

4 to 6 jalapeño peppers, seeded and finely diced (optional)

4 to 5 medium to large avocados, pitted, flesh diced

Herdez green salsa mixed with mayonnaise and Valentina salsa picante for serving

Shrimp-a-Mole

Two classic appetizers—shrimp cocktail and guacamole—in one! This simple yet intriguing appetizer takes regular guac up a notch with the addition of succulent shrimp bits and zippy cocktail sauce in lieu of salsa to bind it all together.

Serves 4 to 8

- 8 ounces jumbo (10/15) shrimp
- Salt
- 4 to 5 large ripe avocados, pitted
- 1 medium white onion, finely chopped
- 2 to 3 tablespoons finely chopped cilantro leaves
- ½ cup spicy-hot horseradish cocktail sauce, such as Kelchner's or Beaver Brand Extra Hot
- Juice of ½ fresh lime
- Tortilla chips for serving

Boil the shrimp in a medium saucepan with salted water. Let cool, then peel, devein, and cut them into ¼-inch chunks.

Smash the avocado flesh in a large bowl. Add the shrimp, onion, cilantro, cocktail sauce, and lime juice and stir to combine. Cover and refrigerate for 1 hour. Serve with tortilla chips.

Shrimp & Octopus Ceviche

Ceviche—wherein citric acid "cooks" raw seafood that is mixed with onions, peppers, cilantro, and any number of other ingredients—is popular throughout Baja, and odds are, if you're staying at a fishing lodge, it's the first thing you'll be served when you step off the boat at the end of the day. There are virtually no limits to the types of seafood you can use, nor the vegetables you may add. Dorado (mahi-mahi) are plentiful and they are one of the fastest-growing fish in the ocean, so they end up in many ceviche dishes. The most prized fish for ceviche might just be wahoo. And for a unique combination of both texture and flavor, I especially like shrimp and octopus ceviche.

Serves 4

2 to 3 limes

3/4 cup finely chopped red onion

2 finely chopped radishes

1 medium jalapeño pepper, seeded and finely chopped

1/4 to 1/2 pound octopus, cut into 1/4-inch chunks (3/4 cup)

12 jumbo shrimp, peeled, deveined, and chopped into 1/4-inch chunks (1 cup)

Juice of 1 lemon

1/2 cup chopped unpeeled English cucumber

6 cherry tomatoes, quartered

1/2 cup chopped cilantro leaves

Coarse sea salt

Tajin seasoning (optional)

Tortilla chips for serving

Squeeze the juice of 2 of the limes into a glass bowl. Stir in the red onion and let sit for 10 to 15 minutes (the lime will make the onion less pungent). Then mix in the radishes and jalapeño.

Add the octopus, shrimp, and lemon juice and stir well, making sure the shrimp and octopus are well-coated. Add the cucumber and tomatoes, and stir again. At this point, you want to make sure there is enough juice to coat everything but not so much that the ingredients are swimming in juice. If you need more, add the juice of the third lime now; if you don't, leave it be. Add the cilantro, a pinch of salt, and/or a few dashes of Tajin seasoning. Transfer everything (especially the juice) to a more compact airtight container and refrigerate for at least 1 hour before serving the chilled ceviche with tortilla chips.

BELIZE

Fishing for Permit

KIRK DEETER

“Don’t call the alligator a ‘big mouth’ until you have crossed the river.”

—BELIZEAN PROVERB

I thought I was starting to get really good at this fly-fishing deal.

Then I started chasing permit.

Actually, my first dedicated permit-fishing excursion was hexed, if only because it went so perfectly well.

The first time I ever went permit fishing was with a guide in Belize. The guide saw a permit's signature black-sickle fin slicing along the flat, so he killed the engine of the panga boat we were fishing out of and told me to hop overboard and bring my rod.

We were planning on chasing just bonefish that day, so I only had an 8-weight with a small shrimp fly tied to a 10-pound leader . . .

No matter. "Let's go!" he whispered.

I took three steps out of that boat, fired a lucky forty-foot cast that landed near the fish. I then made several strips of the line and watched in amazement as that tail deliberately tilted and the fish ate my fly. I set the hook (with a strip-set, just as I had been taught), and I was in business! Less than ten minutes later, I landed permit numero uno.

First permit I ever saw. First cast I ever made to a permit. Fifteen-pounder landed to hand and released unharmed. *No problemo.* (But in our haste, I had forgotten my camera.)

Nothing to this permit stuff, I thought, *this isn't nearly as difficult as all the hoopla makes it out to be.*

I paid for that blasphemous thought, because over the course of the next seven days on those flats, I saw no fewer than forty other permit feeding and tailing—some looked like silver strobe lights blinking beneath the water surface. I made dozens of other casts that landed in the zone (some I thought were surely even more perfect than that first cast), and I repeatedly came up empty. I was deeply humbled. I deserved it.

On the Water

In the fly-fishing lexicon, there are many fish species purported to be the "fish of one thousand casts": muskellunge, wild steelhead, Atlantic salmon (depending on where you are), and others.

I've fished for them all.

But sight fishing with a fly rod—when you see the fish before you make the first cast, formulate your approach, and hope for the best—is tricky business. And doing so when chasing permit stands apart as the most challenging and ultimately rewarding (if you're lucky . . . and make no mistake, luck has a *huge* role to play) feat any fly angler might endeavor to tackle.

If you're foolish (or brave) enough to play the permit game, Belize is undoubtedly one of the best places to do it in the entire world.

That said, if you've grown up a trout angler, and you dream about taking that fly-fishing game to saltwater for the very first time, Belize is probably the perfect place to do that

PREVIOUS: The Belize Barrier Reef is a UNESCO World Heritage Site. **OPPOSITE:** Belize is about sight fishing on the flats with shrimp and crab fly patterns. And you might see the fish one hundred yards away (or more). If you're lucky, that fish could be a permit. And only if you're really lucky and good, you just might land one.

ABOVE: Permit, the dock, and a typical bonefish (the ghost of the flats). **OPPOSITE:** Keep that rod tip high! Any permit or bonefish can wrap you around a coral head and cut your fly line in an instant.

also—it's one of the best saltwater fly-fishing destinations worldwide for both newbies and seasoned veterans.

So Much to Explore

This small Central American country (formerly British Honduras) was the first place my wife and I chose to visit as I decided to venture into the salt for the first time, because Belize might just also be the best saltwater fly-fishing destination in the world to bring along a non-angling companion (or, in my case, one who is "not quite as interested in fishing as I am") for a number of reasons.

For the curious, Belize offers more tropical "side-adventure" opportunities than anywhere else. Roughly only the size of Massachusetts, Belize can accommodate pristine flats fishing, of course, but also some of the best scuba diving and snorkeling along the second-largest barrier reef in the world (second only to Australia's Great Barrier Reef). One can also explore Mayan ruins, take jungle excursions to caves and inland blue holes, go bird-watching, float down rivers, visit markets, even get a luxurious spa treatment at any number of jungle resorts in the Belizean interior, and much more. If you go to Belize and only fish or dive or snorkel offshore, you're cheating yourself out of one of the best jungle experiences to be had in the northern hemisphere. I recommend tacking a few jungle days onto any Belize fishing trip.

As for the fishing, Belize offers different opportunities and challenges. The party scene is in the town of San Pedro on Ambergris Caye, an island usually accessed via a short-hop flight from Belize City. But don't underestimate the fishing around Ambergris. El Pescador Lodge is probably the smartest bet for any angler who wants to taste a bit of all that fishing has to offer, in addition to some local culture and nightlife.

Personally, I like getting away from it all and being on the reef, some thirty miles or so offshore. The boat ride from Belize City is like a portal to a parallel universe—one far removed from crowds, traffic, bleeping phones, and Zoom conferences. Turneffe Flats Lodge caters to this crowd of anglers as well as divers. And there are vast schools of bonefish in this area. Though typically not monster-size, the bonefish throughout the Belizean flats are not fussy and perfectly suited for dabblers and aficionados alike.

The more interested you are in the chase for permit, the farther south in Belize you may want to venture. Placencia is considered permit central for Belize, but Turneffe Atoll and Ambergris Caye offer plenty of shots at permit during most months. (*Shots* . . . nobody is brave enough to promise that permit will eat your flies anywhere.)

If tarpon is your game, the Belize River is where the big boys tend to hang, though, again, you can catch silver kings off Ambergris and out on the atolls often. But if you're tarpon-fixed, I'd go to the Belize River Lodge. That's where the resident fish and the big boys live.

On the Table

Food in Belize is an adventure in and of itself. And like everything else here, Belizean cuisine is a comforting mix of many cultural influences—part Caribbean, part Latin American, with heavy amounts of Creole (locally *Kriol*), English, American, and even a dash of Asian influences mixed together for good measure.

Those last moments are the most tenuous. You made the cast . . . you fought the fight . . . but can you at least touch the leader, maybe even land the permit? This is where heartbreak and hero shots both happen.

Caribbean spiny lobsters can be found in abundance along the barrier reef in Belize, but be sure to mind all regulations and closed seasons.

A fresh-caught, grilled snapper might be the dish of the day along the coast, while street tacos are hard to pass up as you stroll through the inland jungle town of San Ignacio. Stewed chicken is my favorite.

Among the first lessons to be learned about Belizean cuisine is that "beans and rice" and "rice and beans" are two distinctly different dishes, and you'll find those everywhere. In Belize, rice and beans are both staple food items. They are eaten daily throughout the country. But "rice and beans" tends to be the bigger production, often served with Sunday dinner in most (if not all) Belizean households. While individual recipes vary, rice and beans are cooked together in one pot, typically with coconut milk or oil and spices. Onions, peppers, and garlic are optional and based on individual family recipes.

On the other hand, "beans and rice" are cooked separately. The beans tend to be cooked with the same ingredients as rice and beans with the addition of some pork (maybe even a pig's tail) for flavoring. The beans are then served on top of a helping of white rice.

Lesson two: Fry jacks are another staple that usually take the place of toast or muffins alongside fried or scrambled eggs, bacon, sausage, and fresh fruit on a breakfast plate. While there are different twists on recipes, the appeal of fry jacks is that they're incredibly basic, and most involve only a handful of ingredients—all-purpose flour, shortening, baking powder, a pinch or two of salt, and water—then they're usually fried in oil (typically vegetable oil, but coconut oil works too). A good fry jack is meant to complement and soak in the flavors around it rather than be the featured attraction.

Lesson number three: Marie Sharp's hot sauce is served with just about everything in Belize—at breakfast, lunch, and dinner. There are several different varieties, but my favorites (and the most popular) are the Famous Original and Fiery versions, though I can't tell much difference between the two. They are carrot-based habanero pepper sauces that are actually flavor enhancing, and not just "hot for the sake of hot only." Marie Sharp's still makes its sauces with fresh ingredients in the Stann Creek region south of Belize City. I think it's the best hot sauce I've ever tasted, so I still regularly load up on five-ounce bottles (you can easily order it online if your local grocer doesn't carry it), and I pack a bottle in my kit for every fishing trip I take. Marie Sharp's will make the blandest food more than tolerable, and I suppose if I were marooned somewhere and had to eat my boots, I could probably do it if I had a bottle of Marie Sharp's.

A lot of fishing is a moveable feast that you take with you wherever you subsequently travel, and in the case of this dash of Belizean cuisine, I mean that quite literally.

Belizean Stew Chicken

This is a traditional family feast that makes the whole house smell good as the chicken simmers in an array of spices. It's the ideal representation of the cultural melting pot that is Belizean cuisine. Serve with rice & beans, and fried plantains (recipes follow).

Serves 4 to 6

2 tablespoons achiote powder

2 tablespoons white vinegar

2 tablespoons Worcestershire sauce

2 tablespoons ground cumin

1 teaspoon dried oregano

1 teaspoon dried thyme

3 pounds bone-in chicken thighs, skin removed

2 tablespoons coconut oil

1 tablespoon light or dark brown sugar

1 white onion, finely chopped

1 green bell pepper, finely diced

6 cloves garlic, crushed or chopped

2 cups low-sodium chicken broth

1 bay leaf

Coarse sea salt and freshly ground black pepper

2 to 3 strips cooked bacon (optional)

Marie Sharp's hot sauce for serving

In a large bowl, mix the achiote, vinegar, Worcestershire, cumin, oregano, and thyme. Add the chicken pieces and coat completely.

In a large Dutch oven over medium heat, melt the coconut oil and brown sugar. Stir together until completely blended. Add the chicken, reserving the remaining marinade. Brown the chicken on both sides, about 5 minutes per side. Transfer to a plate.

Add the onion, bell pepper, and garlic to the pot and cook until the onion is translucent, stirring frequently, about 10 minutes.

Add the chicken broth, bay leaf, and any remaining marinade to the pot. Stir together. Return the chicken thighs to the pot and bring to a boil. Reduce the heat to low and simmer, covered, until the chicken is tender, about 1 hour, stirring occasionally. Season with salt and pepper, then add crumbled bacon, if using. Serve family-style with hot sauce on the side.

Rice & Beans

1 cup dried red kidney beans

1 tablespoon vegetable oil

1 medium white onion

4 cloves garlic

1½ cups coconut milk

2 cups white rice, rinsed in cold water

1 teaspoon paprika or achiote

1 teaspoon dried thyme

Marie Sharp's hot sauce

Rinse the kidney beans and soak in a bowl of water overnight.

Warm the vegetable oil in a large pot over medium heat. Sauté the onion and garlic in the hot oil until the onion is translucent, about 10 minutes. Add the coconut milk, 2½ cups water, drained beans, rice, paprika, and thyme and bring to a boil.

Reduce the heat to low and simmer, covered, until the rice is cooked, about 20 to 30 minutes. Serve the hot sauce alongside.

Fried Plantains

2 ripe plantains (see Note)

2 to 3 tablespoons coconut or vegetable oil

Coarse sea salt and freshly ground black pepper

Peel the plantains and cut on the diagonal about ½ inch thick.

Heat the oil in a large frying pan over medium heat. Add the plantains and brown them on both sides, 3 to 5 minutes per side. Transfer to a plate with a slotted spoon and season with salt and pepper.

Note: The plantains for this dish should be soft to the touch and the skins should be yellow and brown.

MARIE SHARP'S
BELIZE
THE FAMOUS
MARIE SHARP'S

BRAZIL

Jungle Angling in the Amazon Basin

KIRK DEETER

"Even more complex and dangerous than the river itself were the fishes, mammals, and reptiles that inhabited it. Like the rainforest that surrounds and depends upon it, the Amazon River system is a prodigy of speciation and diversity, serving as home to more than three thousand species of freshwater fishes . . . By comparison, the entire Missouri and Mississippi river system that drains much of North America has only about 375 fish."

—CANDICE MILLARD

I have been on many long flights over South America. What always strikes me as I look out the airplane window is just how vast, dark, and mysterious the Amazon rainforest seems, even in comparison to the open ocean. You can gaze for hours on nothing but deep, dark landscape—some of the last remaining lightly touched wilderness on the planet. From thirty-five-thousand feet above, at night especially, it seems like there's absolutely nothing there.

Of course, nothing could be further from the truth. There's more life packed acre by acre from the jungle canopy to the forest floor in the Amazon than anywhere else in the world. And this jungle even pumps life into other parts of the earth. The Amazon rainforest, while it is certainly—ever-increasingly—threatened by the encroachment of civilization, is one of the de facto "lungs" of the planet. It's here where the plant life converts more carbon dioxide into oxygen than anywhere else.

When your feet are on the ground (or you are in a boat on the river) in the jungle, the darkness literally bursts into a stunning array of color, sound, and earthy, almost spicy smells. There's *so much life* there, it's bewildering.

And the jungle experience is indelible. Long after I return home from a jungle adventure, as I lay my head on a pillow to sleep at night, I can still hear the insects buzz and the monkeys scream. It's actually soothing—like a natural lullaby sung in a whisper by Mother Earth.

Fly fishing in the jungles of South America today is what the golden age of the Big Five on African safaris was a century or more ago.

Wide open.

Abundant.

Still being discovered and explored. Deeply understood by very few.

If you really want to experience the ragged edge of the fly-fishing world, you should endeavor to become a jungle angler. But be warned—once you experience the deepest rainforests and pull on fish like these, well . . . you'll never be the same again. You'll never think of fly fishing for trout in the same context, nor will you even think about saltwater fishing for bonefish, tarpon, or permit in the same light.

On the Water

The quarry (and this merely scratches the surface):

Arapaima: Mighty, prehistoric fish that seem like a freshwater version of tarpon, except when you hook one; it's just as likely to attack the boat and thump you with its tail as it is to jump and bound away.

Payara: The "vampire fish" looks like a piscatorial version of the saber-toothed tiger, and fights like no other. Watch your fingers.

Wolffish: Nasty, toothy, ugly critters that often share water with electric eels. They aren't terribly difficult to hook, because they eat most

PREVIOUS: Certain rivers in the Amazon system are ideal for sight casting. **OPPOSITE:** There are various subspecies of peacock bass, each with distinctive colors and characteristics, from the butterfly peacock to the enormous *Chicla temensis* strain that can tip the scales at well over twenty pounds.

things around them, but they're tricky to land and release.

Piranha: Yes, they can strip a carcass clean in a matter of minutes when they swim in schools, but what the angler really has to worry about is them eating the fish you just hooked before you can land it. Some piranhas are actually pretty good dinner fare.

Yatorana: Lightning sleek, they are the bonefish of the Amazon. Fast, wily, and often pretty selective, you can sometimes get them to eat the grasshopper flies you use in Michigan or Montana off the river surface.

Pacu: The permit of the freshwater jungle. Similar in shape and profile but darker in color, they can be just as frustrating and difficult to land as the permit. But sometimes they'll eat berries that drop into the river. Maybe the best fish for sight fishing in the jungle.

Peacock bass: There are many different brilliantly colored and supremely aggressive species of peacock bass, and they're all wonderful. A wild peacock bass from South America would eat any North American bass for lunch.

If You Liked *That*, My Friend . . .

My personal fascination with jungle angling evolved over time, and it actually started with a brown trout fishing trip to Tierra del Fuego in Argentina (following the same darn fish that got me into fly fishing in the first place to one of the furthest points in the world I could imagine). I was writing for *Field & Stream* magazine at the time.

As I sat at a table in a Buenos Aires steak restaurant after the trip and the night before flying home to the States, Marcelo Perez (who had invited me to fish the Rio Irigoyen, the world's southernmost trout river) said: "I have another adventure in mind. We've found a place in Bolivia where there are giant

OPPOSITE: Arapaima (*top and bottom right*) and payara. **TOP:** Camp on the Xingu River. **BOTTOM:** A peacock bass tries to hide, but the telltale spot on its tail gives it away.

dorados. If you think you might want to write a story . . ." Natives consider these golden fish with ferocious teeth and black spots to be one of two sons of Tupã the sun god, the other being the jaguar.

"Sure, I'm in. I'll go. When?" I interrupted.

Six months later, I found myself landing in Santa Cruz, Bolivia, in the middle of the night, where I was scooped up by Marcelo and a team of South American explorers. We spent three weeks in country, first provisioning in Santa Cruz, then driving through the night to Trinidad to earn access and buy-in from the Indigenous Tsimané people (many signed the agreement with thumbprints). We then flew in a Cessna to an airstrip cocaine runners had cut into the jungle near the Indigenous village of Asunta and spent two weeks exploring and camping in tents in the jungle. There were often fresh jaguar prints pressed into the sandy playas where we camped.

The whole experience scared the heck out of me. Intensely aware of the impending presence of anacondas, freshwater stingrays, and other nasty critters, I think I spent 90 percent of the time staring at my feet. But I also realized that jungle fishing was on an entirely different level than anything I had done before.

I wrote the story for *Field & Stream*, which earned some accolades and simultaneously put the company Untamed Angling and fly fishing in South America on the map. As such, I also became one of the *hermanos de selva* (brothers of the jungle), which remains one of the greatest sources of pride I've ever had as a fly fisherman, a writer, an editor, or anything else.

The Jungle Anglers

Once you start down the jungle-fishing path, one adventure leads to another. Perhaps no fisherman in the world understands the Amazon like Rodrigo Salles, who grew up fishing the interior of Brazil with his grandfather. Rodrigo invited me to make more stories, and I subsequently found myself in places I had read about in books that chronicled the ill-fated quests to discover El Dorado and Teddy Roosevelt's expedition along the Rio da Dúvida (River of Doubt) that now bears his name. I never imagined actually being there myself.

The paradox of the jungle is that it seems like a veritable Shangri-la, with macaws flying overhead, monkeys swinging among the branches, flowers blooming, and butterflies fluttering along each riverbend playa.

But the dark truth is that it's difficult for any organism to survive here, and many creatures—from tiny parasites and bugs to fierce jungle cats—would just as soon eat you if given half a chance. I once watched a harpy eagle fly overhead with a screaming spider monkey clutched in its talons. It was a stark lesson on how the jungle food chain worked. Over the centuries, many thousands of humans have perished, seemingly (sometimes literally) swallowed by the landscape and the animals that live therein.

Rodrigo and Marcelo created their unique company, Untamed Angling, specifically to take adventuring anglers deep into the heart of the Amazon—with an uncanny shroud of safety and comfort that would have been completely implausible just a few decades ago. They fish places like the Xingu River, where Percy Fawcett and his entire

PREVIOUS: An arapaima will attack your boat and make spectacular jumps. **OPPOSITE:** Many American anglers expect jungle rivers to be muddy and are surprised to realize how clear some of them can be.

expedition perished in search of the Lost City of Z, and the Rio Marié in the northwest corner of Brazil, where one can live aboard a posh, custom riverboat to chase the vaunted *Cichla temensis* strain of peacock bass, which can tip the scales at an astounding twenty pounds or more.

The magic that allows the outsider angler to experience these adventures, unharmed, is that Untamed Angling has solidified partnerships with Indigenous communities. They've found a way to forge relationships, so sport fishing is now a viable economic driver, enough that it protects a way of life and preserves the landscapes in the face of constant threats like mining, logging, cattle grazing, and other commercial ventures that would otherwise destroy the rainforest.

Out On the Edge

And that's how I ended up flying to a dirt airstrip in a place more than a hundred miles from the nearest paved road, among the Kayapo—the guardians of the rainforest. I had bought a soccer ball and some cleats to offer as gifts upon my arrival (I have learned that there is nowhere on earth where the popularity of the "beautiful game" is not appreciated, especially in Brazil) and, despite the language barrier, I was accepted as a friend.

Our Kayapo guides ferried us downriver, portaging boats around challenging rapids, until we arrived at an austere yet remarkably efficient camp, replete with bedrooms, makeshift indoor plumbing, and even a lounge where we could sit, sip cocktails, and listen to bossa nova music.

The next morning, I awoke to find one of the Kayapo women painting my face and arms in traditional patterns. Then we set off to fish.

After stringing up an 8-weight fly rod and tying on a streamer fly, I waded into the surprisingly cool, crystalline currents and starting making casts. From bank to bank, it seemed like I was fishing a trout stream, like I had done thousands of times before.

Then a tapir emerged from the jungle, and waded across the river, about fifty yards from where I stood.

I waited for a while in silence and just looked around.

How in the heck did I ever end up here? I wondered.

Then, after several minutes, I loaded up and made another cast.

On the Table

Brazil is another food paradise: There are many complex flavors from natural ingredients, including those from the rivers and jungle. In a jungle camp, you experience many fish dishes, meat stews, even beef and sausages roasted on spits and skewered. There are abundant berries, root vegetables, and leafy greens. There's so much to choose from—with profiles from mellow to spicy—all from a literal melting pot of influences from the Portuguese to Indigenous traditions. Brazil is also seeing a very vibrant and quickly evolving cosmopolitan epicurean renaissance. Much of Brazilian cuisine is regional, and based on what's most readily available in that area. Regardless of where you are, however, you can count on at least some type of complex stew. The drinks are juice-based and delicious.

For this, I chose (with Rodrigo's help) some dishes that any home cook can create . . .

OPPOSITE, CLOCKWISE FROM TOP: Wet-wading for peacock bass; a hooked arapaima lunges; macaws are a common sight in the jungle.

Butterfly Peacock Bass Salad
with Grapefruit Vinaigrette

I met Chef Leandro Ettomi on a jungle adventure to fish the Rio Marié in northwestern Brazil. According to Chef Ettomi, this dish combines clean Amazonian flavors with Japanese technique and balance.

Serves 4

1¾ pounds butterfly peacock bass fillets or tilapia

8 sheets nori seaweed

Salt

10½ ounces carrots, peeled and chopped

2 ripe avocados, pitted and flesh removed

Juice of 2 limes

Freshly ground black pepper

10½ ounces zucchini

1 tablespoon mirin

1 tablespoon sake

1 tablespoon sesame oil

Juice of 2 grapefruits

1 tablespoon Dijon mustard

Extra-virgin olive oil

Bring a large pot of water to a boil over high heat.

Cut the fish fillets into 8 sticks approximately 3 inches long and ¾ inch wide. Wrap each piece individually with a sheet of nori. Group four wrapped sticks together and roll them tightly in plastic wrap. Refrigerate until ready to cook.

Once the water is boiling, salt it and add the carrots. Cook until tender, about 10 minutes. Once soft, transfer to a blender and blend until smooth. Set aside and clean the blender.

Place the avocado flesh in the blender with the lime juice and blend until creamy and smooth. Season lightly with salt and pepper and reserve.

Using a mandoline or sharp knife, slice the zucchini into thin ribbons. Place the ribbons in a medium bowl with the mirin, sake, and sesame oil and let marinate for 10 minutes.

In a small bowl, whisk together the grapefruit juice, mustard, and a drizzle of olive oil until emulsified. Season with salt and pepper.

Bring 2 inches of water in a high-sided skillet to 176°F, as measured on an instant-read thermometer. Remove the fish rolls from the refrigerator and gently poach them in the water for 15 minutes. Remove and allow to cool slightly before slicing into medallions approximately ¾ inch thick.

Arrange the marinated zucchini ribbons on each of four plates. Place the sliced fish medallions over the zucchini lengthwise. Add spoonfuls of the carrot and avocado purées to each plate. Finish with a generous drizzle of grapefruit vinaigrette.

Poling a skiff in the jungle in search of peacock bass.

Glazed Pork Belly
with Roasted Pepper Purée

According to Chef Ettomi, this dish is a vibrant balance of richness and brightness—the lacquered pork is deeply savory, the purée smooth and smoky, and the pickled onions add a pop of acidity. A modern Brazilian twist on a classic comfort combination.

Serves 4

7 tablespoons white vinegar

2 tablespoons sugar

About 9 ounces red onions, thinly sliced into rings

7 tablespoons soy sauce

Scant 3½ tablespoons apple juice

Scant 3½ tablespoons apple cider vinegar

3 tablespoons honey

2¼ pounds pork belly

2¼ pounds sweet potatoes, peeled and cut into ¾-inch cubes

1 pound red bell peppers

5 ounces boiled potatoes

2 tablespoons extra-virgin olive oil

Preheat the oven to 300°F.

In a bowl, combine the white vinegar and sugar. Add the onions and let them pickle until ready to serve.

Combine the soy sauce, apple juice, apple cider vinegar, honey, and scant 3½ tablespoons water in a bowl. Whisk until fully blended. Set the glaze aside.

Place the pork belly in a cast-iron skillet and roast for 3 hours, basting with the glaze every 20 minutes. The glaze will slowly caramelize and lacquer the surface of the meat. Increase the oven temperature to 400°F.

Put the sweet potatoes in a single layer on a baking sheet and roast until golden brown and tender, 20 to 25 minutes. Increase the oven temperature to 500°F.

Place the bell peppers in a single layer on a baking sheet lined with foil and roast until the skins are charred and the flesh is tender, about 10 minutes. Once cool enough to handle, peel the peppers, remove the seeds, and place them in a blender with the boiled potatoes. Blend, then add the olive oil while blending. Process until the purée is silky smooth.

To serve, slice the pork belly into thick strips, about 1 inch wide. Arrange the strips on each of four plates with the sweet potato cubes and a quenelle or ring of roasted pepper purée. Garnish with the pickled red onion rings.

CATSKILLS

Fishing the Catskill Rivers for Brown Trout

MATTHEW SUPINSKI

"There are deeper gorges, greater streams, and higher mountains but in no other place is the combination so blended into a harmony so perfect as to form such tempting bits for the camera or the brush."
—EDWARD F. BIGELOW

If the almighty created a template for what a trout stream should look like it would be based on one in the Catskills. Its free-stone and ice-cold tailwater wonders have everything that trout and the aquatic insects they feed on need. Over the ages, gorgeous canyons of large sedimentary and volcanic rock have carved out enticing river pools and eddies, and long, gravely riffles and gentle flats. Aquatic greenery, like water-cress and duckwort, garnish these hallowed waters and emanate from its cold, spring-fed sources. Or the icy flows come from the frigid, calcareous-rock-carved depths of reservoirs that created these perfect wild trout factories. Here they swim happily and rise ever so gently and selectively to feed on an endless flotilla of mayflies that skitter across the water like flailing sailboats.

This leads to the ultimate temptation for the trout angler to seek out and cover every inch of these waters, since every river reveals its nuances through each river bend. Hence trout is forever king in the Catskills. It will never be dethroned or have second billing. And because of that, almost every major book on fly fishing for trout originated, or had strong attachments to, this true cradle of American fly fishing. It's a shrine we must forever embrace and honor until the last trout still swims in the legendary Cairn's Pool on the iconic Beaverkill.

PREVIOUS: Floating the Catskill tailwaters and even the lower Beaverkill when it is high is a great way to cover water and approach trout lying in deep pools and runs where wading is impossible. **OPPOSITE:** Angler casts on the hallowed ground-zero Neversink tailwater. **ABOVE:** A brown trout most likely bulge feeding with its back and fins sticking above water. Catskill browns and rainbows are known for feeding where insects are in the stillborn/emerger state.

On the Water

Over the many decades that I have been coming here, and now call it a second home, I have learned to love the Catskills' hidden secrets, which reveal themselves slowly over time—and only in small, never-ending, intoxicating doses. My reintroduction to this area came when I made an impulsive trip to visit a beautiful lady I had just met who would eventually become my wife. I had forty-eight hours off from my food and beverage job in D.C., and an invite to her family's summer home in the Catskills. It had been at least fifteen years since my last visit to these hallowed grounds. As my exit on the Quickway came up, I found the Katrina Falls Road and couldn't wait to get out and stretch my legs and explore. Looking back at it today, that most memorable trip embedded in my soul the two things that I will love until the day I die: the wonderful lady I married and these soul-captivating mountains and legendary trout rivers that flow through them.

TOP: Walt and Win Dette, fly-tying legends in the Catskills. Winnie's dad owned the Riverview Inn where, in Ferdon's Eddy on a cold spring day, he ushered in the invention of the Hendrickson fly by Roy Steenrod. Their great-great grandson, Joe Fox, still runs Dette's Fly Shop in Livingston Manor, a must-stop for everyone coming to the Catskills! **BOTTOM:** The indigenous brook trout with its fall colors is a sight to behold. **OPPOSITE, CLOCKWISE FROM TOP:** J. G. Miller with a beast of a wild Delaware brown; the Hendrickson nymph; a stunning *Isonychia* mayfly.

Inspiring a Passion for Brown Trout

It was a true epiphany when I became enthralled with these magnificent fish. In my old Red Ball rubber hip-high wading boots at eight years old, and standing on a frozen, snowy bank in April on Elton Creek in the Southern Tier of western New York's Alleghany Mountain range, my first brown trout caught me. It was a ten-inch beauty—full of red dots with white circles. Its warm brown and gold eyes looked down at its mouth where it was hooked, and it had a gorgeous butter-scotch belly. I called for my father to take a picture of me and my catch. His Leica camera was an old war relic that he carried with him wherever he went. It was my first "hero shot."

The addictive drug called fly fishing for trout was fully manifested in me by my teenage years. It was then that my father and I started to take yearly Memorial Day trips to drive east to hit the mayfly hatches on the iconic Catskill river shrines to trout.

The hallowed waters of the Beaverkill River were our destination. Back then it was the queen of all those royal waters (it still is today). Here, I got my first truly large brown trout during the Gray Fox mayfly hatch downstream from the Junction Pool, which is known as Barnhart's Pool. We fished each run and pool hard from morning till dusk. We threw nymphs and traditional wet flies like the Quill Gordon, Hendrickson, Queen of Waters, Light Cahill, Breadcrust, and Hare's Ear during non-hatch periods. We waited for the first mayfly to hatch, or spinners to fly, as we watched the surface for the first rise. The dry fly and matching the hatch is a sacred ritual to the Catskill fisher's game. At night, we would sit by a campfire telling stories about flying saucers, ghosts, and my dad fighting German soldiers during the war.

The whole dance was about trying to catch the elusive and at times very snooty Catskill brown trout that saw lots of flies from

CATSKILL FLY FISHING
CENTER & MUSEUM
1031
OLD ROUTE 17
MUSEUM & GIFT SHOP
10am - 4pm

top-quality fly anglers from all over the East Coast. I was always captivated by the legend of the giant Beamoc brown trout, a leviathan that had two heads, as a result of being confused about which river to swim up. It was said to haunt the waters of the Junction Pool, where the Beaverkill and Willowemoc converged. With its giant prehistoric kype, that mythical big brown embodied the elusive aura of the Beaverkill's big browns that I dreamed of catching.

No trip to the Catskills was complete without a trip to watch the famous Dettes tie flies. Another treat on every trip was enjoying the prime rib at the iconic Antrim Lodge, which my dad loved.

OPPOSITE, CLOCKWISE FROM TOP LEFT: A must-stop! The Catskill Fly Fishing Center and Museum; Ceballos's Isovicarium, a deadly modern-traditional fusion that combines the *Isonychia* and March Brown as an emerger/dun Compara style; a guide's lunch and snooze on a cold spring day. **ABOVE:** A Hendrickson mayfly flotilla.

The New Sporting Chic

The birth and rise of the iconic Catskill trout tradition is tied to the turn-of-the-nineteenth-century accumulation of wealth. Here, the booming entrepreneurs of the Industrial Revolution started a leisure market of wealthy New York elites arriving by train to explore the trendy scenic mountain retreats. They discovered the sporting and fashionable charm of fly angling, and both men and women alike would wear the finest Abercrombie and Orvis outdoor clothing while making an important and proper social statement. It became the chic thing to do.

The beautiful indigenous brook trout was the main catch of the anglers back then. The sporting abilities of the newly emerged Catskill socialite angler were not as refined as those of the locals. Thus, the locals became the guides, teaching them how to swing a set of tandem wet flies to fool the brook trout. This was the deadly way to fish for them, and sadly hundreds of wild, native brook trout were killed and hung from the trophy poles outside each hotel and private club.

With the pace of killing, it's no wonder that the brook trout were soon eliminated from the Catskill rivers. By the early 1880s, due to angler devastation, tanneries, and acid factories polluting the rivers, the brookies were all but gone—except for those found in small, remote, and tough-to-fish cold-water mountain brooks and tributaries. Then came a savior, or perhaps a forever-dominating curse of the native trout, depending on how you view it. In 1886, Aden Brook, a tributary to the Neversink, received the first planting of German brown trout. Other Catskill rivers immediately followed with plants of the browns. Everything in fly angling in the Catskills would soon change in a big way.

Tactical Evolution for the German Browns

The German brown trout introduced into Catskill rivers had to swim in fast, cascading, boulder-strewn waters—some very cold—with great fluctuations in flows. Thus, they weren't in the gentle flowing spring creeks of ideal temperature like in the Hampshires of England, where fly-fishing tactics had their birth. This is of serious historical significance because the Catskill rivers dictated a new style of selective fly-fishing presentation and fly patterns that would eventually evolve there.

This transition in tactical presentation and fly patterns in Catskill fly angling was a direct result of the new super-wary and selective German browns, which were tough to catch. With ice-cold, fast-flowing spate rivers occupied by predominantly brook trout, one can easily see how tying three gaudy wet flies on a leader can sometimes produce three brook trout on a catch! The aggressive demeanor of these chars is due to their volatile habitat. Brook trout are known for their extreme lack of wariness to begin with. They thrive in river conditions with fast, cold, oxygenated waters that have small windows of foraging opportunity or means to grab food. Floods, droughts, and anchor ice take their toll on a trout's livelihood, and thus they must take a meal any time it is available. Aggressiveness to forage with less discrimination about food forms is inbred in the genetic behavioral structure of brookies.

On the other hand, a brown trout, in a perfect ecological environment like English chalk streams, proceeds about its daily feeding with ease, scrutiny, and comfortable wariness. Those conditions allow a food supply in ample

Tough to find in their original feral places, brook trout are still the heart and soul of eastern fly fisherman all along the Allegheny Mountain range.

numbers and diversity 24/7, twelve months a year. This is why it becomes a very selective creature that analyzes prey with extremely refined accuracy to selected foraging details. Needless to say, an angler will experience refusals to the fly or bait offerings if all presentation details are not perfect. When the brown trout made its Catskill debut, it was scorned for its being photophobic with a stubborn demeanor. Anglers were unable to fill basket creels to the brim, which just added to the scorn.

Enter Theodore Gordon, the father of American selective trout angling. As a result of his correspondence with the British angling icons of the time, like Frederic M. Halford, George Selwyn Marryat, and G. E. M. Skues, Gordon tweaked the English flies into a whole new silhouette, profile, and sparseness designed for the fast and tumbling Catskill waters. He became a prolific fly designer, entomologist, fish behaviorist, and overall tactical master. He studied the ways of the trout in the Catskills, and his writings influenced a new age of angling masters and fly tyers like Roy Steenrod. The days of the fish-killing trophy poles were over, and a new connoisseur of trout fishing was emerging—one who was interested in the theoretical, mental challenges and sporting enjoyment trout fishing in the Catskills provided.

From the Trout Stream to the Kitchen Connoisseur

The Catskills' trout streams, from freestone to tailwaters, can bestow a cruel and harsh learning curve. The complex habitat has tremendous insect hatches and food-forage diversity a trout angler must understand and master. Couple this with the tactical-presentation diversity these waters demand, and they are truly at a PhD level to learn and master. Fly tying, tactics, and hatch study are musts for the trout angler here.

Trout are busy and productive creatures that make humans look lazy. They must continually forage in hopes that a full belly is coming soon. On my *Hallowed Waters* podcast, Dr. Robert Bachman of Penn State and

LEFT: Theodore Gordon, the father of American fly fishing. Here with his "lady friend," as he alluded to her. **OPPOSITE:** The classic freestoners like the Beaverkill and Willowemoc are the hallowed waters where American fly fishing got its start.

I discussed in-depth the selective foraging behavior of trout in a stream where he did his thesis work. He drove home the point that there is no thought or reasoning to a trout's daily foraging escapades. He said each river has a limited number of "best seats in the restaurant niches" that are prime feeding lies for the trout. Yet I can't help but wonder that a trout has some inkling, some intuition, that if it swims up to the next riffle, drops down a few pools, it might intercept a bounty of spring's first big mayfly feast or some other prey. Fact is, some trout can get very large if they venture downstream and find new feeding opportunities. It can compare to when we go around a corner and find the most awesome and delicious little hole-in-the-wall bistro. Often venturing out, expanding our taste preferences by exploring and trying new things, leads to great rewards.

To this day, when summer calls for our return to the Catskills from our home in Michigan, I count every day until that Route 17 exit comes up and we are back in its high, cool elevation—something the flat landscape of Michigan is deprived of. I spend my days perusing my dances with trout as I fall in love all over again

ORVIS
864
MADE IN USA

with some of the most beautiful wild browns on the planet. The mind games of the trout stream cricket we play is still a visual shtick of experiencing a fish's nods and refusals. But most important, it's about the well-earned hook-ups and catch. I tie and invent a few new fly patterns there each year, just so I know that I still have my touch. And yet what remains unchanged over the decades is the joy of paying my dues on the water as a stalking, selective trout master—something I forever aspire to be.

On the Table

New York's Italian Comfort Food

New York has the third-largest population of Italians outside of Italy. The early immigrants were responsible for introducing and perfecting Italian-American cuisine. My bond with Italian food started in my youth growing up in Niagara Falls in an Italian neighborhood; the aromas coming from my friends' homes were incredible. Garlic permeated the air, along with the strong scent of fresh herbs like basil and oregano. There, marinara and ragu sauces simmered, and osso buco and whole stuffed fish and poultry baked in the ovens and slow cookers. Making and cooking pasta was like serving communion at church—every noodle was worshipped.

From the local pizza joints on every corner that the Napolitano immigrants started to the delis hanging Parma hams and sausages, delicious food was everywhere. Italian sub shops used thin-sliced old-world-style cold cuts like soppressata and mortadella, and baked delicious breads.

Catskill Italian

In the feral environment of the Catskills, you can find venison, fish, and fowl, along with foraged green edibles and wild mushrooms like chanterelles and morels. There are also boutique breeds of locally raised free-range cattle and pigs. All are used by many talented chefs and indulged in by foodies. Yet it is the venturing spirit of the Italians who came up the Hudson from New York City and spread their delicacies all over the Catskills and New York State that is formative. Italian chefs learned to love the Catskills, with its fishing and hunting opportunities. Some of the best Catskills restaurants have Italian influences—and even high-quality thin-crust New York–style pizza can be found in the most remote mountain hamlets. Every time I arrive and enter our summer cottage, the first thing I ask my mother-in-law is "Who's making the best pizza around here these days?" One year it was in a sleepy hippie hamlet called Mountaindale. The winding road to get there is scary, with hairpin turns falling off a cliff. You always seem to see a black bear or bobcat cross the road. Surely they must all be drawn in by the scent of the oven's vents permeating into the woods. And the pizza . . . it's so worth it.

This area has a strong allure, but I have seen things go from good times to more depressed times and then back again. Catskills winters are harsh. They take their toll on its people and tourism. Perhaps the Catskills should always be about the wild and untamable.

Catskill brown trout come in various designs based on their genetic lineage, wild vs. stocked, water types, and nutrition. This is a Neversink brown that looks something like a landlocked salmon. Edwin Hewitt introduced Atlantic salmon from Canada into the upper Neversink. They are still stocked in the reservoir and are known to run up the river in the fall.

Eggplant Caponata

This is a stew-like and meal-worthy caponata with bay scallops, calamari, and shrimp.

Serves 4

- 5 tablespoons extra-virgin olive oil
- 1 large eggplant, diced
- 2 ribs celery, diced
- 1 medium yellow onion, chopped
- 3 cloves garlic, minced
- 2 red bell peppers, seeded and diced
- Coarse sea salt
- 1 pound bay scallops
- 1 pound calamari, sliced
- 1 pound medium (41/60) shrimp, peeled and deveined
- 1 pound ripe Roma tomatoes, seeded and chopped
- 3 tablespoons capers in brine, drained
- 3 tablespoons sliced or chopped black olives
- 2 tablespoons sugar
- 3 tablespoons red or white wine vinegar
- Freshly ground black pepper
- Baguette for serving

In a large skillet over medium heat, warm 2 tablespoons of the olive oil. Sauté the eggplant until tender. Transfer to a bowl.

Add another 2 tablespoons olive oil to the skillet, heat, and add the celery and onion. Cook until softened, about 5 minutes. Add the garlic and cook until fragrant, about 30 seconds, then add the bell peppers and ½ teaspoon salt. Cook until the bell peppers are tender, about 8 minutes.

Add the remaining tablespoon olive oil and return the eggplant to the pan. Cook for another 5 minutes, or until all of the vegetables are very tender. Add the scallops, calamari, shrimp, tomatoes, capers, black olives, sugar, and vinegar and simmer until the seafood is just cooked through, about 3 minutes. Season with salt and pepper, and serve immediately with pieces of baguette.

HATCHES
a complete guide to fishing the hatches
of north american trout streams
Bob Nastasi
CORTLAND
444
CLASSIC
WORLD FAMOUS FLY LINE
CATSKILL
FLY TYERS
GUILD

Route 17 Lasagna

Route 17 is the heart and soul of the Catskills. Called the Quickway by locals, it was built in 1924 and has been the major route to the Catskills ever since. It crosses over all of the major trout streams in the area. I named this delicious lasagna after the road.

Serves 6

1 pound lasagna sheets

Coarse sea salt

1 pound lean ground beef

1 pound hot or sweet Italian sausage, casings removed

2 tablespoons extra-virgin olive oil

8 ounces portabella mushrooms, sliced

1 small red bell pepper, seeded and chopped

1 (32-ounce) container ricotta

1 large egg

4½ cups grated Parmesan cheese

2 cups fresh spinach or arugula

Easy Tomato Sauce (recipe follows) or 2 (24-ounce) jars sauce

2 pounds fresh mozzarella, cut into 16 slices

Dried oregano

Finely chopped fresh parsley leaves

Preheat the oven to 375°F.

Bring a large pot of salted water to a boil and cook the lasagna sheets according to the package instructions, then drain.

In a large skillet over medium heat, break up the ground beef and sausage and brown, about 8 minutes.

When cooked through, drain and transfer to a medium bowl. Set aside.

Heat the olive oil in the skillet and sauté the mushrooms and red pepper until softened but not browned, about 6 minutes. Add to the bowl with the meat and stir to combine.

In a separate medium bowl, mix the ricotta with the egg and 1 cup of the grated Parmesan.

Bring a small pot of water to a boil and quickly blanch the arugula or spinach in hot water. Drain and when cool enough to handle, squeeze out the liquid. Stir into the ricotta mixture.

(RECIPE CONTINUES)

Line the bottom of 13 x 9-inch baking dish with a layer of noodles. Layer half of the ricotta mixture on the noodles, then half of the meat mixture. Cover with ½ jar of sauce. Top with half of the remaining Parmesan and 6 slices mozzarella.

Top with another layer of noodles, then repeat with the remaining ricotta, meat mixture, ½ jar sauce, Parmesan, and 6 slices mozzarella. Add another layer of noodles, ½ jar sauce, and the remaining mozzarella.

Bake, uncovered, until browning on top, about 45 minutes. Let stand for at least 15 minutes, then sprinkle with parsley, slice, and serve.

Easy Tomato Sauce

Makes about 3½ cups

1 tablespoon extra-virgin olive oil

3 cloves garlic, minced

1 (28-ounce) can diced tomatoes

1 (28-ounce) can crushed tomatoes

1 (6-ounce) can tomato paste

1 cup dry red wine

¼ cup sugar, plus more as needed to cut acidity

2 tablespoons dried oregano

2 teapoons dried or 2 tablespoons fresh basil

Crushed red pepper (optional)

Warm the olive oil in a large saucepan over medium heat. Sauté the garlic until fragrant, 30 to 45 seconds. Add the diced and crushed tomatoes and the tomato paste and stir to combine. Simmer for 1 minute.

Add the wine and stir to combine. Stir in the sugar until dissolved.

Add the oregano and basil and a pinch or two of crushed red pepper, if using.

Simmer on low heat until thick and the flavors have melded, about 45 minutes.

Peter Supinski on the Neversink at dusk during rusty spinner time.

The Homestead Apple

THE HOMESTEAD RESTAURANT + LOUNGE
AT THE ELDRED PRESERVE, ELDRED, NEW YORK
RECIPE FROM PASTRY CHEF OLIVIA WELLINGTON

The Homestead has been our family's restaurant in the Catskills for several generations. It has been an iconic steak and seafood supper club on the banks of the holy waters of the legendary Neversink for almost a century. It is now nestled in at the Eldred Preserve—a Catskill-forested setting with trout ponds and locally grown and harvested cuisine. To make this dish, you will need a kitchen scale for measuring ingredients, six small silicone sphere- and apple-shaped molds for assembly, and a candy thermometer for the caramel and glaze.

Serves 6

APPLE COMPOTE

60 g local maple syrup

20 g Pollinator Bourbon

0.5 g fine sea salt

2 local apples, peeled and finely diced

5 g gelatin sheets

SALTED CARAMEL DULCEY MOUSSE

110 g sugar

20 g water (for caramel)

8 g gelatin sheets

190 g Dulcey chocolate, in discs or roughly chopped

190 g heavy cream

1.5 g fine sea salt

20 g unsalted butter, softened

440 g heavy cream, lightly whipped

DULCEY CHOCOLATE GLAZE

10 g gelatin powder

60 g cold water

150 g sugar

25 g water (for caramel)

180 g water (for dilution)

160 g Dulcey chocolate, in discs or roughly chopped

150 g glucose syrup

100 g sweetened condensed milk

6 slices good-quality toasted cinnamon raisin bread, preferably The Homestead's, for serving

Edible flowers, gold leaf, or apple powder for garnish

Make the compote: Bring the syrup and bourbon to a boil in a medium saucepan. Add the salt and apples. Simmer for about 2 minutes. Soak the gelatin sheet in water until soft. Stir in the softened gelatin until dissolved. Pour into the sphere-shaped molds and freeze.

Make the mousse: In a high-sided medium saucepan, caramelize the sugar in 20 g water until amber.

Soak the gelatin sheet in water until soft. Place the chocolate in a medium heatproof bowl.

Gently whisk the cream and salt into the caramel. Add the gelatin and butter, then pour the caramel mixture over the chocolate. Let sit, then blend until smooth. Cool slightly, then fold into the whipped cream. Fill the apple-shaped molds halfway, then insert one frozen apple compote into each. Fill the rest of the mold with the remaining mousse and freeze.

Make the glaze: Bloom the gelatin powder in bowl with 60 g chilled water.

In a high-sided medium saucepan caramelize the sugar in 25 g water. Add 180 g water to stop cooking.

Put the chocolate, glucose, milk, and gelatin in a medium heatproof bowl. Pour the caramel into the bowl and blend until smooth. Cool to 95°F.

Dip the frozen mousse apples twice and let set.

To serve, place each glazed apple on a slice of toasted cinnamon raisin bread. Garnish with edible flowers, gold leaf, or a light dusting of apple powder.

COLORADO

Fishing the High Country for Cutthroat Trout

KIRK DEETER

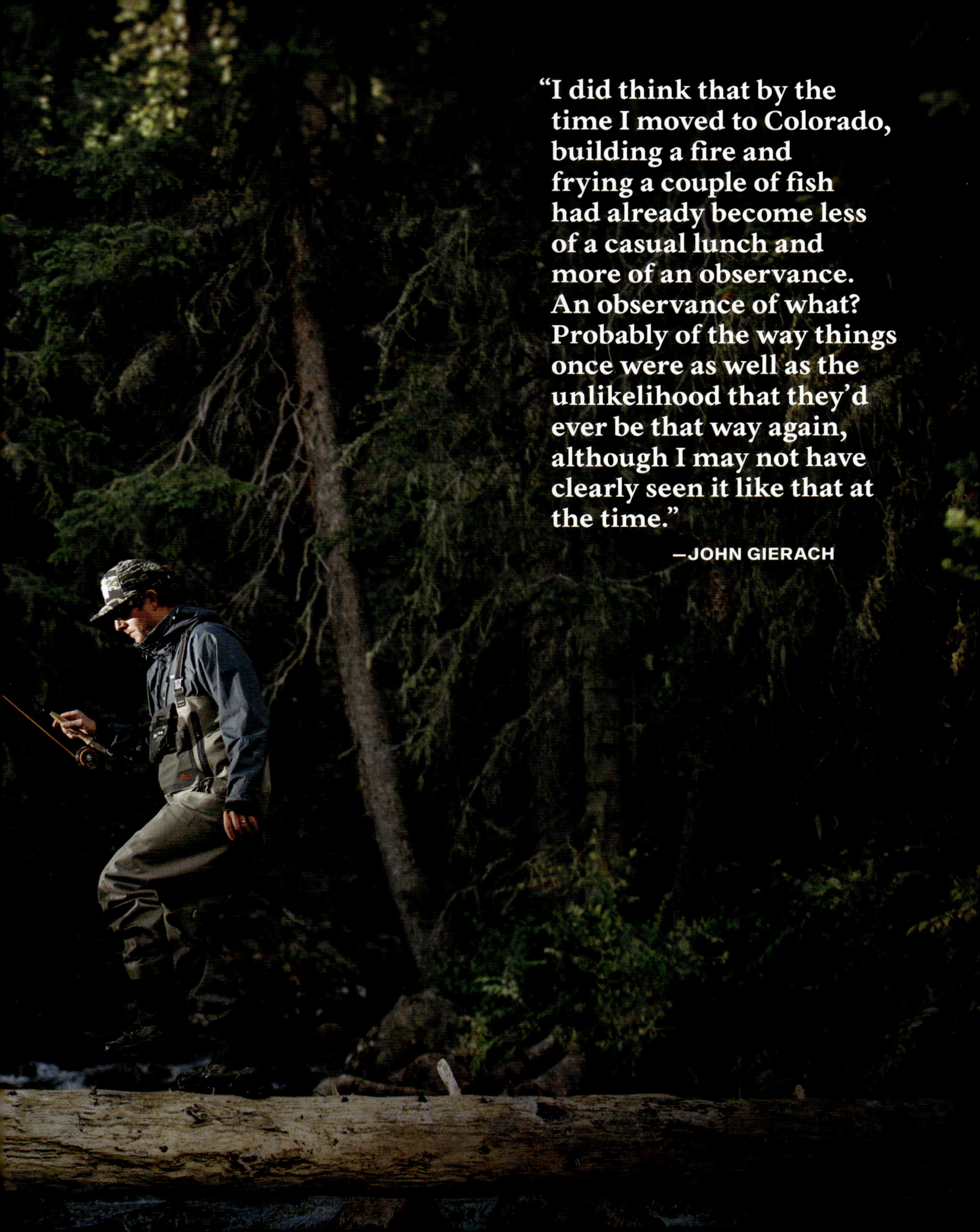
"I did think that by the time I moved to Colorado, building a fire and frying a couple of fish had already become less of a casual lunch and more of an observance. An observance of what? Probably of the way things once were as well as the unlikelihood that they'd ever be that way again, although I may not have clearly seen it like that at the time."
—JOHN GIERACH

PREVIOUS: Treading the fine wading line in search of rising trout. **ABOVE:** Geoff Mueller connects on Piney Creek; Colorado has different strains of native cutthroat trout, including the Colorado River cutthroat (*center*) and the greenback (*bottom*). **OPPOSITE:** The release of a hefty cutty caught somewhere (secret) in the Gore Range of central Colorado.

Having traveled all over the world to write stories about fly fishing, I am often asked, "Where is the favorite place you've ever fished?" My answer has always been the same—I love wherever I am at the time. My heart is in Michigan where my roots are . . . I'm enthralled with New Zealand . . . I'm addicted to saltwater flats . . . bewildered by the jungle . . . and just darn proud that Alaska is part of the United States.

But at the end of the day, I live where I live with good reason. And I live in Colorado.

I am told that if you took Colorado and somehow pulled it flat with all its craggy peaks laid on an even plain, it would occupy a space at least as large as the state of Texas. I don't know if I actually believe that, but I can attest to the fact that the up-and-down factor of the Colorado landscape is the allure. If you're willing to hike, maybe climb a bit, the Centennial State has more hidden rivulets and babbling creeks than an angler might hope to experience in a lifetime. Having huffed and puffed my way around the mountains and into the creeks and rivers since I was a teenager, I feel like I'm still only scratching the surface.

On the Water

There is something special about fishing the headwaters of some of the most iconic rivers in America . . . the Colorado, the Arkansas, the Platte, the Rio Grande . . . everything literally flows downhill from here. As you fish these waters, there's a level of profundity if you pause long enough to think about it. That snow that falls on the fourteeners in the

middle of Colorado is the vital water source that extends in all directions.

East of the Great Divide, the North Platte and South Platte eventually conjoin to create the shallow, marshy waterfowl haven—the Platte River—that twists through Nebraska and pours into the Missouri River. The mighty Arkansas River can be leapt across in a single bound up by Leadville. The Rio Grande forms in the high country above Creede. And the Colorado River pours westward from the Divide, where it turns into one of the most vital waterways in North America (and one of the most contested).

Each of these watersheds held its own genetically unique strain of cutthroat trout. In the Platte River drainage, it was the "greenback." The Colorado River still has its distinctive strain of Colorado cutties, at least in the high-country tributaries, if not in the mainstem itself anymore. The Rio Grande has its own strain of Rio Grande cutthroat trout, and the Arkansas had what's now believed to be its own extirpated strain of yellowfin cutthroat trout. Yet another distinct strain of San Juan River cutthroat trout was only recently revealed through DNA analysis.

The trout fisheries are as diverse as the fish themselves. Cheesman Canyon on the South Platte, where school-bus-size boulders break up the river currents, is one of the most popular trout fisheries in America. Because it's a mere hour or less from downtown Denver (the urban metroplex with the most fly anglers, per capita, of any city in the world), the South Platte sees its fair share of pressure. But if you go after four p.m. when most of the guide trips have ended—or especially if you go in late September during the first serious snowfall of the year—that river can still surprise you. It's the kind of place where you might wonder if there are any trout at all, until the snow falls, the *baetis* mayflies hatch, and the river surface starts to bubble like a tureen of soup with all the rising trout.

CLOCKWISE FROM TOP: Releasing a native cuttie; a Frank Smethurst Mouse Pattern; the Royal Wulff.

Springing out of the mountains above Aspen and the Reudi Reservoir are the Roaring Fork and Fryingpan Rivers, where, if you hit it just right on a soggy, rainy day in early August, the green drake flies look like an armada of tiny sailboats and the trout go nuts.

The Mother's Day caddis hatch on the Arkansas River around Salida is legendary (though if you wait until actual Mother's Day, you'll probably miss the show).

The Yampa River meanders through Steamboat Springs, and some of the best fishing holes can be found right in town. But you need to watch out for the tubers floating by in the summer months.

I think the Animas River near Durango is probably the most underrated river in Colorado, and perhaps the entire Rocky Mountain West. Black ants and beetles are usually the ticket during much of the season.

Meyers and Gierach, Friends and Mentors

One of the most scenic float trips an angler can take anywhere in the world is down the Gunnison River Gorge. The put-in, the Chukar Trail, is a steep climb down to the river that's best to horse pack into. The gorge section is just downstream of the Black Canyon. Now a national park, the Black Canyon is so steep that they say you could set the Empire State Building in the river bottom, and its spire still wouldn't reach the canyon rim. Most people like to float this stretch in June for the stoneflies, but I like September better, after the tourist crowds have thinned and the grasshoppers become the bill of fare.

I remember once camping in the canyon with buddy Paul Zabel and Charlie Meyers, then the outdoors editor for the *Denver Post*, who became my writing mentor and a dear friend. One night during a three-day float down Gunny Gorge, a ring-tailed cat climbed out on a tree limb above our campfire, seemingly as rapt in the yarns Charlie spun as Paul and I were.

Every August, Charlie and I also made predawn pilgrimages to fish in South Park on the reservoirs during the *callibaetis* hatches. We'd kick about in float tubes, catching football-shaped rainbow trout that had gorged on summer bugs. We also hatched the idea to write *The Little Red Book of Fly Fishing* together. Sadly, Charlie passed away before that book was published. But there's now a monument dedicated to him—the Charlie Meyers State Wildlife Area—appropriately on the "Dream Stream" section of the South Platte, between the reservoirs where we used to fish together. I don't fish there often, but I do visit now and then just to think about Charlie.

John Gierach was another great one, and another Colorado connection. I got to edit the last thirty-three fly-fishing stories he wrote, as he contributed them to *TROUT* magazine. Those Gierach essays, matched with wonderful paintings by artist Bob White, weren't just "content." I was a fan, like everyone else. I just happened to be editing the magazine.

Blue-Lining

The funny thing is, both John Gierach and Charlie Meyers were never that into the "iconic" Colorado fishing spots that get written up in magazines or shown in videos or Instagram posts. Instead, they were more about exploring the semi-obscure, sometimes even anonymous creeks and streams that might or might not hold large trout.

North Boulder Creek in Dream Canyon

TOP: Hiking above treeline in search of native cutties. **BOTTOM:** Gore Canyon on the Colorado River, where a moose encounter is common. **OPPOSITE, CLOCKWISE FROM TOP:** High Country lake casting; releasing a wild Colorado trout; floating canyons.

I feel more and more the same way the more I fish. This has become its own special brand of fly fishing with its own cultlike following.

Blue-lining is the art of looking at a topographic map (or the app you can now download to your phone) and hiking in, up, and around those mountains and down into the valleys, and figuring out if there are any wild trout living in any of the dozens of waterways either without names, or with redundant ones like "Deer Creek," "Bear Creek," "Blue Lake," or "Trout Lake." There must be at least a dozen "Bear Creeks" in Colorado alone. Most often the fish are in these places, but sometimes they aren't and that's just fine.

When you do find them, sometimes they'll be native cutthroats. Oftentimes, they'll be remnant—now wild and naturally reproducing—populations of browns, rainbows, or even brook trout that were originally put in these spots to be sustainable food sources for the mining camps that dug for precious metal ore a century or more ago.

And when you do find them, these fish eat gaudy dry flies, like Humpies, Royal Coachmen, Trudes, and Goddard Caddis. You can tie on a dropper nymph, like a Copper John (created by another Colorado fishing legend, John Barr), but sometimes that seems too easy.

Worth Hiking For

I fondly remember one early fall trip when I was cutting my Colorado fly-fishing teeth in the Telluride region of southwestern Colorado. Zabel, our friend Duncan Coker, and I drove several miles up a dirt road past where the pavement ended. Then we hiked a few miles into a creek (I won't name it specifically, but I gave a pretty strong hint a few paragraphs ago) that fed the Dolores River, somewhere near the old mining town of Rico.

We made camp, and then spread out to go fish. I walked up on a beaver dam. It made a large pool upstream, and the creek dropped a few feet below the dam. I stood in the creek and stared at eye level across the pool as scads of wild cutthroat trout—most of them sixteen inches or longer—slurped small mayflies off the surface.

I tied on a Parachute Adams, unfurled a cast with a 3-weight rod, and immediately connected to a fat trout. I did that three or four more times, then moved on, even though the other fish were still rising with gusto. Suddenly, I heard an elk bugle on the hillside, and I decided I'd rather listen than fish.

Yeah . . . this is why I live here, I thought. Things may never again be the same in Colorado, but they're pretty darn special right now.

On the Table

Colorado is one of the most dynamic foodie states in America. You might not think of Colorado as an agricultural mecca, but you'd be mistaken. This is far more than cattle country. Some of the juiciest, best cantaloupe in the world are grown around Rocky Ford. Many of the best peaches on the planet are grown in and around Palisade. Flavorful potatoes come from the San Luis Valley. And there are other staple crops like red beets—heck, Colorado is even the nation's capital for growing carnations.

These recipes are highlights of Colorado cuisine: They are staples for celebratory or fish-camp dinners (we have quiche for breakfast) . . . and dishes that I make a point to serve when fishing friends visit. They're what my friends would say I'm famous for.

Elk Tenderloin
with Whiskey Cream Sauce

Elk meat is the ultimate organic, lean protein. The backstraps and tenderloins are considered the prized cuts, and usually reserved for special occasions. Hunting your holiday feast is a cherished rite for many Coloradans, but if hunting is not your deal, there are plenty of ways to buy responsibly grown elk meat, either through mail order or at the butcher's. But remember, it's bad form to overcook an elk tenderloin.

Serves 6

If frozen, thaw 1 (12- to 16-ounce) tenderloin to room temperature. Lightly coat with olive oil, and sprinkle with salt, pepper, and perhaps garlic powder. (You do not want to over-spice elk meat; you want to augment its wonderful natural flavor.)

Elk tenderloin should be served medium-rare, with an internal temperature of no more than 125°F. So, you can either use a sous vide method (placing the meat in a sealed bag and submerging it in a water bath with a specifically controlled temperature, 120°F) and then briefly toss on a hot grill to sear the outside and seal in flavor . . . or, you need to regularly check the tenderloin on the grill or smoker with a meat thermometer.

Let the meat rest after cooking for 10 minutes, then slice into ½-inch-thick medallions.

Serve with the whiskey cream sauce, lightly dolloped on the medallions or served alongside, and the roasted-beet salad.

Another good complement to elk tenderloin is the berry-based glaze we recommend for halibut in the Alaska chapter (page 36).

(RECIPE CONTINUES)

Whiskey Cream Sauce

1 shallot, finely chopped

2 cloves garlic, minced

1 cup light sour cream

½ cup bourbon whiskey

1 tablespoon prepared horseradish

In a small bowl, whisk together the shallot, garlic, sour cream, whiskey, and horseradish. Refrigerate until ready to serve.

Roasted-Beet Salad

Most people don't realize that Colorado is the beet capital of America.

Serves 8

6 whole beets

2 cups arugula

1 cup candied walnut halves, or pepitas or crushed lightly salted pistachios

1 cup goat cheese, crumbled

Balsamic glaze to taste

Preheat the oven to 350°F.

Wash and dry the beets, then wrap them in foil. Place on a small baking sheet and roast until tender, 45 minutes. Once cool enough to handle, peel and dice them.

Arrange the arugula on a serving platter and top with the beets. Sprinkle with the walnuts and goat cheese crumbles. Drizzle with balsamic glaze and serve at room temperature.

Colorado Pork Green Chili

The beauty of this dish is that it's an all-day deal. Smother it on eggs for breakfast, or eat it as a side with a salad or sandwich. But after a raw, cold day rowing a boat or fishing in the high country, nothing beats a hot bowl of green chili with warm tortillas or corn muffins on the side to dunk into it.

Serves 8 or more, depending on whether it's a side or a main course

2 tablespoons chili powder

1 tablespoon garlic powder

1 tablespoon onion powder

1 teaspoon coarse sea salt, plus more to taste

2 teaspoons freshly ground black pepper, plus more to taste

1 (3-pound) pork shoulder roast

Vegetable oil (optional)

1 large white onion

6 to 8 cloves garlic, minced

4 cups low-sodium chicken broth, plus more as needed

2 pounds store-bought roasted green chilies, chopped, preferably Big Jim Medium-Hots from New Mexico

2 (14.5-ounce) cans fire-roasted diced tomatoes

1 tablespoon ground coriander

1 tablespoon ground cumin

2 teaspoons smoked paprika

1½ teaspoons dried oregano

1 (12-ounce) can Coors Banquet (optional)

2 tablespoons cornstarch

Finely chopped cilantro for serving

Sliced green onions or scallions for serving

Lime wedges for serving

Crema Mexicana, grated Campesino cheese, or sour cream for serving

Preheat the oven or a temperature-controlled charcoal or wood-fired grill to 325°F.

In a small bowl, mix 1 tablespoon of the chili powder, the onion powder, garlic powder, salt, and black pepper. Coat the entire roast with the rub.

Put the roast in a high-sided cast-iron skillet or roasting pan and cook until the internal temperature reaches 150°F on an instant-read thermometer, about 3 hours. Alternatively, place the roast in a high-sided cast-iron skillet, and cook in a wood-fired, temperature-controlled smoker or grill for 3 hours (I use apple or mesquite wood).

Once cool enough to handle, use a knife and fork to pull the meat apart into bite-size chunks and shreds (you don't want to cut the pork into cubes).

Lightly coat the bottom of a large Dutch oven with some of the roast drippings (or do this with vegetable oil). Heat over medium-low, then add the white onion. Sauté until translucent, about 5 minutes, then add the garlic. Once the garlic is fragrant, about 45 seconds, add the shredded pork and stir.

After 2 minutes, add the chicken broth and cook for 1 to 2 minutes. Stir in each of the following ingredients separately: green chilies, diced tomatoes, the remaining 1 tablespoon chili powder, the coriander, cumin, paprika, and oregano. Taste carefully (it will be hot) and season with salt and black pepper.

Cover the pot, reduce the heat to low, and simmer for 2 hours, stirring occasionally and checking the thickness of the chili. If the chili is too thick (it should still be soupy), add the beer or more broth or water.

In a small bowl, mix the cornstarch with ¼ cup lukewarm water. Just before serving, pour this cornstarch slurry into the chili, stirring to incorporate. Let simmer for another 10 minutes, then serve.

Garnish with cilantro, green onion, and lime wedges. To mitigate the heat, drizzle with a little crema Mexicana, add some grated Campesino cheese, or dollop with sour cream.

Colorado Fire-Roasted Hatch Green Chili Quiche

Even though Hatch green chilies are from the Hatch Valley in New Mexico, they are an adopted staple in many Colorado recipes. This quiche replaces the Denver omelet as my Colorado breakfast favorite.

Makes 2 quiches; serves 12

2 (9-inch) frozen or fresh deep-dish pie crusts, thawed according to package instructions if using frozen

10 large eggs

2 cups whole milk

2 cups diced ham or crisp, cooked chopped bacon

1½ cups shredded cheddar (or a cheese blend)

¼ cup shaved Parmesan

1½ cups chopped green onions or scallions

2 cups fire-roasted Hatch green chilies (see Note), cut into nickel-size pieces

Preheat the oven to 375°F .

Bake the thawed crusts for 7 minutes, then cool. (If using fresh pie crusts, do not prebake them.) Place the pie crusts on baking sheets lined with parchment paper.

In a large bowl, beat the eggs with the milk. Stir in the ham, cheeses, green onions, and chilies.

Divide this egg mixture between the pie crusts evenly and bake until the center of the quiches have set, 50 to 55 minutes. Let cool for 10 to 20 minutes before serving.

Note: Roasting your own Hatch green chilies is easy, but you can also buy them online or from your grocer's freezer section. Avoid canned chilies as they lack the flavor of fresh or frozen.

Marvel 8-'91

Peach Pie

1 cup sugar

3 T. flour

1 egg

1 T. butter

Slice 2-3, cups fresh peaches.

Mix dry ingredients

Add beaten egg + peaches.

Pour into unbaked pie crust

Dot with butter

Bake 350° until done

Crust

2 cups flour

2/3 cup Crisco plus 2T

T water

PALISADE PEACH PIE
THIS IS MY GRANDMOTHER'S RECIPE—PALISADE PEACHES IN AUGUST ARE A MUST-HAVE.

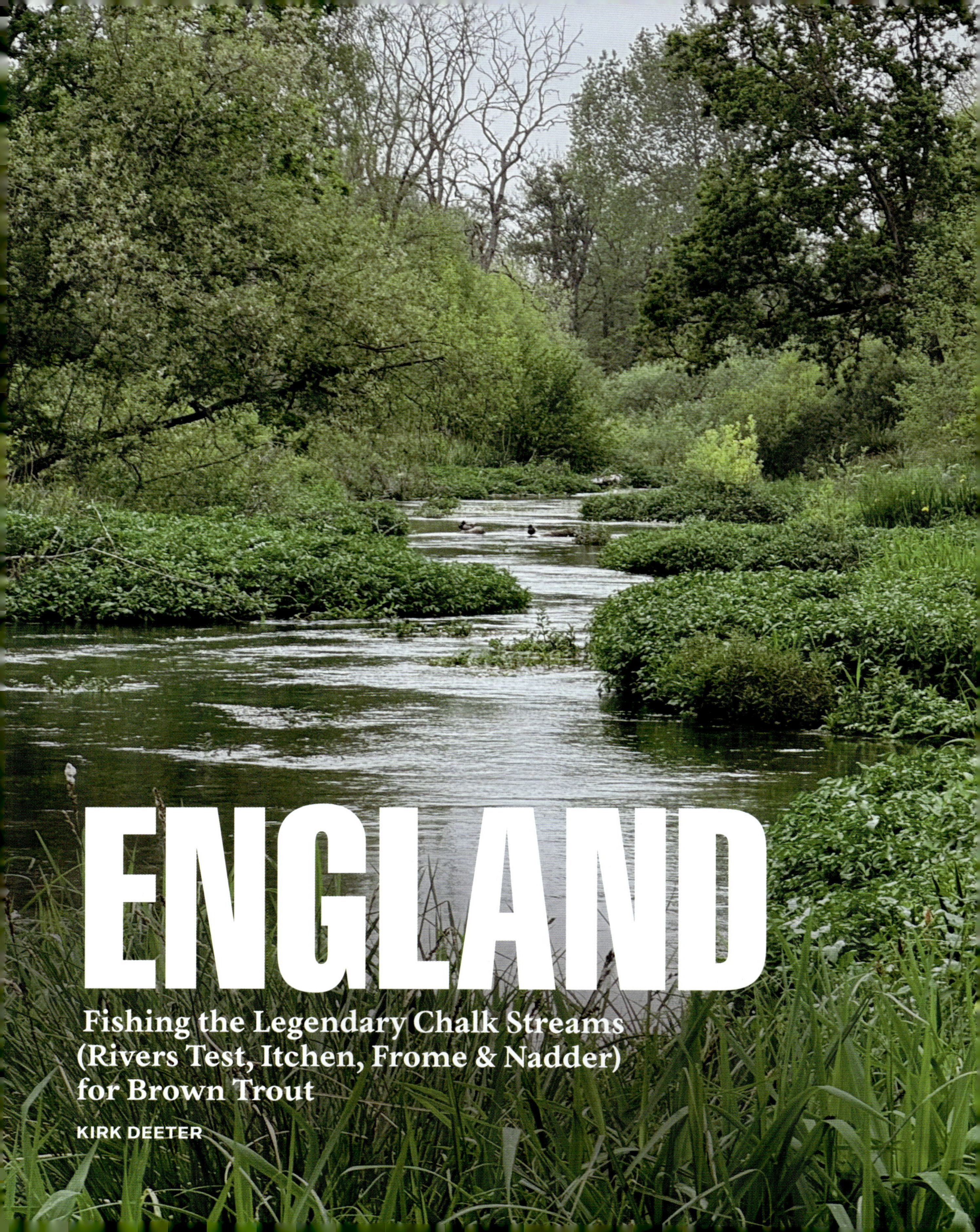

ENGLAND

Fishing the Legendary Chalk Streams (Rivers Test, Itchen, Frome & Nadder) for Brown Trout

KIRK DEETER

"Rivers and the inhabitants of the watery element were made for wise men to contemplate, and fools to pass by without consideration."
—IZAAK WALTON

ORVIS

I had caught my eighth brown trout of the afternoon, so I sat on a bench along the River Itchen and just watched the fish eat mayflies.

This is where it all began, I thought, trying to frame the significance of that moment. This is the world's cathedral of fly fishing.

Some will say that, like golf, fly fishing originated in Scotland. The truth is, it might all have started half a world away, at least five centuries earlier than we all thought. There is now proof that the Indigenous peoples of the Amazon Basin in Brazil fashioned bird feathers to hooks chiseled from shells in order to catch fish. Was that some sort of fly fishing? Probably.

Dame Juliana Berners, a fifteenth-century English nun, was credited with being the first to publish on fly fishing after she wrote *A Treatyse of Fysshynge wyth an Angle*. She most certainly found her inspiration near St. Albans in Hertfordshire.

However, the real thunder that forever changed the world of fly fishing, as much or more than Sir Isaac Newton's apple changed physics, happened right along the Itchen in Hampshire where Izaak Walton found inspiration to write *The Compleat Angler* in 1653. He is now entombed in nearby Winchester Cathedral where stained-glass windows and even an altar artfully celebrate fly fishing, marking some of the very first, and far from the last, intersections of religion and angling.

PREVIOUS: Walking along a feeder stream to the River Test. **THESE PAGES:** Guide Steve Dowling (*opposite*) releases a healthy chalk stream brown. Dry-fly fishing took off in southern England, which still proudly celebrates this tradition like nowhere else.

On the Water

There are roughly three hundred chalk streams in the entire world, and most of them are in England—the others are in Normandy, France. They are fragile marvels of nature, pumping pure, consistently cool waters from deep within the earth through layers of ancient sediment.

Centuries after Walton fished these rivers, in the late 1800s and early 1900s, this is where Frederic M. Halford honed and advocated purist dry-fly-fishing techniques, and where G. E. M. Skues engaged him in gentlemanly debate, professing the value of using nymph flies that imitate insects in their larval forms. You can still stay at the Grosvenor Hotel in Stockbridge and enjoy a pint or two in the pub where these two would have it out.

Today, the vast majority of chalk streams are privately owned and managed, and thus require access fees in order to fish the best beats. The property owners and hired river-keepers maintain the rights to dictate how these waters get fished, vis-à-vis gear, flies, methods, catch limits, and fishing hours. (Hence, the reason I was "benched" after my eighth fish.)

The fishing, in prime season, is predominantly dry-fly, and is often very technical, requiring an ability to match hatches and make difficult casts and presentations. This is not a place to visit in order to stack up numbers or go trophy hunting. Rather, it's a place to honor and respect. The true value of fishing here has more to do with tradition and appreciation of the water itself than anything else.

When conditions cooperate, typically mid-May into early June, large green drake

THESE PAGES: May is the prime month to fish "drakes" in southern England. The combination of gin-clear water, large mayflies, and eager brown trout creates a spectacle that's unmatched anywhere else in the world.

(*Ephemera danica*) mayflies make for otherworldly dry-fly action. Thus, for true aficionados of fly fishing, there are no more hallowed waters on the planet. These rivers are simply stunning in their natural beauty, as are the brown trout that swim in them. The tuned-in angler can literally feel a connection to sacred history with every cast.

Holy Waters

Ever since I got hooked on fly fishing as a young man, I dreamed of fishing the chalk streams of England. It had always been a bucket-list destination, and the more I poured myself into the sport, the more I felt an (almost) holy obligation to make a pilgrimage to fish these rivers. But I spent thirty-plus years back-burnering this trip in favor of other trout-fishing adventures. After all, there are many exciting and interesting places to catch trout in this world. So, England waited while I explored the Rocky Mountain West, then branched out to fish in Alaska, Chile, Argentina, New Zealand, and many other places.

There's an old (probably overused) adage that says an angler goes through a cycle, in that they first want to catch a fish, then they want to catch a lot of fish, then they want to catch a big fish, then they want to catch a lot of big fish—and then, they don't really care about catching fish, they just appreciate being where they are, and they focus on the "why" more than the "how" or the "how big" or "how many."

I think one can make a case that the odyssey many traveling trout anglers experience in their lives tracks along that same continuum—in my case, from Michigan to Montana, Alaska to Argentina (and beyond). But ultimately, when I clearly cared most about the "why," I made the chalk stream trip happen, and I am proud and grateful to have closed the circle and fished these fabled streams, because it turned out to be one of the most rewarding, interesting, and fulfilling fishing trips I've ever taken.

Granted, I had to check some of my "American angler ideology" at the door. This is straight-up, unabashed, pay-to-play fishing, and Yanks like me, who are proud of our public lands and fisheries and don't necessarily like to be told what we can fish with, when we can fish, and how many fish we can catch (and release) just need to understand that.

On the other hand, I must admit that watching a blanket drake hatch at two p.m. during a bright, cloudless afternoon, and watching scads of healthy wild brown trout munch those bugs with almost reckless abandon, made it seem pretty obvious what a clear trout stream *could* be like without the minions pounding the heck out of the fish by whatever means possible, whenever they felt like it. The guides who work these waters—all of whom were truly top-notch anglers with years of hard-earned experience—seemed to agree that if these rivers were to go "public," it would take less than a couple weeks to effectively destroy the fisheries and the hundreds of years of history they represent.

Also, know that all chalk streams are not clear enough to see through, even though the Bombay Sapphire gin distillery is on the River Test with reason. Some, like the River Kennet, River Nadder, or River Frome (pronounced *froom*) have darker substrate and are referred to as green or dark chalk streams. The point being, while the water is still sourced the same way and has the same temperature characteristics, you cannot sight fish on these rivers with the same effect that you can on the Test or Itchen, where you can spot trout in the

OPPOSITE: You fish a bit, you rest a bit. Maybe have a cup of tea . . . all part of proper English fishing. But when the bugs hatch and the fish are on, that'll bring out the best in you. English dry-fly fishing is very much "top of the game."

TOP: Sarah Deeter shows a hard-earned brown she caught on the River Nadder. **BOTTOM:** The River Test is to fishing what St. Andrews and Augusta National are to golf. **OPPOSITE:** The brown trout here are picky indeed . . . but they also fight like English bulldogs.

clear currents. In these rivers, you look for rise forms and drop a fly where you see the rings on the surface. With the right cast that works.

The English Way

As for the fish themselves, while the brown trout is indeed native to the British Isles, most of the fish in the chalk streams are planted, though many are also "wild" descendants of browns that were put there generations ago. Locals understandably don't use the term "native" often, and while some Atlantic salmon might still trickle into the lower beats on the Test and elsewhere, the salmon heyday is in the past.

Another thing to know going in is that 90 percent or more of your casting will happen from the bank. Only on certain beats will you actually need waders (unless you opt to wet-wade, but the water is always *cold*) and actually approach the trout by wading in the stream. The chalk streams all have carefully manicured and maintained walking paths beside their banks (often steep) with warming huts and even benches spaced along the way.

This is strictly "opportunity" fishing, and if you think you can plow up the middle of the river, blind-casting, using a bobber and weighted nymph, you will be sorely mistaken. It's far better to sit on one of those benches and watch the water, and wait, sometimes for hours. The desired action usually happens, and when it does, the dry-fly fishing goes off. Do not cheat yourself, or disrespect the fishery, by being impatient.

In sum, fishing the chalk streams really boils down to the four essential elements of great fly fishing: foremost, the water; then the fish; then the bugs; and, ultimately, the angler's ability to make a good cast and dry-fly presentation. This is one of the few places in the world where those four factors still matter in equal measure.

If you appreciate and understand those things, and if you can make good casts, you might just be lucky enough to catch eight big, healthy wild brown trout on size-12 dry flies in a day. Of course, if you appreciate where you are, and respect who might have trod the same paths from which you make those casts, it all has immensely greater significance. And that's as good as it gets.

If that's not good enough, get back in the angler continuum, and explore and catch, and measure, and do all that stuff in other places.

But eventually, the "how many" will be less important than the simple "how" and "why" of fly fishing. The "why" will inevitably lead you to the chalk streams of England.

OPPOSITE: The Itchen winds its way through Winchester. **ABOVE:** You'll often have an audience of sheep in the pastures that line many chalk streams.

On the Table

England still gets a bad rap for having bland food, but the truth is far from that, especially in the countryside. There's been a renaissance of farm-to-fork culinary adventure, especially in the past few decades as classically trained chefs have taken up residence. Winchester, where the Itchen flows toward the sea, for example, is a legitimate foodie destination now, and it hosts the largest farmers market in the UK twice a month.

Many of the chalk streams are literally part of the food and beverage scene, as watercress grows in such abundance during the summer months, riverkeepers set aside weeks—usually after the prime mayfly hatches have subsided—to cut the vegetation in the river. If they didn't do this, any hooked fish would almost certainly burrow in and break off a fly. The ancillary benefit of all this is delicious watercress soups and salads.

The water is famously "gin clear," and the local distilleries are there to prove it. It's worth visiting the Bombay Sapphire distillery on the River Test, if only to smell the dry botanical ingredients like juniper and lavender before they're infused into the gin.

When I want to go back to this place in my mind and with my taste buds, it's classic pub fare of fish and chips, mushy peas, and Eton mess for dessert, which was what I had many times after fishing. I sprinkled in some modern updates to these classics.

Fish & Chips
with Mushy Peas

Serves 4

Canola oil for frying

1 heaping cup all-purpose flour

1 tablespoon paprika

1 tablespoon garlic powder

1 tablespoon baking powder

1 teaspoon fine sea salt

1 teaspoon ground white pepper

1 large egg

1 English pub ale, such as Fuller's ESB, Boddington's, or Newcastle Nut Brown Ale

4 (6-ounce) skinless cod fillets

Tartar sauce for serving

Malt vinegar for serving

Lemon wedges for serving

In a Dutch oven fitted with deep-frying thermometer, heat 1 inch of canola oil to 375°F over medium-high heat.

In a medium bowl, whisk the flour, paprika, garlic and baking powders, salt, and pepper.

Add the egg and stir to combine. Slowly add the beer while whisking with a fork. Blend until the batter is lump-free but not runny (it should be the consistency of pancake batter).

Right before cooking, wrap the cod in paper towels to absorb excess moisture.

Once the oil comes to temperature, coat the fillets completely with batter and carefully place in the oil. Cook until crispy and golden brown, about 10 minutes.

Serve hot with tartar sauce, malt vinegar, lemon wedges, and mushy peas. If you like, add on "chips" (French fries to us Yanks; see Supinski's fries on page 229). If you want, sprinkle the chips with truffle salt.

Mushy Peas

2 tablespoons unsalted butter

3 cloves garlic, minced

1 (16-ounce) bag frozen peas

3 tablespoons whole milk

2 teaspoons lemon juice

1 tablespoon finely chopped mint leaves (optional)

Fine sea salt and freshly ground black pepper

Melt the butter in a medium saucepan over medium heat, then add the garlic and cook until fragrant, about 45 seconds. Add the frozen peas and cook until softened, about 5 minutes.

Transfer half of the peas to a food processor with metal blade, add the milk, and process until pureed. Return the pureed peas to the saucepan and stir in the lemon juice and mint, if using. Season with salt and pepper. Mix well and serve.

Eton Mess

This famous British staple, originally created to serve students at Eton at the annual cricket match against the Harrow School, is simple, flavorful, and refreshing.

Serves 6

2 pints fresh berries, preferably strawberries, stemmed and coarsely chopped

Drizzle of freshly squeezed lemon juice

1 cup heavy cream

2 to 3 tablespoons confectioners' sugar

1 teaspoon pure vanilla extract

3 cups store-bought meringue (you can buy on Amazon or from Trader Joe's), crushed

Put the metal bowl of a stand mixer into the freezer for a few minutes to chill.

Place the berries in a bowl and drizzle with lemon juice (this will keep them looking fresh).

Return the chilled bowl to the stand mixer and fit with the whisk, then whip the heavy cream and confectioners' sugar for 3 to 5 minutes, until desired consistency. Fold in the vanilla.

Layer the ingredients in tall sundae, parfait, or half-pint glasses (use your imagination): Berries, crushed meringue, whipped cream . . . berries, crushed meringue, whipped cream . . . berries, crushed meringue, whipped cream.

FLORIDA KEYS

Fishing the Flats for "Silver Kings"

KIRK DEETER

"They migrate, as many fishes do, and when we touch or intercept these migrations, we sense, subliminally, the dynamism of the biosphere: tarpon migrate by season, season is a function of planetary movement, and so on. Which is no more than to say you can face bravely those accusations of loafing when you have ruined a month chasing tarpon, racking your brain to understand their secret, sidling lives."

—THOMAS MCGUANE

I often daydream about trout fishing. But my night dreams usually involve tarpon.

It's been that way since, many years ago, I got my first glimpse of a "silver king" bursting above a placid, mangrove-lined flat, as if it were a living molten-metal lightning bolt on the other end of my whistling line.

On the Water

I was fishing with my buddy Al Keller—me a wet-nosed writer chasing an adventure angle, and he an equally green fishing guide from southwestern Florida. We were ripping across Sunday Bay in the Ten Thousand Islands when Al suddenly killed the motor and told me in an urgent whisper to make myself ready. Somehow, he had seen three tarpon "laid up" a few hundred yards away, hovering just under the glassy surface. As I tiptoed toward the bow of Al's flats skiff, I caught a glimpse of them myself. They looked like iron-gray torpedoes suspended in the water column.

Al had scurried onto the poling platform, and he push-poled us gently into range. Neither of us uttered a word until just after I fired my first cast toward one of the fish that had drifted slightly apart from the other two.

PREVIOUS: The best saltwater flats in America are found off the Florida Keys. **LEFT, TOP TO BOTTOM:** Keys guide Bear Holeman helps to land and release a tarpon. **OPPOSITE:** Tarpon . . . *Magalops atlanticus* . . . the "Silver King" . . . may not be at the top of the oceanic food chain, but for the fly angler there is no higher aspiration, nor respected quarry. When you can tie into a fish that might be older than you . . . that's certainly cause for pause and deep respect.

"They eat with their mouths, not their tails," Al snickered. (This would be the first of thousands of lessons in humility I'd learn in the tarpon game.)

Having figured out which end was which, I let loose another cast, which somehow found the zone despite the fact that my heart was hammering and my knees were knocking.

That fish turned its head toward the fly, made three deliberate sweeps of its tail, opened its bucket mouth, and sucked that black-and-purple tarpon bunny fly down like nobody's business. The whole thing unfolded like a slo-mo black-and-white highlight reel, and even now, years later, I can close my eyes and play that clip like it happened yesterday.

Now, to my meager credit, I had done my homework, and had read up on tarpon fishing enough to know that setting the hook like you might do with a trout was the kiss of death. Tarpon, while they're not toothy critters, do have hard, bony mouths; as such, one must strip-set the fly, which can be tantamount to trying to drive a finish nail into a cinder block by pulling on a string. But I gave that line a few hard tugs and then let loose. As my reel started to whine, I knew I was in business.

What I wasn't ready for was the sheer shock of watching the gill-rattling jumps that soon followed. That's not just a visual thing. It's also audible. And you don't just hear the rattle, you *feel it* in your chest. Then, you just admire the swoosh as the tarpon takes flight, and when it crashes back into the water sending echoes over the flat, you suddenly realize that this craziness is an entirely different game than anything else in the world of fly fishing.

OPPOSITE, TOP: The real attraction of fishing for tarpon is that you can tie into huge fish in shallow water. It's visual, audible, and sensory overload in the best way. **BOTTOM LEFT AND RIGHT:** Tarpon, as well as snook, love getting into the mangrove flats. (The bird is a Goliath heron.)

Silver Kings

The great writer and filmmaker Guy de la Valdène once described a tarpon trip with Thomas McGuane (whose novel *Ninety-Two in the Shade* still stands in my mind as the definitive work on Florida Keys fly-fishing and guiding culture) and Richard Brautigan (who penned *Trout Fishing in America*, an equally influential tome). De la Valdène said that when Brautigan saw his first hooked tarpon bolt above the surface, he was left in a near catatonic state.

The more you fish for tarpon, the more that seems perfectly understandable.

As for me and that first foray with Al Keller, I fought the fish valiantly for a while, had the pleasure of watching many leaps, and felt the mighty tug. It made my body sweat, my hands cramp, and my muscles ache. Ultimately, I made a rookie mistake and let the fish wrap my line around a mangrove root and, alas, it broke off.

Although it didn't seem so at the time, it wasn't a failure. In fact, because far more tarpon are hooked than actually landed—and because, after all, tricking a tarpon into eating at all is the hardest part—tarpon crazies have come up with a special description for hooking, but failing to land, the fish. They call it jumping tarpon. As in: "How did it go today, Pete?" "Oh great, we *jumped* three tarpon!" "Fantastic!" Which is another way of saying, "We didn't catch any fish, and we punted the ones we managed to hook, but we're going to say we won the game anyway."

I don't have a problem with that. Although talking about how many trout or bluegills you "jumped" doesn't work as well.

Nevertheless, jumping that tarpon became an inspiration that opened my eyes to a new world that was far more captivating than anything else. It only made me want to chase *Megalops atlanticus* more.

The Allure of the Silver King

Of all the fish you might endeavor to catch with a fly rod, there has never been, nor, in my mind, will there ever be, one that can "change your world" in an instant, forever, more than the tarpon will. Part of that is, of course, the thrill of the chase itself.

But the larger part is all about the beast. You see, while tarpon aren't particularly sexy fish—they look like overgrown herring—and their oily, greasy flesh makes them far less than a delicacy, they are nonetheless special when you understand more about them.

In an evolutionary sense, they are among the last remaining dinosaurs of the sea. And by cross-sectioning the otoliths (like fishy eardrums) during necropsies of caught tarpon, scientists have learned that, much like gauging the age of a tree by measuring its rings, they could see that tarpon can live to ages of eighty years or older.

Thus, it's quite possible that the silver king you might hook on the other end of a fly line is significantly older than you are. And to get that old, in environments rife with birds that eat juvenile fish, bull sharks, red tides, micro-plastics, and other pollutants, that beast has to be one damn resilient fish.

Lessons in Humility

I once had the honor of fishing with Bill Curtis, the guy who actually invented the poling platform, from his yellow skiff named *The Grasshopper*. I hooked a monster tarpon only to see it break my line like a cobweb because I'd let my line snag on a cleat on the boat deck. Bill said, "That's okay, son. That's not the first time that's happened."

If you put the fly (a shrimp, a baitfish imitation, whatever) in front of a tarpon, it will eat it.

Two days later the Keys schooled me again, this time with a permit. While fishing off of Curtis Point (named after Bill) near Biscayne Bay, we saw a giant permit swim into range. As I stood on the bow of Bill's boat that fish reflected like a giant garbage can lid under the water surface.

I loaded up and made what I thought was the absolute perfect cast—sixty feet, gently dropping the fly *just a tad beyond* that cruising fish. I made a few strips of the line, and that permit abruptly wheeled away and bolted. Heartbroken, I looked over my shoulder to ask Bill what I had done wrong. He had already climbed down off the poling platform and was mumbling under his breath.

"Permit aren't used to their food attacking them," he said.

I did manage to redeem myself by landing a tarpon the next day.

Years later, I also redeemed myself with Al Keller by catching three, hundred-plus-pound tarpon in a single morning, though I broke one of his rods on the second fish. He forgave me, and we're still close friends and fishing buddies.

Birthplace of Flats Fishing

There is, of course, so much more to fly fishing in southern Florida. In my mind, the most underrated fish of any to be caught in the ocean is the snook. They don't have big teeth, but they have sandpaper-like mouths, so if you come home at the end of the day with your thumbs gritty, as if they've been filed with an emery board, you know you had a good day.

Then there are redfish and sea trout, and snapper, grouper, sheepshead, and more.

For the fly angler, a bonefish, tarpon, and permit caught in the same day is a "grand slam." If that's on your bucket list, the Keys are a good place to do it.

Most of all, fishing here is about history and culture, not just Hemingway . . . or Parrotheads . . . or partygoers. I'm talking about the guide culture. There's a big-time difference between the guide who knows where to use a spinning rod with live shrimp bait, and those who truly know the game of saltwater fly fishing. The best saltwater fly guides in the world are those who live (and last) in the Florida Keys. And, trust me, they know it.

LEFT: Releasing a juvenile tarpon. This fish can live to be eighty years old or older. **OPPOSITE:** A Key West fish house shows the typical catches of the day. When the grouper is fresh, that's option "A."

On the Table

There might be no more refreshing drink after a long, hot day on the flats than a mojito. After all, from Key West you are closer to Cuba than you are to mainland Florida, and the recipe is simple (1½ ounces clear rum, freshly squeezed lime juice, club soda, mulled mint leaves, and a glass full of crushed ice; garnish with fresh mint for sniffing and serve in a pint glass).

I also think of "refreshing" in the context of food, especially after spending several hours baking under the sun on the flats. I like tastes that are light, tangy, and often spicy. Most of all, I like endemic flavors—stuff that drops a pin right in the place where you're sitting down to eat it.

When I'm in the southernmost reaches of Florida, it's all about blackened grouper with homemade slaw, usually in sandwich form. It's all tangy on the taste buds, but also intriguing and inviting.

And how in the heck could you enjoy fishing in the Keys without a bit of key lime? Having been around that block many times, I've found that these little finger-food-size bars pack the flavor minus the ostentatious meringues and such that seem a bit like overkill.

This is a genuine angler's meal . . .

The Everglades
TIBOR REEL BY TED JURACSIK

Blackened Grouper Sandwiches
with Coleslaw

I grew up trout fishing in Michigan. My father-in-law introduced me to saltwater fly fishing in Florida, and I remain grateful on so many levels. We'd come back to the dock, whether we'd been skunked or not, and gather the family to head for a simple dinner of grouper sandwiches, with tangy slaw and chips on the side. Even now, although he's gone, when I wrap up a day on the Florida flats, I still head off to find a good grouper sandwich. I couldn't imagine doing it any other way.

Serves 4

2 tablespoons paprika

1 tablespoon garlic powder

1 tablespoon onion powder

2 teaspoons sugar

1 teaspoon coarse sea salt

1 teaspoon freshly ground black pepper

½ teaspoon cayenne pepper

1 pound wild-caught grouper, cut into 4 pieces

2 tablespoons vegetable or canola oil, or butter

Potato or brioche buns

Lettuce

Tomato slices, pickles, and salt and vinegar chips (optional)

Mix the paprika, garlic and onion powders, sugar, salt, pepper, and cayenne in a small bowl. Season both sides of the grouper with the mixture.

Heat the oil in a large cast-iron skillet over medium. Place the fish in the pan and cook until it starts to curl, about 3 minutes per side.

Serve on buns with lettuce and coleslaw, tomato slices optional. Include a pickle, additional coleslaw, and salt and vinegar chips on the side of each sandwich.

Coleslaw

⅓ cup apple cider vinegar

2 tablespoons sugar

½ teaspoon celery seed

Salt and ground white pepper

1 cup mayonnaise

½ head green cabbage, thinly sliced

1 cup shredded carrot

½ cup finely diced red onion

Combine the vinegar, sugar, celery seed, a seasoning of salt and pepper, and the mayonnaise in a small bowl. Mix the cabbage, carrot, and red onion in a large bowl. Add the mayonnaise dressing and stir until the cabbage mixture is thoroughly coated. Chill for at least 1 hour for the flavors to set.

Key Lime Bars

Sure, it may seem cliché, but there's just something about key lime pie, and it does not taste any better than it does on a hot, sunny day in the Keys themselves. This recipe for smaller-size bars will put you right there, no matter the season, and no matter where you actually happen to be at the time. It's like eating bites of sunshine.

Serves 9

CRUST

5 tablespoons unsalted butter, melted, plus butter for baking pan

9 honey graham crackers (1 sleeve)

¼ cup sugar

FILLING

2 (14-ounce) cans sweetened condensed milk

6 large egg yolks

1 cup bottled key lime juice

1 tablespoon lime zest, plus more for garnish

Lime wedges for garnish

Whipped cream

Preheat the oven to 350°F and butter the bottom of an 8-inch square baking pan.

Make the crust: Place the graham crackers in a zip-top bag, seal it, and crush them with a meat tenderizer or rolling pin until crumbs are the consistency of sand. Transfer the cracker crumbs to a medium bowl with the sugar. Stir until mixed evenly into the crumbs.

Add the melted butter and blend together with a fork. Again, the mixture should resemble grainy sand.

Press the crumb mixture into the bottom of the prepared baking pan. Make sure the crust is flat and even. (If packed too tightly the crust can be hard; too lightly and it can fall apart.)

Bake the crust for 10 minutes. Let it cool completely, at least 30 minutes, before adding the filling.

Preheat the oven to 325°F.

Make the filling: In a large bowl, whisk the condensed milk, egg yolks, key lime juice, and lime zest. Pour over the cooled crust.

Bake until the filling is just set but still a little jiggly, 20 to 30 minutes. Cool to room temperature, then refrigerate until fully set, about 2 hours. Cut into 9 pieces, then plate and top with a wedge of lime and a dollop of whipped cream.

Garnish with lime slices, zest, and whipped cream. Cut into 9 squares and enjoy.

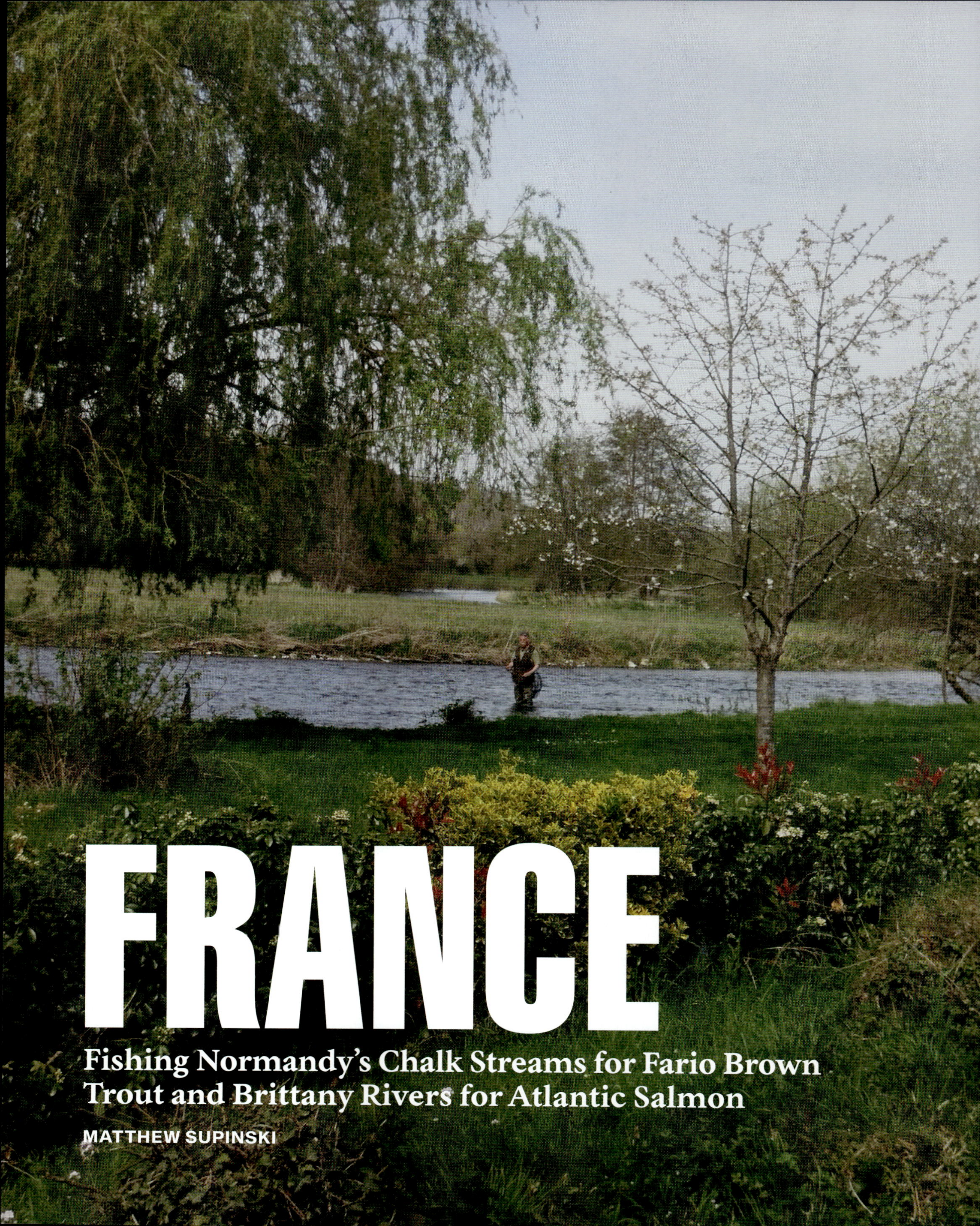

FRANCE

Fishing Normandy's Chalk Streams for Fario Brown Trout and Brittany Rivers for Atlantic Salmon

MATTHEW SUPINSKI

"In chalk streams, rivers rising in chalk and with abundant weed, the stock of food is equivalent to the larder of an extremely luxurious restaurant. The fish has too great an abundance to choose from. The menu does not interest it. It likes to choose 'a la carte' those dishes which appeal most to its appetite or greed."

—CHARLES RITZ

The millrace at Aclou, near Brionne in Normandy, France, still spills pure and icy spring water, as it has for centuries. There Charles Ritz spent many a night watching the River Risle's trout rise to mayflies and sedges. Or if he was quick, out of the corner of his eye he could catch them flashing and grubbing for scuds and pale watery nymphs in the weedy channels. Here at dusk, after a day's fishing, Ritz often sipped fine cognac and smoked Cuban cigars with his good friend and confidant, Frank Sawyer, inventor of the time-honored Pheasant Tail nymph fly pattern. Ducks and kingfishers meandered in the mix at the mill pool, especially when the large *Ephemera danica* mayflies were heavy on the water. They relished them equally as did the gorgeous, red-spotted fario brown trout that swim here. Especially at dusk, as the cadence of the mill's waterwheel seduces and puts one into a rare and truly intoxicating calm, this place has the ability to make one's stresses and anxieties disappear. You will want to stay in this enchanting French pastoral setting forever.

France has a stunningly diverse ecology, so it's unfortunate that many visitors only go to the touristy Parisian sites, eateries, and monuments. There, one often ends up having very hectic and often less-than-memorable experiences commonly associated with any

PREVIOUS: The hallowed chalk stream waters of the River Risle in Normandy in early spring. **OPPOSITE:** Mills are synonymous with chalk streams and limestone spring creeks around the world. **TOP:** The meadows of the Risle are loaded with terrestrials all summer. Here, the author's rubber-legged Letort Cricket. **BOTTOM:** The magnificent "Mayfly Danica." the genesis fly that inspired fly fishing for the legendary Dame Juliana in the late 1400s.

large city's impatient inhabitants and frenzied tourists. But the moment you leave the urban madness, you quickly breathe a sigh of relief and feel the true French country (*campagne*) vibe—a charm you unmistakably get from this magnificent breadbasket of France and Europe.

I believe that only the French can continually produce and seduce a foodie's palate, no matter what they cook. They never fail to romance and satiate your taste buds with their finest delicacies, produced by the long history of iconic French chefs that have hailed from all its amazingly food- and spirit-rich appellations. Those chefs have inspired nouvelle cuisine, comfort bistro fare, and peasant styles of nose-to-tail worship. Here, nothing is wasted and the entire animal is used as Auguste Escoffier preached.

On the Water

The sea-to-table bounty from the Normandy and Brittany coastal waters just adds to the cornucopia of culinary opportunities. The succulent Bélon oysters, scallops, mussels, and lobsters, along with various fish like the chef's-choice turbot, sole, pollack, and sea bass, give a chef unlimited possibilities. But, most important for the angling sportsman and culinary connoisseur alike, it's all about the Atlantic salmon, which swam up the Seine and Risle by the hundreds of thousands centuries ago. With its waters now cleaned up from centuries of pollution, Paris can witness Atlantic salmon swimming throughout the city once again. *Vive la Saumon!*

My interest in this special part of France came from reading Ritz, the famous hotelier and fly-fishing author. As a corporate hotelier and food and beverage director, I was inspired by Ritz's passion for fly angling and cane-rod building, combined with his epicurean taste for the gourmand lifestyle. The Ritz Hotel in Paris was home to many iconic French chefs, among them perhaps the finest of them all, Escoffier.

Our senses of taste and smell are often associated with joyful experiences we remember the rest of our lives. In France, those wonderful aromas seem to come from wherever you are. They may hit you when you are wading and Euro nymphing a mountain trout stream in the Pyrenees, or as the water flows under the bridges through the main street of an old mountain town and you catch a whiff of a boulangerie or café. Or a particular scent might permeate the quaint cobblestone streets lined with butcher-shop charcuteries and bustling brasseries.

A Chalk Stream Passion

As a member of the food and beverage management team at the prestigious Shoreham Hotel in Washington, D.C., I helped implement the magnificent vision of the Omni corporate top brass: to recreate a true Parisian brasserie in the capital city. The iconic French chefs at the time, like Paul Bocuse, Jean-Louis Palladin, Alain Ducasse, Guy Savoy, and Jacques Pépin, were relaxing formal nouvelle cuisine and creating peasant-style comfort eateries. Our team traveled to Paris to experience true Parisian restaurant landmarks. The result of our efforts was an authentic brasserie we named Café Monique. As my passion for authenticating and improvising gourmet comfort food styles from around the globe grew, so did my appetite for chalk stream spring creeks and their super-selective trout. This became an obsession during that Washington tenure.

CLOCKWISE FROM TOP: The true wild and indigenous chalk stream fario of the River Risle that took a French Spider-Hewitt style; Guillaume Chauvelot, whose family have been pioneers and living the river for a century; a beautiful golden butter brown that was fooled on a March Brown extended body.

ORVIS

In the nearby pastoral Amish country of the Cumberland Valley, icy-cold limestone spring creeks flowed. I spent every waking moment outside of the hotel pursuing its highly sassy trout with flies I tied and crafted as passionately as the brasserie dishes and fine service we created. My limestone mentors, Shenk, Proper, and Marinaro, insisted I visit their identical duplicate streams across the pond like the Rivers Test and Itchen in the Hampshire countryside of England, which I did and loved. But a Pezon et Michel bamboo rod I purchased, inscribed with Ritz/Sawyer Parabolic in its cane finish, along with my readings of their books about the River Risle in Normandy, fueled my interest to explore there.

My Holy Grail

On a gorgeous summer morning, heading northwest from Paris on the N13 after our hotel group tour, I couldn't help admire the stark medieval architecture of the Renaissance in the beautiful town of Evreux. Monasteries and abbeys dotted the countryside, where Limousine and Guernsey cows grazed. And to add to this fairy-tale countryside, an occasional old-school wooden farm cart full of hay or produce and led by horses clopped down the cobblestone roads. Near the town of Nassandre, not far from Aclou, my host Guillaume met me, and we drove to his quaint country house, a bed-and-breakfast. Here flowed my Holy Grail: the famous Risle with its beautiful wild fario brown trout. Fario was a name given to the true indigenous strain of European stream brown trout that were brought to America in 1884 from the Black Forest of Germany.

A chalk stream/limestone spring-creek brown trout, no matter where it's found, has a moveable feast of rich and diverse food to sustain it year-round.

CLOCKWISE FROM TOP: Frank Sawyer, the legendary ghillie and nymphing icon, probed his River Avon in England and the Risle in France, where he tested out his nymph and rod design theories with his partner, Charles Ritz; Sawyer's original Pheasant Tail designs; Marinaro/Baltz Jassid.

When we arrived at the bed-and-breakfast, the finest charcuterie plate I ever tasted greeted me, with a side of rich country butter shavings and a fresh-baked baguette; I was in gastronomic heaven. I experienced for the first time a rabbit and pork pâté en croute with pistachios. The goose liver foie gras was sumptuous. And rounding out the board was a fruitwood-smoked trout fillet. Garnishes included cornichons, sweet peppers, and pickled mushrooms. Rich Camembert wedges completed the feast. It was the most perfect and delicious cold dinner plate I have ever tasted. A few snifters of local brandy and a fine cognac gave me a warm buzz.

The next morning Guillaume briefed me on what to expect as I explored his estate's river beats. It was late summer, and the cool days and rainy season were about to begin. The Risle fario were a perfect study in indigenous wild trout that evolved to be stubborn. They looked very similar to the Letort Spring Run brown trout I hunted in Pennsylvania, with spaced-out spotting and big scarlet-red dots. They also appeared very fat and healthy, as I watched a few grub in the weedy shallows near the small bridge I hid on. One thing I have always preached: Approach the stream with a low profile and stalk slowly, like a heron. The soggy ground near the chalk streams sends vibrations to the fish's lateral lines across great distances and alerts the fish to your presence—one sloppy stumble and you can quickly send them for cover and make them passive to the fly for the day. I also did a sampling of the stream's gravel and vegetation to determine their primary food sources, which can vary from one chalk stream to another. As expected, the stream's vegetation was full of scuds, which accounted for the very rotund girths of the trout I saw. Since most of the larger mayfly hatches were over for the season, the gravel and weeds were teeming with iron blues: blue-winged olive *Baetis* and *Drunella* mayfly nymphs. It was time to get busy.

TOP AND BOTTOM: Blue-winged olives (BWOs) come in *Baetis*, *Drunella*, and *Epeorus* forms. They are the heart and soul of spring-creek/chalk stream hatches. Called iron-blues by the British, they emerge all year long—especially on cloudy days.

The European spring creeks, on prime real estate, run through nicely manicured lawns, gardens, and millhouses. Next to the stream, a thin strip of shrubbery and vegetation is always left by each river's caretaking ghillies, to allow for aquatic insects that are molting as well as terrestrial ones like beetles, ants, grasshoppers, and crickets to exist as trout food. I was glad I brought my limestone-spring-creek box full of Sawyer's pheasant tails, scuds, CDC blue-winged olive dries, and a handful of Jassids and ants; a few cream midges, sedges, and Caenis/Tricos were tossed in. The French are masters of meticulous detail—I used to buy French Tortue tippet material at the Yellow Breeches Outfitters shop back in the 1980s. Their tippet spool sizes were super-small diameters (from -8x to 11x).

I crawled along a beat on my hands and knees where fish were rising to some extremely small minutiae I couldn't identify. I saw some mating clouds of what I thought were tricos (what Brits call the white curse) along the banks. My Pennsylvania limestone days taught me to tie #28 midges by the boxload, and I was happy my eyes were trained for the task.

My first few casts with #24 Caenis/Trico–style spinners went ignored. I saw two very nice browns come up and refuse them. I was shocked. Usually when trout were taking minutiae, smaller and sparser was always better and immediately accepted, but not that day. I tried again over several other fish that were sipping, and once again nothing. I then tied on a tried-and-true Vince Marinaro standby, a #20 Jassid. This iconic fly imitates an ant, a leaf hopper, small beetle or terrestrial, perhaps midge of some sort. To a wild trout it was buggy food.

As I walked very gingerly along the banks, I noticed one good bulge of a rise tight by an overhanging willow. It was one random rise, and I immediately cast my Jassid in its feeding lane and gave it a quick twitch, then dead drift. The water boiled, and I was into a very good fish. It bore along the weedy undercut bank and knew exactly where to go when in trouble. The stiff cane rod with strong Tortue material turned the fish from heading into one cluttered weed channel after another; all of them would have spelled immediate disaster.

The big brown made one exceptional leap, with weeds hanging off the leader. I knew it would take a miracle to land this beauty without breaking off. I kicked off my Wellington boots so I could jump into the stream's weed banks by the shore to keep the brownie away from one less obstacle. On a wing and a prayer, I performed a ballet act of a jump and a net job any ghillie would have been proud of. The beautiful nineteen-inch French chalk stream fario of my dreams lay breathing in the water of my net as I snapped a few shots with my beat-up Nikon SLR and Kodachrome. My mission was accomplished. I know my chalk-stream master, mentor, and hero, the greatest of them all, Vince Marinaro, was smiling down on me from heaven at that moment. (I have now caught chalk stream brown trout in seven countries around the globe and on two continents.)

I had a wide smile as I walked through the pasture back to the country house. A cute Bouvier herding dog became my streamside friend as it led me back, realizing a meal was to be had. Waiting for me to toast and celebrate my fario victory was a bottle of Calvados that I had purchased. I also had a few local craft beers I kept chilling in the cold river. The blonde beers there were amazing, especially the ones with cinnamon.

Early spring is a rite of seasonal passage for the trout stalker celebrating opening day. With leaves yet to bud, the Risle's trout turn their foraging activity toward the first blue-winged olive hatches, when the first rising trout is a celebrated sight.

CLOCKWISE FROM TOP LEFT: Châteaux, Victorian villas, and royal estates were built since feudal times on trout and salmon rivers in Europe. Here, the gentlemen anglers often sip cognac, smoke cigars, and wait for the royal drake mayfly of the evening hatch to appear and watch trout feed before they get into a casting position; the historic mill at Aclou where Charles Ritz, Frank Sawyer, Ernest Hemingway, and Arnold Gingrich spent many days watching trout rise; fresh red chanterelles are a French forager's gold; a true local country pâté en croûte is served and enjoyed with fine wines.

On the Table

Where Sauces and the Sea Are Worshipped

Chef Marie-Antoine Carême in the early 1800s, and Escoffier a century later, made sauces supreme in French cooking. Every trained culinarian must perfect the family of mother sauces like espagnole, velouté, béchamel, and tomate, along with hollandaise and mayonnaise. Early and contemporary French gourmet cooking comprises daughter variations of these along with mirepoix and jus de veau lié (thickened veal stock). All the luscious ragus and meat, fowl, and venison dishes had these succulent rich sauces, with fresh herbs and spices adorning them.

Though an hour's drive from the coastline, Normandy is closely tied with the delicacies from the channel and Bay of Biscay in Brittany. Herring still come up the Seine and are treasured delicacies. But for millennia the distinguished Saumon du Atlantique was the fish of the kings and queens. On Brittany rivers, such as the Ellé, Léguer, Scorff, Sélune, and Aven, small runs of Atlantic salmon can still be caught on the fly in the summer months. Though mainly grilse, smaller one-winter-at-sea salmon, or *castillon* as the French call them, are truly the most prized fish for a French chef. They have been known to poach whole fish and decorate them for grand occasions like weddings and coronations. Pâtés, terrines, mousses, and galettes, along with baked-en-croute styles, have been cherished salmon delicacies.

At a quaint L'Auberge farmhouse inn restaurant near the Risle, where I had dinner on that trip, the chef-owner said his grandfather and his father before him were famous for getting their hands on the first fresh salmon of the spring. Those salmon swam up all the tributaries as far up to the Alps, where they once spawned in the mountain headwaters. The aristocracy of the land barons, kings and queens, and prime ministers and their dignitaries all received the first spring salmon that swam back to their natal rivers.

In those castle and country estates, as the fire cracked, music played, and wine and cognac were poured, the grand chef du maison brought out the platters first of salmon, with its pinkish-red meat from an amazingly rich diet of crustaceans, eels, and herring that it consumed in the high seas. It was usually poached or roasted, with perhaps a succulent dill-dijon beurre blanc, and garnished with the wild mushrooms of the spring. A mélange of baked new spring potatoes with onions, rosemary, garlic, and celery seed accompanied the salmon. Finally, accoutrements of sautéed asparagus and fiddleheads in cognac with fresh dill completed the feast. Appetizer cold platters were always the riches of the sea, with pickled herrings, prawns, oysters, gravlax, and fruitwood-smoked trout or pike. These gourmet celebrations of the first fish coincided with the season of morels, white truffles, and various other wild fungi.

Onion, Bacon, Gruyère & Wild Mushroom Tart

À LA NORMANDIE

A succulent quiche-style country dish that fuses all those delicious country favorites together. Feel free to swap in a store-bought pastry crust.

Makes 1 (9-inch) tart; serves 4 to 6

PASTRY

2½ cups all-purpose flour, plus more as needed

1 teaspoon coarse sea salt

1 cup (2 sticks) cold unsalted butter, cut into ½-inch pieces

3 tablespoons ice water, plus more as needed

FILLING

6 slices thick-cut bacon

3 large sweet onions, thinly sliced

2 cups sliced wild or cremini mushrooms

Coarse sea salt and freshly ground pepper

7 large eggs

1 cup heavy cream

½ cup shredded Gruyère

1½ tablespoons freshly grated Parmesan

1 teaspoon minced rosemary leaves

¼ teaspoon cayenne pepper

Pinch nutmeg

Make the pastry: Preheat the oven to 450°F.

Whisk the flour and salt in a large bowl. Cut in the butter using a pastry blender until the mixture resembles fine cornmeal. Pour in the water slowly, while kneading the dough into a firm ball. Pour in additional ice water as needed if the dough is too dry or additional flour if too moist.

Divide the dough in half. On a lightly floured surface, roll out one of the dough halves into a round slightly larger than a 9-inch pie pan. (To freeze the other dough half, wrap tightly in plastic wrap and place in a zip-top freezer bag. To use from frozen, remove from the freezer bag and thaw at room temperature.) Fit the dough in the pan and fold over and crimp the edges. Bake until the crust just starts to turn lightly brown, 10 to 12 minutes. Set the pastry shell aside and reduce the oven temperature to 375°F.

Make the filling: Cut the bacon into small pieces and cook in a medium skillet over medium heat until crisp, about 6 minutes. Using a slotted spoon, transfer the bacon to a plate lined with paper towels. Set aside.

Discard all but 3 tablespoons of the bacon fat. Add the onions and mushrooms to the fat in the pan and cook over low heat until the onions caramelize and the mushrooms are browned and tender. Season with salt and pepper; let cool.

In a large bowl, whisk the eggs with the cream. Crumble in the bacon, then add the onions, mushrooms, cheeses, rosemary, cayenne, and nutmeg. Season with ½ teaspoon salt and ½ teaspoon pepper.

Pour the filling into the pastry shell and bake until the custard is set, about 25 minutes. Transfer to a rack and cool slightly before serving.

Cedar-Planked Atlantic Salmon
with Dijon-Dill Beurre Blanc & Caramelized Wild Mushrooms

This delicious recipe celebrates the ritual of the first salmon and is best served with potatoes and asparagus (recipes follow). Prior to cooking the salmon, soak the cedar planks according to the package instructions.

Serves 4 to 6

SALMON

2 (1½-pound) sides Atlantic salmon or 4 (6-ounce) fillets, pinbones removed

Extra-virgin olive oil

Chardonnay for sprinkling

1 lemon

About 4 tablespoons Trader Joe's Salmon Rub or homemade rub (see Note, next page)

SAUCE

1 large shallot, minced

1 bunch fresh dill, leaves finely chopped, plus more for garnish

1½ cups Chardonnay

¾ cup heavy whipping cream

4 tablespoons unsalted butter

1 teaspoon Dijon mustard, plus more to taste

¼ cup finely chopped parsley leaves

1 lemon

MUSHROOMS

1 pound mixed wild mushrooms or 1 pound chanterelles, trumpets, boletes, shiitakes, porcinis, or morels, chopped

½ cup Chardonnay

2 tablespoons unsalted butter

Dash balsamic vinegar

Pinch dried thyme

Pink salt and freshly ground black pepper

Make the salmon: Brush the salmon with olive oil, sprinkle each side with Chardonnay and a few squeezes of lemon, then coat with the salmon rub.

Put 2 soaked cedar planks on a gas grill on medium-high. Close the lid and when the temperature reaches 375°F to 400°F, place a side of salmon on each plank. Close the lid again and grill until the salmon is still somewhat pink in the middle and flakes, 15 to 20 minutes. Be careful not to overcook the salmon.

Make the sauce: To a medium saucepan over medium heat, add the shallot, one-quarter of the dill, and the Chardonnay. Lower the heat and cook until reduced to 2 tablespoons, 5 to 7 minutes.

Add the cream. Reduce to ½ cup, 5 to 7 minutes.

Remove from the heat and whisk in the unsalted butter. Stir in the mustard, taste, and add more, if desired. Add the parsley and several squeezes fresh lemon. Cover the sauce to keep warm.

(RECIPE CONTINUES)

Make the mushrooms: In a large skillet on low heat, add the mushrooms, Chardonnay, butter, and balsamic vinegar and slowly cook until the mushrooms are browned. Add the thyme and season with salt and pepper.

When ready to serve, top each side of salmon with the some of the sauce and all of the mushrooms. Garnish with fresh dill, serve any remaining sauce on the side, and enjoy with the potatoes and asparagus.

Note: You can make a homemade rub using 4 tablespoons each of brown sugar, smoked paprika, dried thyme, salt, and pepper. (Any leftover rub can be stored in an airtight container for 1 week.)

Country-Style Baked New Potatoes

16 medium red new potatoes, thinly sliced

2 medium white onions, thinly sliced

Extra-virgin olive oil

1 full sprig rosemary, leaves minced

Pinch celery seed

Pink salt and freshly cracked pepper

Preheat the oven to 400°F.

In a 9-inch round baking dish, arrange the potato and onion slices upright like a tian, placing an onion slice between every 2 potato slices. Generously drizzle with olive oil.

Sprinkle with the rosemary, celery seed, salt, and pepper. Cover with foil and bake for 40 minutes to cook through.

Remove the foil and bake until slightly crispy, another 5 to 10 minutes. Serve immediately.

Roasted Spring Asparagus

2 bunches large purple asparagus, trimmed

Extra-virgin olive oil

Pink salt

Balsamic vinegar

Preheat the oven to 400°F.

Place the asparagus in a single layer on a large baking sheet and generously coat with olive oil. Sprinkle with pink salt.

Roast until tender and beginning to crisp, about 7 minutes (they are also excellent grilled).

Drizzle with balsamic vinegar and serve.

Pistachio Crème Brûlée
with Orange "Trout Roe Caviar" Pearls

ALLENBERRY RESORT & PLAY HOUSE BOILING SPRINGS, PENNSYLVANIA
RECIPE FROM CHEF REBEKAH BOWERSOX

The limestone/chalk stream legends of Pennsylvania used the Allenberry Resort and Playhouse, on the banks of the historic Yellow Breeches Creek trout stream, as command central. On its banks my wife, Laurie, and I got married as many of our guests came off the river in their fishing waders. The inspiration to fish the chalk streams of France and England came from these limestone legendary mentors of mine like Marinaro and Shenk. Today, it is a destination resort for every trout fly fisher: the food is superb!

Makes 6 (4-ounce) servings

PISTACHIO PASTE

1 cup unsalted pistachios, shelled, plus more, crushed, for garnish

½ cup sugar

⅔ cup almond flour

Drop almond extract

Amaretto as needed

PISTACHIO CRÈME BRÛLÉE

3 large egg yolks

⅓ cup sugar, plus more for caramelizing

½ cup pistachio paste

1 cup whole milk

1 cup heavy cream

2 drops almond extract

ORANGE "TROUT ROE CAVIAR" PEARLS (OPTIONAL)

Canola oil

3 cups orange juice

3 tablespoons sugar

1½ teaspoons agar agar

Yellow food coloring

Preheat the oven to 300°F.

Make the pistachio paste: Bring 4 cups water to a boil. Add the pistachios and cook for 2 minutes; strain. When cool enough to handle, rub with a kitchen towel to remove the brown peel. Place the pistachios in a medium bowl.

In a medium saucepan fitted with a candy thermometer, combine 2 tablespoons water with the sugar and bring to a boil over medium-high heat. Wash down the sides of the pan with a silicone brush and cold water to prevent crystallization. Boil until the temperature reaches 245°F, then pour onto the pistachios, mix with a silicone spatula until the syrup crystallizes and the pistachios become "sanded."

(RECIPE CONTINUES)

Add the almond flour and almond extract, then transfer to a food processor fitted with the metal blade and process into a paste. (If it is too thick, add amaretto while processing.)

Make the pistachio crème brûlée: Whisk the egg yolks and sugar until light yellow.

In a medium saucepan, warm the pistachio paste with the milk, heavy cream, and almond extract; bring to a boil.

Pour the hot liquid into the egg-sugar mixture, whisking constantly until smooth, and strain through a fine-mesh sieve into a large measuring cup.

Pour the mixture into six ¾-inch-deep ramekins. Place the ramekins into a baking dish and fill with water halfway up the sides of the ramekins. Bake until just set, 30 to 40 minutes. Allow to cool to room temperature, then chill in the refrigerator for at least 2 hours.

Make the orange pearls: Refrigerate a 6-inch-deep container filled with canola oil to at least 44°F.

Combine the orange juice, sugar, agar agar, and food coloring in a medium saucepan fitted with a candy thermometer. Bring to 194°F.

Cool the mixture to 100 to 110°F. Transfer to a squeeze bottle and slowly drip dots into the cold oil. Allow to sit in oil for 2 minutes, then strain the pearls and rinse with cold water.

Meanwhile, top the crème brûlées with a thin layer of sugar and torch until caramelized (alternatively, briefly place under a broiler until caramelized). Top with crushed pistachios and the "trout roe" pearls and serve.

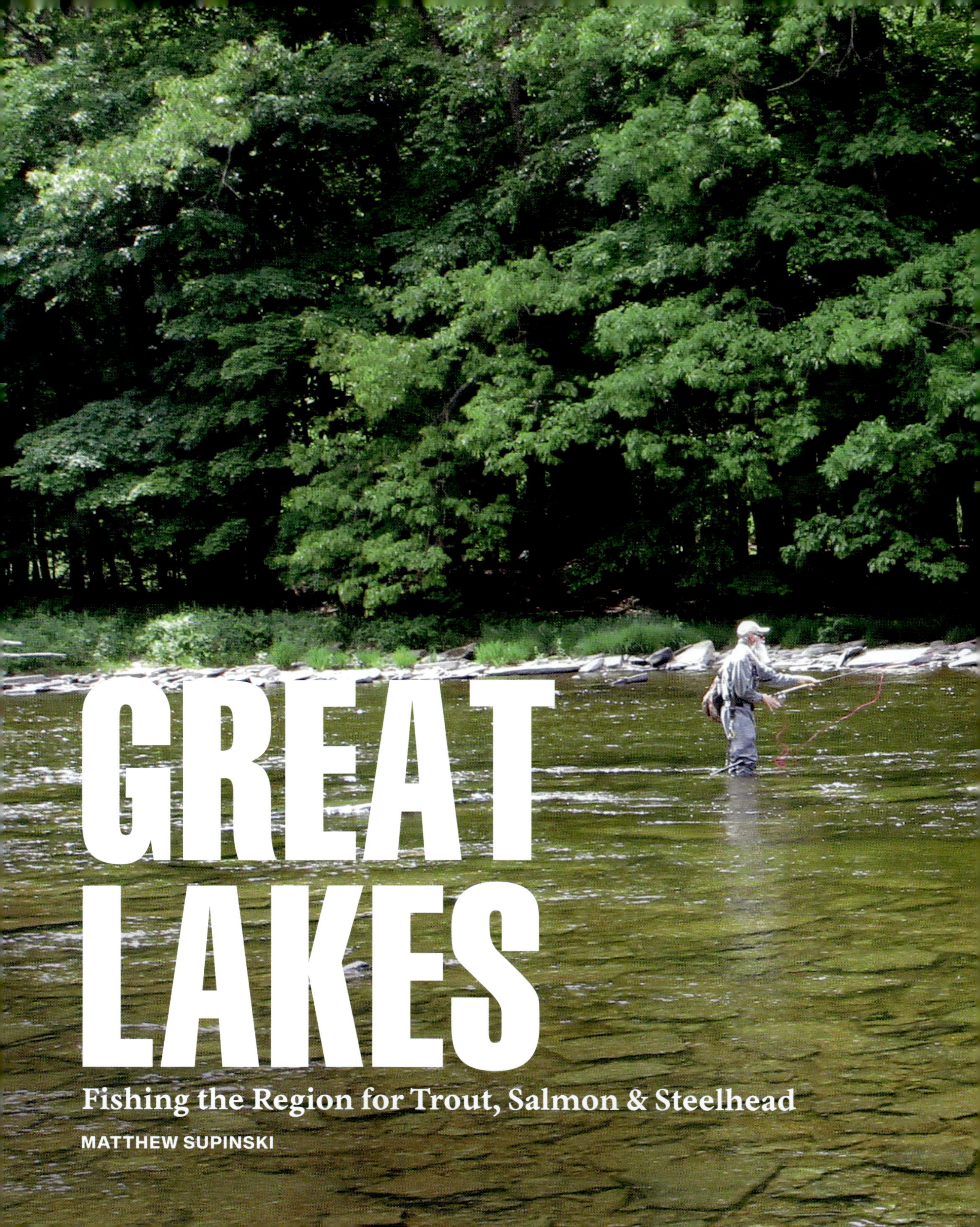
GREAT LAKES
Fishing the Region for Trout, Salmon & Steelhead
MATTHEW SUPINSKI

"The Great Lakes Basin holds hard to winter. Five inland seas carry enough water to flood the continental United States to a depth of ten feet, and for many months the upper layer of these vast sweetwater pools bear ice. Hundreds of millions of tons of ice take a long time to melt."
—BOB LINSENMAN

I am a Great Lakes man. The Great Lakes have been part of my spirit since birth. I was born and raised on the mighty Niagara at the Falls. Here, at one of the Seven Natural Wonders of North America, billions of gallons of azure water cascade downward 150 feet into a violent, thunderous crescendo. The Great Lakes, with enough water to flood the United States to a depth of ten feet, siphons through a narrow river and gorge, and creates a spiritual sanctuary Indigenous people once worshipped as a god. As a young boy, we pretended to be pirates, using discarded wooden doors and planks from cargo ships in a canal by the Niagara rapids, named Three Sisters Islands. I played on the sandy beaches of Lake Ontario during social picnics with other immigrant families. We stuffed dead alewives that washed up on the beach into the backs of teenage girls' bathing suits as they sunbathed with their eyes closed. At age eleven, I caught my first steelhead rainbow trout on the Cattaraugus Creek tributary of Lake Erie, where my uncle lived. There was a smokery on the beach that had the most amazing smoked whitefish and blue pike.

It is the ethnic immigrants and Indigenous people who are the heart and soul of the Great Lakes. They are a hearty bunch willing to withstand the brutally harsh winters, as the early French fur trappers, explorers, and Jesuit missionaries did. To endure blizzards that dump twelve feet of snow at a time, with blistering below-zero temperatures, takes a special type of person. Yet it is still a place where the four seasons can be experienced with all their luster and beauty, as when the forests in fall are ablaze in color. But it is the fishing and the food that are always paramount here.

PREVIOUS: Paul Moore lays out a nice tight loop as he explores the salmon/steelhead waters of New York's iconic Salmon River. **OPPOSITE, TOP:** New York's Zoar Valley and Cattaraugus Creek is home to the spey master/author Rick Kustich. The "Catt" is one of the most iconic steelhead rivers in the Great Lakes, and where the author caught his first steelhead. **OPPOSITE, BOTTOM:** The most perfect Great Lakes brown and steelhead specimens from the author's Gray Drake Lodge portion of the Mighty Muskegon in Michigan.

On the Water

There is perhaps no other place on the planet that has the freshwater sport fishing diversity of the Great Lakes. It is a world-class destination for all cold-water trout and salmonids, along with warm-water species like bass, pike, muskellunge, and perch. From the genesis of their formation, the Great Lakes were indigenous waters for the char family of lake and brook trout. Overharvesting and pollution decimated their populations. Along with that came an alewife explosion as they swam up from the Atlantic Ocean. Alewives, a sardine-like fish, invaded all the Great Lakes, and their populations exploded. At the same time, the lake's alpha predator, the lake trout, saw their numbers declining at an alarming rate. In the 1960s, Howard Tanner and the Michigan Department of Natural Resources imported and stocked Pacific salmon—first coho and Chinook—that ate the alewives in massive numbers. Soon anglers were catching these salmon in trophy twenty-to-thirty-pound West Coast sizes.

Today anglers spend billions of dollars annually in this robust sport fishery, since the fish are now naturally reproducing in the wild.

The fish continue to run upstream to spawn annually, and all anglers cherish them in droves, including fly fishers who have modeled techniques from their Pacific Northwest brethren. You can argue that today the greatest steelhead rainbow trout fishery exists in the tributaries of Lakes Erie, Michigan, and Ontario, where anglers of all methods can catch multiple steelhead in one outing. While Pacific salmon are the jewels of the charter boat fishery, the chrome and pink steelhead are the pinnacle of every river angler, especially the fly angler.

My Steelhead Dreams Come True

When I was a boy, my dad and I would fish the beautiful trout-stream tributaries of the Zoar Valley in the spring. We chased brown trout and little rainbows. But we didn't know those beautiful little rainbows were lake-run steelhead in the pre-smolt phase. Those fish were part of the great California trout transplant into Lake Huron and Michigan's Au Sable River in 1876. The rainbows of steelhead genetic bloodlines later spread throughout the Great Lakes to include other plants from Washington State and Oregon.

Our very first encounter with the giant silvery rainbows—*srebrny pstrąg*, as we called them in Polish—was with a huge chrome and pink, most likely a spawning female, in the shallow gravel of Clear Creek in April. I tied a Micky Finn streamer on the heaviest trout tippet I had. She swiped at it immediately and broke me off instantly. I was devastated and cried the whole ride home.

A scenic natural wonder of the Great Lakes, the Pere Marquette River of Michigan is where Joliet and Father Marquette led missionaries, explorers, and fur trappers as they charted the entire inland lakes and Mississippi river systems for France. Here, the first brown trout from Europe came in 1884, and they are now wild and self-sustaining.

FINATIC

My dad and I eventually became passionate in pursuing these magnificent rainbow beasts in our home waters of the Niagara, where they swam from Lake Ontario. We also had an invite from my dad's boss to use a small cabin on the shores of Georgian Bay, off Lake Huron in Ontario, Canada. There, we found some little trout streams, like Beaver and Big Creeks, that had the big lake-run rainbows running up them. We spent long days chasing them as we picked morel mushrooms and ate streamside lunches.

This steelhead obsession particularly took hold of me, as I went on to guide for thirty years and eventually wrote *Steelhead Dreams*. It takes a special love to spend days on end swinging a fly or dredging a nymph or egg fly on these beautiful waters for the tug of one of these often-elusive unicorns. It is truly a Zen-like calling. As I wrote in *Steelhead Dreams*: "The art of steelhead fly-fishing lies in the transcendental, almost existential realm an angler takes on when waiting patiently for the tug of the 'big pull, the big grab!' It becomes a process of ultimate mind discipline—a meditation of a thousand-cast mantra to a fish that does not need to feed in the river like trout on a daily basis. The enticement of the fly to pique a steelhead strike response is an innate tradition and process born out of complex issues. Natal imprinting to food forms, predator-prey relationships explored in its hunting of the big lakes and oceans, and procreation-driven aggression are perhaps the strongest behavioral strike modifiers."

As one grows and matures in the angling arts, and in the passion and pursuit of chasing steelhead, one continuously delves into and explores all the new fly patterns and techniques, such as swinging a fly spey-style and tactical nymphing that can be applied to catching these fierce, hard-fighting fish. Along with all the science of run timing, and reading the water and fish behavior, it can get very complicated. But what gets you hooked

OPPOSITE: A fall steelhead crushes the author's intruder and catches its breath before the release. Keeping fish wet is the responsible way to insure a bright steelheading future. **TOP:** A Loch Ness Monster–like landlocked Atlantic salmon in a Michigan glacial lake chases the author's bait-fish streamer with a vengeance near the surface. **BOTTOM:** One of the most beautiful leopard-spotted wild browns from a Michigan river one will ever catch.

for life is usually that very first steelhead you catch, hold in your hands, and get to see up close with its stunning pastel colors of Monet's paintbrush.

For me it was on a cold, snowy afternoon during Thanksgiving weekend on a Lake Erie tributary. It was a typical gloomy and overcast late-fall day along the Erie shoreline. My uncle Michael, whom we were visiting, was playing in a polka band that Saturday afternoon, and my parents were attending the event, so I pleaded with my father to let me go fishing on my own. Though my mother was against it, my dad granted my wish. Since I was not yet of driving age, he drove me and dropped me off by the New York State Thruway bridge on the reservation waters of Cattaraugus Creek. On a previous trip a few weeks before, I saw a very talented elderly man catch a nice steelhead near the bridge abutment. With my fiberglass fly rod, I started my usual progression of offerings that learning steelheaders practice in their novice stage. I started with real salmon eggs in a wedding veil, called a spawn sack, then fluorescent orange spinners, then some bright wet fly streamers. I put on a Polar Shrimp, a recent addition to my fly arsenal that I learned to tie from Eddie, the bait and tackle shop owner who was a mediocre fly-tying steelheader.

I patiently probed my offerings through each pool and run, and as is typical in the Great Lakes regions, the weather demons unleashed a very quick, strong Arctic clipper. The winds started to howl across the open gravel riverbed terrain. Then the sheets of pelting lake-effect snow came. I wasn't prepared for it. When we left the house it was sunny and somewhat pleasant, so I wasn't expecting such a dramatic change. Luckily for me, there was the Thruway bridge that I took shelter under, and with it was a nice steelhead pool. As I shivered, I propped my fly rod on a stick like I did when I fished worms for trout. I let the fly just sway in the pool as I shivered and awaited my father. I trusted he would see that the weather had changed and come back to get me.

Just then a huge crimson-cheeked, kyped male steelhead jumped in the pool, as I quickly noticed my rod was bending off the stick and headed for the pool. I grabbed it and had one of the fiercest battles with a trout I ever experienced. I was panicked and started to shake, knowing my skills to fight something this large were limited. After a good brawl, the fish made an error in escape and ran up on the gravel beach. I pounced on it like a bear with a net. It was mine! Now recalling that special moment, it was the most magnificent beast I have ever seen. It had such a richness of magenta and other colors of the rainbow against a silver and green background. With an old Leica camera my dad gave me, I snapped my first pictures of a Great Lakes steelhead, then let the fish go. I was beaming with joy when my dad arrived. I was hooked for the rest of my life on these magnificent migratory wonders, which today embody the heart of the Great Lakes experience.

OPPOSITE, TOP TO BOTTOM: Spey-swinging big intruders and sculpins for early winter steelhead is often a slow and deep presentation; a crimson-red buck (male) steelhead caught by Pere Marquette master Tommy Lynch; Niagara Falls, one of the Seven Wonders of the World, where the author grew up. **TOP:** Brown trout kypes (croc jaws with teeth) get ferocious. This Pere Marquette brown has a lower overbite that many very senior browns will develop as they get closer to spawning. **BOTTOM:** Senyo's Belly Button Lint.

115 PROOF
OLD FORESTER
KENTUCKY
1920
PROHIBITION STYLE
DOMAINE CHANSON
CLOS DES FÈVES
MONOPOLE
BEAUNE PREMIER CRU

On the Table

Ethnic Diversity and the Beauty of Comfort Food

The most powerful force that unites all Great Lakes people is the beauty of their ethnicities—from old-world European and North African immigrants to more recent immigrants from South and Central America. From Toronto to Buffalo, Cleveland to Milwaukee, for those of us who grew up there or visited this melting pot, it was the weekend ethnic festivals, church carnivals, and large cooking and beer tents I personally remember the most. We had a German club called Edelweiss. Polish clubs had their Falcons and Kosciusko bingo halls. Greek Hellenic clubs had some of the best festivals with gyro and spanakopita street vendors. The food was amazing.

Above all, in this land of great waters existed the passion for eating fish. The Catholic Lenten Friday papal decree of no meat mandated its appeal. Thus, the Friday fish fry became a sacred ritual and tradition everyone enjoyed, regardless of religion. American veterans and ethnic clubs, church halls, and off-the-beaten-path mom-and-pop restaurants specialized in fish fries. The indigenous walleye pike, whitefish, and perch were most commonly used. But as their populations declined and fish became pricey, it was on to the perennial favorites of cod, haddock, and Alaskan and Icelandic pollack.

Take-out fish-and-chips establishments down by the fishing boat docks were usually the best. Our favorite was Hansen's carry-out fish market in Lewiston on the Niagara River. They used haddock, which had that wonderful flaky texture in a light, crisp batter; the fish just flaked off as you smothered it with a delicious tartar sauce. Then there were the outstanding french fries, which I ate with salt, malt vinegar, and ketchup. They were like the ones from the french-fry tents at carnivals.

OPPOSITE: The beauty of a fall day on an Erie steelhead river. Guides take pride in their shore lunches, on this day grilled duck. **ABOVE:** Finding the elusive *Morchella*, a true morel and delicacy, is a foraging art form in the Midwest.

I remember the most remarkable coleslaw with celery seed, horseradish, and vinegar. The indulgent finale? A true custard ice cream. The vanilla-chocolate swirl, topped with hot fudge, was the finest way to end a simple culinary excursion into heartwarming comfort food.

What really fostered my culinary passion was learning how to forage. My dad taught me the artisanal craft, and we picked wild mushrooms, fiddleheads, ramps, and all kinds of wild berries and fruits in the New York State and Canadian forests along Lakes Erie, Ontario, and Huron. He taught me how to shoot ducks, geese, grouse, pheasants, and rabbits in the fall and winter. And, finally, to complete the Great Lakes circle, my wife and I moved to Michigan when I took a job as the food and beverage director of a massive convention hotel. I stayed in the state, but I now fish and guide on the rivers that flow into Lake Michigan and Superior. As a family, we toured the entire coastline of Lake Superior while I wrote two books about these amazing lakes.

Smoked Whitefish, Artichoke & Spinach Dip

Smoked whitefish is a delicacy in the Great Lakes. Combine it with comforting artichoke and spinach dip, and you get this hearty appetizer that you will want to snack on forever.

Serves 4 to 6

1 (8-ounce) block cream cheese, softened

¼ cup mayonnaise

¼ cup sour cream

1 clove garlic, minced

⅔ cup shredded Parmesan

½ cup shredded mozzarella

Freshly ground black pepper

1 (14-ounce) can quartered artichoke hearts, drained and chopped

1 (10-ounce) package frozen spinach, thawed and squeezed dry

1 pound smoked whitefish, flaked

Thin slices baguette, toasted, for serving

Preheat the oven to 350°F.

In a medium bowl, combine the cream cheese, mayonnaise, sour cream, garlic, cheeses, and some pepper. Stir in the artichokes and spinach.

Transfer to a medium crock or baking dish and bake until bubbly, about 20 minutes.

Let cool slightly, then stir in the whitefish. Serve with toasted baguette slices.

Parmesan-Crusted Baked Walleye

This takes the fish fry to a different level, incorporating an East Coast theme. Serve with fries and coleslaw.

Serves 4

1 large shallot, minced

½ white onion, minced

1 cup dry white wine

1 tablespoon dried thyme

1 tablespoon finely chopped dill leaves

3 tablespoons unsalted butter

2 cups oyster crackers, crushed

½ cup mayonnaise

⅓ cup grated Parmesan

4 (8-ounce) skinless, boneless walleye fillets

Zest of ½ lemon

½ cup finely chopped parsley leaves

Tartar sauce for serving

Preheat the oven to 400°F. Spray a baking sheet with nonstick cooking spray.

In small skillet over medium-high heat, sauté the shallot and onion with the wine, thyme, and dill and reduce the liquid by half, 4 to 5 minutes. Whisk in the butter until melted and combined. Stir in the oyster crackers. Let cool completely. In a small bowl, combine the mayonnaise and Parmesan.

Place the fish on the prepared baking sheet. Spread the mayonnaise mixture on top of each fillet. Spread the cracker mixture over the fillets. Top with lemon zest and bake until the fish flakes lightly and the topping is browned, about 20 minutes. Garnish with the parsley and serve with tartar sauce, fries, and coleslaw.

Ultimate French Fries

6 medium russet potatoes, cut into thin wedges

½ cup extra-virgin olive oil

1 bunch scallions, finely chopped

2 teaspoons onion powder

2 teaspoons paprika

2 teaspoons freshly cracked black pepper

Coarse sea salt

Malt vinegar

Place the potato wedges in a zip-top bag with the olive oil, scallions, onion powder, paprika, and pepper. Seal the bag and shake thoroughly to coat. Let sit for 1 hour at room temperature.

Spray an air-fryer basket with nonstick cooking spray. Place the potato wedges in the basket in one layer. Be sure the potatoes aren't overlapping. Air-fry at 380°F until golden and slightly crisp, about 20 minutes. (Alternatively, place them in a single layer on a baking sheet and bake in a preheated 400°F oven for 20 minutes.) Season with salt, drizzle with malt vinegar, and serve immediately.

Nutella-Bourbon Tiramisu

THE VILLAGE BAKE SHOPPE, LEWISTON, NEW YORK

My dad and I would fish the Sand Docks and Art Park piers in Lewiston, often until midnight, for yellow perch and smelt that we would fry and relish on the family's supper table. On Fridays, our whole family would get into the Buick to go for a haddock fish fry and custard down the road from the bake shop. Today, a stop there for their tiramisu is a must!

This delightful recipe combines the classic flavors of tiramisu with a rich Nutella twist and a touch of bourbon! According to Village Bake Shoppe owner Michael Fiore, "We typically make this dessert in a single serving 'cake in a cup' version. This method allows our customers to have a taste in the store, then save the rest for later! We recommend preparing this dessert to fit eight- or nine-ounce clear squat glasses."

Makes several individual tiramisus

ESPRESSO MIXTURE

1 cup brewed espresso or dark roast coffee, cooled

2 tablespoons bourbon (see Notes)

2 tablespoons granulated sugar (optional, depending on sweetness preference)

NUTELLA CREAM

1 cup mascarpone, at room temperature

½ cup Nutella

½ cup powdered sugar

1 teaspoon vanilla extract

1 cup heavy cream

ASSEMBLY

1 (9 x 13-inch) cassata cake, cut in 2 x 3-inch squares (see Notes)

Cocoa powder, for dusting

Chocolate shavings or grated chocolate (optional), for garnish

Make the espresso mixture: Combine the espresso, bourbon, and sugar (if using) in a shallow bowl. If using sugar, stir until it dissolves. Set aside.

Make the Nutella cream: Combine the mascarpone, Nutella, powdered sugar, and vanilla extract in a large bowl. Mix until smooth and well combined.

In a separate bowl, use a hand-held mixer to whip the heavy cream until stiff peaks form. Gently fold the whipped cream into the mascarpone mixture until fully incorporated, being careful not to deflate the whipped cream.

To assemble: Quickly dip the cassata cake squares into the espresso mixture, ensuring they are soaked but not soggy. Arrange a layer of dipped cassata cake in the bottom of your serving glasses.

Spread half of the Nutella cream mixture over the cassata cake squares. Add another layer of dipped cassata cake on top of the cream. Spread the remaining Nutella cream mixture over the second layer of soaked cassata cake. Cover the glasses with plastic wrap and refrigerate for at least 4 hours, or up to a full day in advance, preferably, to allow the flavors to meld. Before serving, dust the top with cocoa powder and garnish with chocolate shavings, if desired.

Notes:

Bourbon: Adjust the amount of bourbon to suit your taste or omit for an alcohol-free version.

Cassata cake: The bakery uses cassata cake for all white-cake order requests. This Italian sponge cake makes a fantastic substitute for the traditional lady finger cookies. If you can't find a plain cassata cake, use a plain sponge cake or lady fingers.

ICELAND

Fishing for Atlantic Salmon and Brown Trout

MATTHEW SUPINSKI

"Imagine your dream stream as you would like it to be. Clean, cold water you can safely drink. Imagine seeing this dream stream alive with salmon. Everywhere you look you see them rising from resting positions or proposing in a steady parade, as they move from the sea to venture farther and farther upstream."

—JOSEPH D. BATES JR. AND PAMELA BATES RICHARDS

There is something very ethereal about flying high above the clouds over the Atlantic Ocean to Iceland. The flight's passengers seem to always be cooing ever so contentedly—polite, smiling, and with a kind warmth that is shown to the random passengers next to them. It must be that ever-present omnipotent sun that comes through the cabin's windows and basks you in a soothing glow. Traveling to Iceland always gives off such a buzzing, radiating vibe of excitement and adventure. For many people, it's a bucket-list destination.

On the Water

My fly-fishing clients and I look forward to the click and pawl screaming drag sounds of our reels. It's then we embrace the ecstatic vibe of the proverbial "fish on!—the tug is the drug." It happens when an Icelandic salmon, resident or sea-run brown trout, or Arctic char takes your swung tube fly and lifts you into a piscatorial ecstasy. Through this excitement my thoughts always turn to Iceland's distant past. I envision its rivers that flow from the glaciers and underground spring caverns. In *The Brown Trout–Atlantic Salmon Nexus*, I speculated that this mesmerizing island could have been where these species evolved millions of years ago.

Iceland is truly a fairy-tale place. And those who visit can't stop singing its superlative accolades. Its gorgeous rivers, turquoise-tinted blue and peat colored, flow and cascade into majestic and breathtaking waterfalls. Hot mineral springs and geysers pop up from the ground, often unexpectedly,

PREVIOUS: Regardless of where they are in the world, Atlantic salmon and their iconic rivers are in exhilarating places. This is the Laxfoss on the Nordura River. **OPPOSITE:** The author had some of his finest days with leaping, hot running salmon on the Bergsnös Pool on the Stóra Laxá. The wild ponies running the valley and following the anglers. They epitomize the free spirit and wonder of Iceland. **ABOVE:** The natural falls seen on almost every Icelandic river due to the rugged topography carved out by volcanoes millions of years ago. **LEFT:** Black and Chartreuse Temple Dog Tube. Tube flies, even the tiniest #14–18s, are deadly on Icelandic rivers. Chartreuse and blue with black show up very well on the volcanic rock, sediment-stained waters.

as you hike through its colorful wildflowers and emerald-green meadows and plains. To bask in its natural spa bath lagoons is a true hedonistic indulgence. To visit this stunning yet stark place is to view what our planet looked like millions of years ago. Here, the geology is a reminder of our primordial past that is still violently replicated by tectonic plates colliding and lifting up ominous, snow-capped mountains and glaciers spewing breathtaking active volcanoes. It's a never-ending show of shock and awe, which lets us know we live on a brutally intense living earth.

The Gentle Vikings

Iceland's history is filled with Nordic Viking tales. These stories of tragedy, mythical gods, Norsemen conquerors, and a violent life stem from the harsh land. Yet surprisingly, today the Icelandic people are so unlike that stereotype, care-free and gentle. They all speak English, so no need to learn any words except *Takk fyrir* (thank you).

Iceland mesmerized me with a powerful magnetic force when I was a young man. It was my first stop straight out of college, on a year-long culinary apprenticeship tour of Europe. I was changing planes in Reykjavík and flying on to Luxembourg. But due to heavy fog, no departures were leaving. On a post-grad budget, I stayed at a youth hostel, but first went to a bar for a beer. The beer turned into many, and I met a beautiful Icelandic girl and thus ended up partying into the night with the local Icelanders. Needless to say, I never made my flight the next day. Turned out her dad was a very wealthy commercial fishing fleet owner and had a summer lodge on an Icelandic salmon river where he entertained clients, such as executives from McDonald's.

The author with his two-handed spey rod fighting a leaping salmon on the Stóra Laxá. The Atlantic salmon is one of the finest fighting game fish on the planet.

He offered me a job helping out his Icelandic chef in the kitchen, and I also acted as a server at dinner. I got to fish the amazing salmon and brown trout waters by the lodge, and I dated his lovely daughter. It was a dream summer for a young man who loves to fly fish and cook wonderful, freshly procured and picked ingredients.

The rivers were teeming with salmon—and we caught many for the chef and the dinner guests. We also cured salmon gravlax-style and cold-smoked them with a dark rum or Scotch whiskey wet cure. When I had hours to myself, I swung black soft-hackled wet flies, imitating the massive Simuliam midge (on Lake Myvtan) swarms. I ate, drank, fished, and played like a Nordic god.

As tourists revel and awe over its natural beauty and cheerful inhabitants, Iceland has its year-round challenges. During winter, its twenty-four hours of darkness and abundant snow can be a brutal pill to swallow. Climate change has also had an impact.

The beauty of Iceland lies in its long summers of constant daylight. On this amazing island, the wildflowers and heather glisten in the endless sun, the geysers blow, the salmon jump waterfalls, and the ducks and puffins feast on the endless solar-generated food bounty of the waters. And all the while, human and fictional-elf sun bunnies bathe in the springs, worshipping the sun like ancient Druids. One cannot talk about Iceland without mentioning the whole elf thing. They are a huge influence in the mythology and stories of the country. The locals claim they see them all

OPPOSITE: The upper beats of the Stóra Laxá. The volcanic rock gorges on Icelandic rivers are breathtaking, but hiking up and down them is only for the fit. **ABOVE:** Arni Baldursson, the Atlantic salmon sensei.

the time. Thus, during the summers in the land of the midnight sun, life thrives endlessly and on every level—even in little elf huts along the volcanic rock grottos. There is love and peace in the air. It is then that the buzz and verve of life in Iceland knows no limits.

ABOVE: When Atlantic salmon come into rivers, they are bright chrome silver with x-spotting. As they get closer to spawning in the fall, the males (*top*) develop strong kypes for sparring with other males, along with beautiful marble spotting like that of brown trout. The females (*bottom*) keep the silver and lavender sheen. **OPPOSITE, CLOCKWISE FROM TOP:** Vala Arnadottir, an eco-influencer, avid spey caster, and fan of *Salmo salar*; guide Jonas and author celebrating a net job at Tungufljot Falls; the vicious kype jaw that fell for an EP Pink Frances Shrimp.

Stóra Laxá: Iceland's Most Stunning River

Arni Baldursson is a swashbuckling Nordic god reincarnated. Leather, shellfish, and fish-scale bracelets and neckwear adorn his suntanned body; he's who would show up at a casting call for a Viking version of Jack Sparrow. His Norseman-like austere looks and warm presence strike you the moment you meet him. I first met Arni thirty years ago when he was showing a photographic portfolio of stunning Icelandic rivers for which his company had fishing rights. His enthusiasm was and is simply contagious and irresistible.

"The Stóra is like a river you dream of when you die and go to heaven . . . it is our most beautiful Icelandic river bar none!" exclaimed Arni over the phone. Arni had fished every salmon river on the island, and I knew he was being truthful. We were talking over details of my upcoming hosted client trip there in a few weeks. "Bring rain! Our rivers are dry!" It usually rains every day in Iceland—and it is also sunny every day. There is usually plenty of water in its rivers. But climate change has reared its ugly head. Now in these countries that historically have had more than ample precipitation, there are droughts as never seen before. Or in some years, there is endless rain and flooding.

When our group landed at Reykjavík airport, we proceeded through customs and had our fishing equipment "deloused" and put through bacterial and fungal cleaning liquids to remove any invasive parasites—more places should practice eco-hygiene. On the van shuttle to Aurora Lodge on the West Ranga

Abel

River, which was our base-camp inn for the Stóra Laxá, we stopped by the fly shop to get last minute supplies. Tiny Icelandic tube flies were being suggested—really tiny ones, #16 to 18. Common for summer and not early fall, this indicated the lowness of the rivers.

The first few days were met by tough fishing because of the low waters. Then the deluge of rains came in a horizontal blistering fashion. One day the winds and rain were so strong we couldn't cast. We could take the sting out with good whiskeys, wines, and vodkas.

Walking on the Moon

Journeying to the very high elevation beats of the Stóra Laxá gorge was like traveling to an enchanted land. Here, cascading waterfalls with salmon trying to jump them kept us fascinated for hours. The water was hypnotic as it swished through the steep volcanic rock cliffs. Looking down into the valley we saw the Laxá River flow and merge into braided island deltas. Valley heathers, mosses, lichens, and endless pastures feed its wild ponies and sheep, which seem to roam everywhere.

What always fascinates me about the fishing in Iceland for Atlantic salmon and brown trout is the tiny size of the flies being swung wet-fly style. Rarely in other parts of the world do you go down to tiny 14 to 16 tube flies and double- or triple-hooked minutiae patterns. The glacial rivers there run very cold and are somewhat sterile, except for some heavy spring-fed rivers like the Big Laxá that is one giant spring-creek-style river with fertility and greater insect and food form diversity

OPPOSITE: Fresh out of the glacial rivers, a perfect chrome Icelandic salmon that fell for the author's Black and Chartreuse. **RIGHT, TOP TO BOTTOM:** Armed and ready, looking down the Stóra Laxá gorge; the goats follow the anglers around like little gnomes; when the Roman's conquered Gaulish Aquitania, they saw salmon leaping the tallest of waterfalls and named them *salar*, or "the leaper."

ABOVE: The author and excellent guide Jonas admire a beautiful male salmon. **OPPOSITE:** Seafood markets are everywhere in Iceland.

that the trout and salmon can prey on. It is those massive midge hatches that provide the imprinted food forms that trigger larger adult salmon to take the fly when they come back from the ocean baitfish hunting grounds. Thus, the smaller swung flies and even tiny dries that imitate the tiny midges are so deadly. Riffle-hitching the tiny flies and tubes adds a wiggling sideways motion to the flies that is quite alluring to the fish, especially on smooth-flowing waters like many parts of the Big and Stóra Laxá.

It's usually the case that, when fishing in a far-flung locale, the best fishing happens at the end of the trip. It was the last day at Tungufljót Falls that the *Salmo salar* gods finally unleashed their blessings. After driving through tiny rivers in Land Cruisers to get to river destinations from the spate of run-off rains, we arrived at a stunning location. The falls sounded thunderous as we hiked down the path opposite them. Between the mist coming off the falls and the heavy deluge of rain, it felt like we were fishing in a vast, spectacular shower. My wife, Laurie, had never spey cast until this adventure, and she was still fishless for the trip. Our magnificent ghillie Jonas saw a few swirling and porpoising salmon tail out, a usual sign of fresh-run, aggressive fish that could be fly takers. With a simple flick of a single spey cast, Laurie's drifting Willie Gunn–German Helmet variant exploded in a take and a leaping salmon. Despite her concern about losing it, she fought it brilliantly, and a fourteen-pound female Atlantic was hers in the net. She was elated beyond description. Several more fish came to the net that day for me, while Laurie just rested on her laurels and enjoyed the show of leaping and fighting salmon that didn't stop in the pouring rain. In the salmon world, good things happen for those who are persistent and patient.

Later that night at the Aurora Lodge, with our chef and all the group's guests, we topped off the day enjoying the chef's Icelandic rack of lamb, in a rich demi-glace–red currant sauce. It was divine. We all toasted to Laurie's salmon and the *Salmo salar* gods on our last night. Both experiences were joys to be celebrated and relished forever—the perfect epicurean angler ending to a memorable trip, *skål*!

Though the fishing over six days was tough because of drought, then too much water, the elixirs that saved the trip were the memorable outstanding meals, Arni's hospitality and hilarious stories, and the congeniality of our group.

On the Table

From Hot Dogs to Fermented Shark: Searching for Identity in Icelandic Food

In a nation like Iceland that is developing its culinary scene, traditional foods such as fermented shark and pickled herring, among other Viking fare, are still evolving to find their niches in today's cuisine. Cooking was and still is for subsistence and practicality, and based on weather extremes and availability.

According to Gunnar Gíslason, "Because of the fallout from the 2008 recession, it just became too expensive to import food. So, we dug deep, focusing solely on Icelandic ingredients. After a year or so, I started to become restless cooking mainly with cod and lamb, two Iceland staples. So, I embarked on a circular field trip of my home country to seek out new ideas. Instead of finding new ingredients, however, I actually discovered age-old traditions and techniques that were dying out. I started devouring history books about how the Icelandic people used to cook, drawing on recipes from my grandparents' generation right back to the Viking age."

There is *kjötsúpa*, a soup of lamb, rutabagas, and mirepoix, that Anthony Bourdain ate on his show while working out with muscle heads. It is known to be an elixir and is eaten to build strong muscles. The cute little puffin duck that can only be hunted in Iceland is a local delicacy and excellent as a smoked dish. And one can't forget the iconic Icelandic hot dogs made with lamb, beef, pork, veal, or even seafood—the beef hot dog probably came to Iceland during World War II when American pilots were stationed there.

Since it is an island-nation in the North Atlantic Ocean, with many rivers and lakes, it is their cod, haddock, pollack, salmon, prawns, langoustines, scallops, and endless fruits of the sea that take center stage. Delicious fish and seafood chowders are a staple, and salmon is cured gravlax-style, cold-smoked, poached, and broiled.

Hearty Icelandic Seafood Chowder

Icelanders live off of fish stews and chowders. This one is loaded with fresh cod, scallops, and shrimp, which are the fruits of the Atlantic and Arctic Oceans.

Serves 4 to 6

- 6 strips thick-cut bacon, chopped
- 2 ribs celery, diced
- 1 medium yellow onion, diced
- 3 cloves garlic, minced
- 1 teaspoon hot sauce
- 1 teaspoon Worcestershire sauce
- 1 teaspoon dried oregano
- 1 teaspoon dried parsley
- 1/4 teaspoon dried thyme
- 1/4 teaspoon coarse sea salt
- 1/8 teaspoon smoked paprika
- 1/8 teaspoon freshly ground black pepper, plus more for finishing
- 1/3 cup all-purpose flour
- 1 cup low-sodium chicken broth
- 3 cups half-and-half
- 1 bay leaf
- 4 (6 1/2-ounce) cans chopped clams, juices reserved
- 1 1/4 cups baby new potatoes, quartered
- 2 pounds skinless cod, haddock, or pollock, cut into bite-size chunks
- 1 pound medium bay scallops
- 1 pound large (16/20) shrimp, peeled, deveined, and quartered
- Chopped parsley leaves for garnish

In a large pot or Dutch oven, cook the bacon over medium heat. When crispy, use a slotted spoon to transfer the bacon to a plate lined with paper towels.

Sauté the celery and onion in the pot until softened, 5 to 6 minutes. Add the garlic, hot sauce, Worcestershire sauce, oregano, parsley, thyme, salt, paprika, and pepper and cook until fragrant, about 1 minute. Add the flour and cook for 2 minutes.

Add the chicken broth, stirring constantly until no lumps of flour remain. Add the half-and-half in the same way. Add the bay leaf and clam juice. Bring the soup to a gentle boil and then reduce the heat and simmer for 20 minutes.

Add the potatoes, increase the heat to medium-high, and bring the soup back to a gentle boil. Cook until the potatoes are easily pierced with a knife, 20 to 25 minutes.

Reduce the heat to medium and stir in the clams, fish, scallops, and shrimp. Simmer until the fish and seafood are cooked through, 5 to 10 minutes. Stir in the bacon. Divide among serving bowls and garnish with chopped parsley and a grind of pepper.

Pan-Seared Sea Scallops in Lemon-Caper Sauce

Sea scallops from Iceland are perhaps the finest on earth. Here, they are pan-seared and served with a delightful lemon-caper sauce with fennel. They are to die for! Serve on a bed of saffron rice (recipe follows).

Serves 4

1 pound (about 14 to 16) large sea scallops

Coarse sea salt

3 tablespoons extra-virgin olive oil

2 tablespoons unsalted butter

4 cloves garlic, minced

½ cup white wine

1 cup low-sodium chicken broth

1 teaspoon lemon zest

2 tablespoons lemon juice

2 tablespoons capers, rinsed

1 tablespoon Dijon mustard

Freshly ground black pepper

Fennel fronds for garnish

Chives for garnish

Allow the scallops to sit for 10 minutes at room temperature. Season both sides of the scallops with salt.

Heat the olive oil in a cast-iron skillet over high heat until the oil shimmers. Add the butter to the skillet. Once melted, sear the scallops until the bottoms are a rich golden brown, about 3 minutes. Flip the scallops and cook the other side until browned, about 2 minutes (be careful not to overcook them). Transfer to a plate with a spatula.

Add the garlic to the skillet and cook until fragrant but not browned, about 1 minute.

Increase the heat to medium-high and add the wine. Simmer for 3 minutes.

Increase the heat to high and add the chicken stock, lemon zest and juice, and capers to the skillet and cook until bubbly, about 8 minutes. Turn off the heat and whisk in the mustard.

Turn the heat to medium and add scallops briefly, just to rewarm. Season with pepper. Garnish with fennel fronds, dill, and chives and serve with saffron rice.

EIMAÐ Á ÍSLANDI
REYKA
SMALL BATCH VODKA
HAND CRAFTED IN ICELAND
TRADITIONALLY DISTILLED & FILTERED THROUGH ANCIENT LAVA ROCKS
DISTILLED WITH RENEWABLE ENERGY
LAVA ROCK FILTRATION
40% ALC/VOL 750ML

Saffron Rice

2 cups cooked jasmine rice

Pinch saffron

2 tablespoons extra-virgin olive oil

2 ribs celery, finely chopped

1 small red bell pepper, finely chopped

½ medium onion, finely chopped

1 (3.8-ounce) can sliced black or chopped kalamata olives

1 (6-ounce) jar marinated artichoke hearts, drained and chopped

While cooking the rice according to package instructions, add the saffron strands to the water. Place the cooked rice with saffron in a large bowl.

In a medium skillet over medium heat, warm the olive oil. Sauté the celery, pepper, and onion in the oil until softened, about 5 minutes.

Add the sautéed vegetables to the rice with the chopped olives and artichokes. Toss together and serve.

Pure nirvana for a salmon angler: sun coming out after a storm, a beautiful waterfall pool with salmon rolling on the surface, and being hooked-up on a good fish (the author is shown).

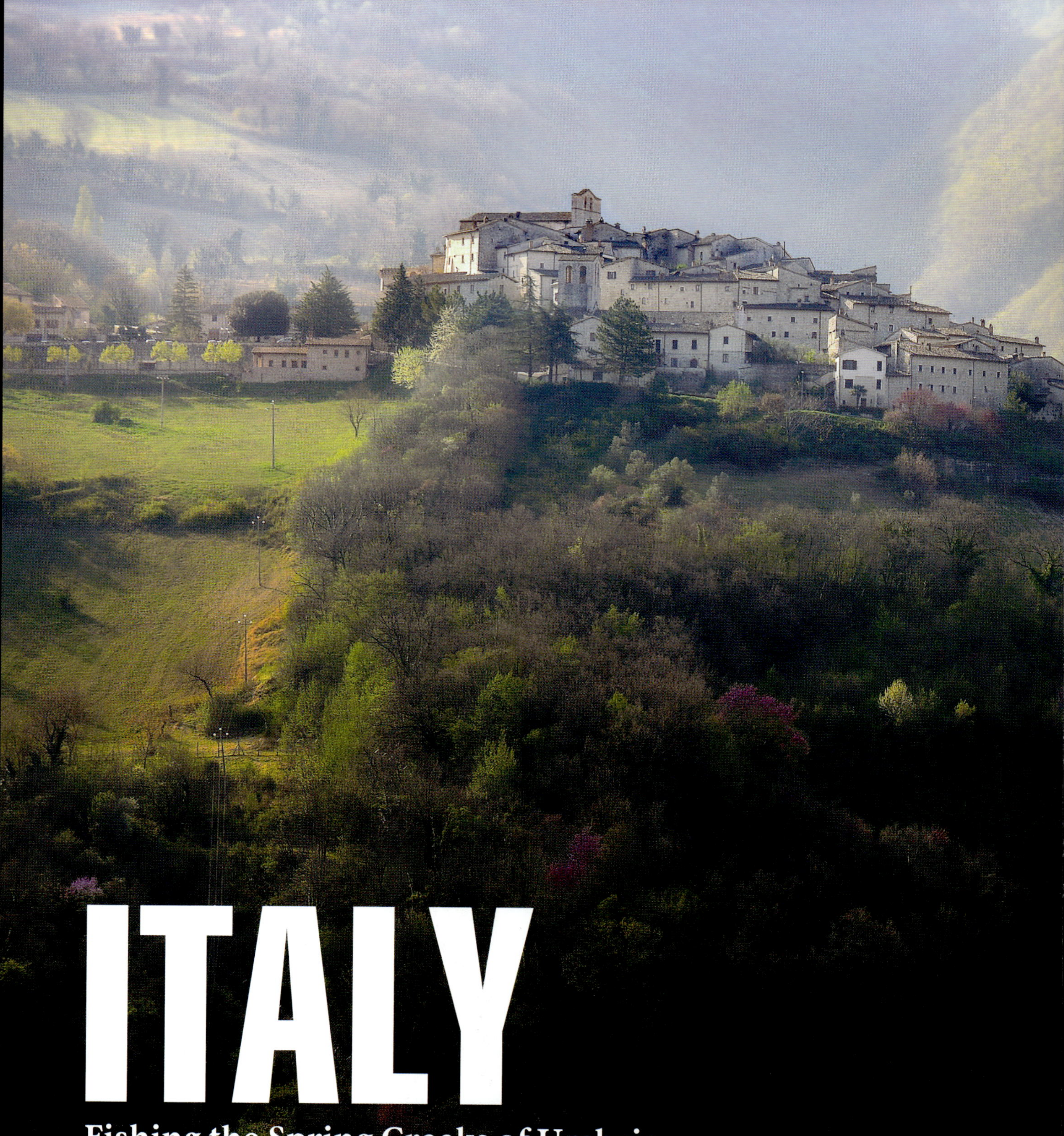

ITALY

Fishing the Spring Creeks of Umbria for Wild Indigenous Brown Trout

MATTHEW SUPINSKI

"They eat the dainty food of famous chefs with the same pleasure with which they devour gross peasant dishes, mostly composed of garlic and tomatoes, or fisherman's octopus and shrimps fried in heavily scented olive oil on a little deserted beach."

—LUIGI BARZINI

The magnificent Nera River, in Umbria, runs icy cold, azure blue, and pristinely clear as it percolates from subterranean caverns through its silty, loamy soils. It runs through narrow gorges and carves through the limestone bedrock, creating beautiful waterfalls and stunning vistas. Winding past the gorgeous steep hills and forests formed millions of years ago, it eventually flows into the Tiber and on to the eternal city of Rome.

Sheep roam the pastures and graze along the narrow winding roads, which lead you to enchanted fairy-tale villages, like one once called Narnia. Today this village in Umbria is called Narni, where pork and wild boar are king. It is here, just an hour's drive north of Rome, that the buried, elusive fungi tuber, white and black truffles, were and still are Roman gold. Here also Perugia chocolates and Pecorino cheeses take on a whole new sumptuous dimension. In this, one of many complex epicurean ecosystems on the planet, some of the finest extra-virgin olive oils and wines were cultivated as early as three thousand years ago.

Aside from these culinary delights, I was after the region's gorgeously colored, indigenous brown trout, with its scarlet-red spots as big as a slice of pepperoni, that sipped mayflies in cold spring-creek waters. It was truly this Roman buttery gold that I wanted in my net. Umbria, for all its riches, is a true treasure on earth that has few equals.

PREVIOUS: Vallo di Nera, one of Umbria's beautiful, centuries-old mountain villages. **OPPOSITE:** An angler high-stick probes the aqua-azure-blue waters of the Nera tailwater/spring creek. **TOP:** An Umbrian brown trout with huge red "pepperoni" dots. **BOTTOM:** An *Ephemera* mayfly, which the author caught his first Nera brown on.

Umbria is one of Itay's premier ice-cold tailwater/spring-creek catch-and-release rivers, where the true fly addict can enjoy the beautiful indigenous wild trout while family members enjoy the breathtaking scenery.

When you go to Italy today you'll find that the Italians have really embraced fly fishing, as compared to years past. Better catch and release management of rivers is starting to take hold and fly-tying is at a very progressive level.

This part of Italy has some of the largest Roman bridges ever built: Ponte d'Augusto is one. Farther up the Nera River valley toward Valnerina, the Mamore Falls rival the beauty of many Icelandic ones. Taking the winding road along the river, you will find the Osteria La Cascata, a quaint waterfall inn with dining overlooking the river and within earshot of the flowing waters. On its gorgeously garnished plates are the rich delicacies of Umbria, which bombard the senses in a true epicurean artistry only the Italians can pull off.

Umbria is a region of many nuances. You'll find stunning stalagmite caves like the ones at Frassisi. In a beautiful retrospective symbiosis, its wild Italian topography of today is a mirror image of its vibrant and volatile geological past. This is the former playground of Italy's saints, where St. Benedict and the most famous naturalist of them all, St. Francis of Assisi, roamed. Stunning cathedrals, castles, and monasteries perch on the jagged hills and exhibit the beautiful Roman and medieval architecture that is so fascinating. In the little villages you can't help but fall in love with the Italian countryside and its warm and truly charming locals. The narrow cobblestone streets run under stone archways, below people's balconies, and into open-air markets of freshly picked pristine produce. Butcher shops display their hanging hams, logs of twined soppressata, mortadella, and other charcuterie. Row after row of wheels of cheeses stack up to the ceilings. In a world that can be tumultuous, life here is still beautiful and simple. It is known as the *la bella vita* (the beautiful life). Nothing here has changed for centuries, and hopefully it never will.

ABOVE: An exultant Luca and a massive Nera brown. Over-the-moon elation is the feeling when one catches a big brown in grappa-clear waters! **OPPOSITE, CLOCKWISE FROM TOP:** With such extreme water clarity, careful wading and stalking are necessary to catch wild trout on the Nera; one of the many large *Ephemera* flies of the European spring creeks; Beetle Succo (Beetle Juice).

On the Water

I first came to know these trout when I was in my mid-twenties, working in cooking apprenticeships throughout Europe. I heard about an amazing trout stream in a town called Trevi, north of Rome. One of my colleagues suggested I contact a man named Fabricio, who owned a small pensione in the hills of Umbria where there was a trout stream. It was a very short train trip from the city. Being American was a big advantage back then. I was a novelty for the country folk wherever I went. The locals would very often invite me into their homes and feed me delicious regional foods. Train station and food court chow got a little boring after a while. But I do admit every station had places where you could get delicious bowls of noodles—with olive oil, butter, cheeses, and herbs, and perhaps with prosciutto, bacon, or local ham. The customary tomato marinara or cream sauces were decadent and powerful flavors—a little dollop went a long way. And then there were the train station wood-oven pizzas and regional sausages on Italian style rolls. They reminded me of Italian-American cuisine from home.

When I arrived at the pensione, Fabricio met me with his unusual-looking Lagotto Romagnolo dog named Gusti, who was a truffle finder. It was May and black truffle season. More important, though, it was also mayfly season on the trout streams of Europe. Here, the mighty *Ephemera danica* mayfly was the dope that fueled the hatch-matching addiction. After a good night's sleep, Fabricio drove me up to Valnerina to meet Luca, an Italian master of the Nera River. It was one of the most frightening drives I have ever taken. The Italians only know one speed, *veloce* (fast), and this is how we traversed the narrow, curving mountainous roads with steep drop-offs. My heart was in my throat the entire drive.

TOP: A perfect Umbrian tailwater/spring-creek fly box has everything. Plenty of mayfly dries, caddis, and stone flies. And don't forget the terrestrials! **BOTTOM:** The spotting on Italian Umbrian browns is remarkable. This one had close to seventy red dots on one side of its body alone—a unique feature. **OPPOSITE:** A tailwater-style spring creek just doesn't get more perfect and azure blue than in Umbria.

Brown Trout on the Nera

Once I saw the water, I was shocked by the clarity and beauty of the Nera. It ran alongside oak, maple, and chestnut groves, with coarse and dense brush tight to the banks—plenty of cover for the beautiful brown trout I was looking forward to tussling with. "Do you have the dry fly that looks like the mayfly?" asked Luca. "Only stone flies I used in Austria," I replied. The river had steep gradients, even though it was a true chalk stream spring creek. I didn't have waders, so I schlepped along the shallow parts along the brush in old Wellies. We found a gorgeous, fishy-looking pool where the trout were rising. The water was ice, but on the hot day it felt good. A mayfly floated past me—a good omen of things to come.

"Two good fish are starting to rise on that far bank. You Americans are good casters; take them!" Luca belted over the sound of the tumbling water. A few mayflies were starting their float procession as I proceeded to cast. I targeted the first good boil and literally with the second cast I was hooked up. "*Enorme trota*, Luca!" I screamed as he ran toward me with the net. As the fish took off down the pool, it made several brilliant leaps. I finally subdued the fish as Luca netted it. "*Congratulazioni Mateo! Bella trota*," I remember him saying while beaming so proudly at his river and the gorgeous, pushing-twenty-inch brownie.

Though the river today is no-kill, back then there were only a few prized larger trout, since most were taken for the table and restaurants. I unhooked my Italian beauty, and remember that *Salmo trutta* slipping out of my hands back into those cold waters.

Later that evening the big bugs subsided, but sedges and olives filled the hatch scene. A few more browns came to hand that day before we called it quits and drove back to where Fabricio waited to pick me up. In hindsight, Luca was one of the most knowledgeable master fly anglers I ever met.

And it was a true honor to experience his Italian brown trout. It is a proud and noble fish that swam the rivers when the Romans built bridges over it. They endured even when Nazi and American tanks rumbled through the country. That fish is forever etched in my memory and is one chapter of my journey that drove me to write my book on brown trout.

Once my most fabulous day was complete, I thanked Luca and offered to return the favor if he ever came to America. Back at the pensione, Fabricio poured me Campari and soda, and the highly potent grappa, as we celebrated and toasted to my Italian trout. We chatted and drank on his balcony well into the night, listening to music and the sound of water. I remember his very poor English and my broken Italian. I'm sure it was comical to listen to, especially as the alcohol kicked in. I will never forget that wonderful experience in Umbria—an enchanting place where time stands still and life is celebrated in every moment.

BELOW: Hunting big brown trout is a lifelong pursuit that has no equal. When that prehistoric-looking fish stares you in the face, you are hooked for life! **OPPOSITE:** An outdoor butcher: The epicurean curing and smoking of meats in Italy is at the highest possible level. **FOLLOWING:** The mountaintop villages in Italy are laid out so beautifully and uniquely—they are architectural marvels.

On the Table

For the Love of Italian Cuisine

My love affair with Italians came at a very young age, growing up in a town dominated by Italian and Polish immigrant families—hardworking factory laborers in Niagara Falls, New York. On both of their sides of the town, you had Catholic churches with names like Immaculate Conception, Our Lady of Fatima, and St. Stanislaus Kostka. But, most importantly, you smelled amazingly tempting foods from butcher shops, deli counters, and smokeries.

In Italy, pastas are usually the first or second course or *primi piatti*, since wild game, veal, beef, lamb, pheasant and quail, and fish and shellfish are the foundation of the entrees. The Italian kitchen is highly structured, from the mother-run family version to the finest trattoria. They take their food very seriously, which is why every dish oozes comfort and deliciousness. When I apprenticed in a small trattoria, the hierarchy of chefs and cooks, and properness of who talks to whom, was very formal. As you never interrupt a mother in her realm when cooking, there they made you aware of your place in the whole protocol very quickly. It was humbling. But the pride, passion, and love put into their cooking, which has been mastered and passed down from each generation, is inspiring. *Buon appetito*!

Mushroom Gratinati
with Crostini

The ultimate antipasto dish: mushrooms, fresh mozzarella and Parmigiano-Reggiano, and tomatoes, which are all synonymous with Italy, especially Umbria. This dish is super fantastic and delicious. Pair with crostini toasted with olive oil, rubbed with garlic, and sprinkled with oregano and basil.

Serves 4 to 6

- 2 cups small grape tomatoes
- 4 tablespoons extra-virgin olive oil, plus more for bread
- Coarse sea salt and freshly ground black pepper
- 2 tablespoons unsalted butter
- 1½ pounds fresh porcini, sliced
- ½ cup freshly grated Parmigiano-Reggiano
- ¼ cup Italian-style seasoned breadcrumbs
- 8 ounces fresh mozzarella, diced
- ¼ cup finely chopped basil leaves
- Store-bought Italian bread or focaccia, thinly sliced
- 2 cloves garlic, peeled and halved
- Finely chopped oregano and basil leaves

Preheat the oven to 425°F.

In a 2-quart baking dish, toss the tomatoes with 2 tablespoons of the olive oil. Season with salt and pepper. Roast until the tomatoes burst, about 15 minutes. Keep the oven on and set aside the tomatoes.

Melt the remaining 2 tablespoons olive oil and the butter in a medium skillet over medium heat. Sauté the mushrooms until they begin to brown. Season with salt and pepper. Add the mushrooms to the roasted tomatoes and toss to distribute.

In a small bowl, toss the Parmigiano-Reggiano and breadcrumbs. Sprinkle about half of the breadcrumbs over the tomatoes and mushrooms. Add the mozzarella and basil and toss together to distribute. Sprinkle with the remaining breadcrumbs.

Bake until the top is golden brown, about 20 minutes.

Meanwhile, brush the bread slices on both sides with olive oil and toast until lightly browned on both sides. Rub both sides with garlic and sprinkle the tops with the oregano and basil. Serve the crostini alongside the gratinati.

Shrimp Scampi Orzo

Though we were in Umbria, Fabricio was from northern Italy, near Venice. Though Umbria is known for thicker, heavier pastas, he introduced me to orzo, which originated in his region. Italians love garlic-flavored pastas that pack a powerful punch, just as truffle adds tremendous flavor. But often truffles are for export, and garlic is used to create pungency. This dish combines the delicious yet simple flavors of garlic, wine, butter, and parsley with beautiful Argentinean red prawns.

Serves 4

2 pounds Argentinean red prawns (or other large shrimp), peeled and deveined

6 tablespoons extra-virgin olive oil

2 tablespoons lemon zest

1 teaspoon red pepper flakes

Coarse sea salt and freshly ground black pepper

8 cloves garlic, minced

4 tablespoons unsalted butter

2 cups orzo

⅔ cup dry white wine

4 cups low-sodium chicken stock

1 tablespoon lemon juice

6 tablespoons finely chopped parsley leaves

In a medium bowl, stir together the shrimp, 2 tablespoons of the olive oil, the lemon zest, red pepper flakes, salt, pepper, and half of the garlic. Set aside to marinate at room temperature. (This step can be done up to 1 hour in advance.)

Add the butter, remaining ¼ cup olive oil and remaining garlic to a medium skillet over medium heat. When the butter starts to bubble, add the orzo and ½ teaspoon salt and cook, stirring often, until the orzo is toasted, about 2 minutes, adjusting the heat as necessary to prevent the garlic from burning. Carefully add the wine—it will bubble—and stir until absorbed, about 1 minute. Stir in the chicken stock, reduce the heat to low, cover, and cook until the orzo is al dente, about 12 minutes.

Add the shrimp in a snug, even layer on top of the orzo, cover, and cook until the shrimp is pink and cooked through, 2 to 4 minutes. Remove from the heat and let sit, covered, for 2 minutes.

Sprinkle with the lemon juice and parsley, season with salt and pepper, and serve immediately.

LOUISIANA

Fishing for Bull Reds on the Mud-Tinted Waters of the Louisiana Marsh

KIRK DEETER

"In America, there might be better gastronomic destinations than New Orleans, but there is no place more uniquely wonderful."
—ANTHONY BOURDAIN

You'll find the gritty fishing soul of Louisiana far from Bourbon Street. Go beyond Vaughan's Lounge and Elizabeth's Restaurant in the Bywater, past Penny's Café in Chalmette (do stop for shrimp and grits, and strong black coffee), and into the heart of St. Bernard's Parish. There's a place there where the city glow is gone, ironically called Hopedale.

Hopedale was more or less wiped off the map by Hurricane Katrina in 2005, and one can still see the empty stilts where homes were blown away. But for any angler in the know, Hopedale, along with the other weathered hamlets that dot the marshy coast, like Venice, Delacroix, and Leeville, are meccas for the best saltwater fly fishing anywhere in America. There are no sandy beaches or high-rise casino hotels along clear azure water here. Just a few shrimpers, crabbers, and some raw, honest fishing.

PREVIOUS: Every spot pattern on a redfish is unique . . . like a human fingerprint. **OPPOSITE, TOP:** Bear Holeman shows off a redfish during his "Dukes of Hopedale" days. **OPPOSITE, BOTTOM:** Josh Fiester with a big bull. **ABOVE:** Travis Holeman preps to cast.

On the Water

The fly-fishing game in the marsh is much like backcountry Louisiana itself—resilient and beautiful in a subtle, primal way. It revolves around ruffian species like black drum, red drum (most often referred to as redfish), sea (or speckled) trout, and sheepshead. The tarpon will roll off the coast at certain times of the year, and if you go far enough offshore, you'll find billfish and yellowfin tuna. Fish under the oil and gas rigs (which are essentially human-made reefs) and you'll find cobia, grouper, snapper, and even wahoo. Lake Pontchartrain sees some wild schools of jacks every so often. There's always *something* in

PREVIOUS: Bear Holeman horses in a redfish as his buddy gets ready to grab it by the mouth with a BogaGrip. **ABOVE:** Louisiana redfish love purple and chartreuse flies. **OPPOSITE:** Post Katrina, the marsh has rebounded in abundance.

Louisiana waters, it's all just a matter of when and where.

The belles of the ball are the redfish. They aren't particularly noble-looking; some even say they're near carp-ugly. But closer examination reveals scales that are undoubtedly a product of evolution, displaying a muted array of earthy tones, a complex mosaic of pinks, browns, yellows and blues, ultimately accentuated by a trademark "false eye" black spot on the tail. Because the black spot (or spots) confuse predators like sharks or porpoises, they strike away from the brain and eyes. Each spot pattern is unique to a redfish, like a human fingerprint.

To the angler, the best attributes of Louisiana redfish are that they eat like hogs at a trough, they grow bigger than redfish do most anywhere else, and they like the skinny water. A redfish can thrive in the marsh whether the water is fifty degrees or more than eighty. They know how to find havens and ride out storms. When the hurricanes bear down on these shorelines, the redfish are often the last to leave the marsh and the first to come back.

Maybe it's because they usually live in more turbid, muddy water, but they don't seem very timid, and they're fairly easy to spot. Even if you don't see their silhouettes through cloudy water, there are other telltales. Sometimes, especially if there's more than one, you can follow their mud trails, where they've been sucking up and crunching small crabs off the bottom. They'll also push a distinct wake and you'll see the "nervous water" move down the shoreline as the fish grazes.

The best telltale is the tail itself. Sometimes, these fish will be so focused on eating they'll tip and tilt with no regard for concealment, their tails flagging in the open air as if they're waving at you and challenging you to a fight. Some of the biggest fish (forty pounds or more) will even swim with half their backs exposed out of water. They ooze up and over

TOYOTA

mud, and burrow into the weeds, almost amphibian in their approach, lazily feeding on shrimp and blue crabs that pour through the spartina grass in retreating currents. Those fish are called crawlers. They'll give you an eyeful. You usually can't gauge how long they are, but they'll often show you how wide they are, which , when it comes to muscle power, is the more meaningful dimension. There's nothing like the initial burst a hooked redfish with "big shoulders" can make.

Not That Tricky

Unlike almost any other fish you might chase in saltwater flats, redfish will often spin around and give you another shot if you make a cast and miss. They aren't always very choosy when it comes to fly patterns (after all, they vacuum up pretty much any living creature, from small fish to crustacean, that they bump into). A purple-and-black fly that loosely resembles a fleeing crab, but also looks like a celestial body (hence its name, Halley's Comet) will usually do the trick.

The larger redfish are called bull reds (though the largest are usually females) or pumpkins, because they appear like reddish-orange globs if you can see them through the tinted water.

Winter is the best season to find the bulls inshore. The only challenge is that, even though redfish might be the most willing players of any saltwater sport fish, conditions must line up just right in order to play the fly game at all. If the wind is wrong, the cloud cover thick, or the water too muddy, even the fattest fish become ghosts. And on those days, you're better off shucking oysters and drinking beer at the boat launch. Having

OPPOSITE: Sea trout. **ABOVE:** Flooded marsh, pelicans, and the late, great Travis Holeman—one of the best there ever was with one of the best bull reds I've ever seen.

experienced enough of those days, I consider that a blessing, because they made me learn and appreciate Louisiana food culture as much as I do the fishing.

A one-day trip to catch bull reds in the Louisiana marsh is a fool's errand. You must dedicate four or five days to any Louisiana redfish venture; if you're lucky, you might get a day and a half of legitimate opportunity. But when everything lines up in the Louisiana marsh, it's heaven. And it will change you forever and alter anything you've ever come to expect or understand about what fly fishing could or should be.

Four Consecutive Casts, One Hundred Pounds of Reds

I'm still haunted by memories of a certain morning when I hooked and landed one hundred pounds' worth of redfish (four fish averaging twenty-five pounds), on four consecutive casts, on topwater popper flies. I was fishing out of Venice at the very bottom of the Mississippi Delta with my friend Frank Praznik, and we motored the skiff down the river channel and turned west into some backwater flats. The morning sun wasn't yet high when we caught our first glimpse of a redfish "laid up" as if napping, just below the surface.

I sent her a wake-up call, dropping a popper fly a few feet in front of her nose, and she exploded on the fly, enough to send noisy shockwaves over the bay. Frank netted her, and we weighed her with a BogaGrip scale: twenty-six pounds. We let her go, and poled around looking for another. It didn't take very long, maybe five minutes. Another cast, another splash, and a twenty-four-pounder in the net.

Two more times. Two more fish—twenty-three and twenty-seven pounds, respectively—and that was how you do one hundred pounds of fish with four fly casts.

Shrimpers taking to the ocean early in the morning.

The next morning, I fished with my friend Captain Gregg Arnold, and we caught a couple more, only these were glued to the bottom. The water was uncommonly clear, and the fish seemed lit up like Christmas ornaments. The fishing here changes every day, which is what keeps you coming back for more. It's impossible to pattern, and, like the best New Orleans jazz, fishing the Louisiana marshes is a constant movement of inspired improvisation.

That's why, after more than twenty years of loving Louisiana (although I've spent many days shucking oysters and drinking beer on the dock, waiting out the weather, for every one day when the fish have lined up perfectly on the marsh), I consider it my saltwater-fishing home, and I wouldn't trade it for any other fishing and eating experience in the world.

On the Table

There are so many distinct flavors to be found in Louisiana—from boudin to broiled oysters, muffuletta sandwiches, and fried shrimp po'boys . . . where to start? Since it isn't always easy to find authentic Louisiana ingredients in different parts of the country (better off ordering crawfish for étouffée online rather than trying to hunt it down in most places), first base should be a straightforward jambalaya that's complex in taste but easy to create. This dish starts with the "holy trinity" of Louisiana cooking (celery, onion, and bell pepper) and takes a turn toward Creole with the addition of chopped tomato. A more Cajun version might skip the tomato and include any toss-up mix of proteins, from alligator to redfish. But I prefer to leave those bull reds swimming in the marsh, so I stick to the reliable flavor combination of shrimp and andouille sausage.

OPPOSITE: Steaming crawfish. **TOP:** Shucking oysters (must be windy out there). **LEFT:** Morning Call beignets and chicory coffee to start the day.

Shrimp & Andouille Jambalaya

Jambalaya is ten meals in one. Part Cajun, part Creole, it has it all. All food groups, and most important, little bits of many of the flavors that define the essence of Louisiana bayou cooking. I've fished and loved the Louisiana marshes for decades, and trust me . . . it's all good! Po' boys, étouffée, muffuletta, boudin, and so much more. But put me on the spot and ask me to offer up a dish that brings me home to the Louisiana marsh, and the answer is very simple: It's "Jambo."

Serves 8 to 10

2 tablespoons vegetable oil

7 ribs celery with leafy tops, finely chopped

1 medium-large white or yellow onion, finely diced

1 green bell pepper, finely diced

1 red bell pepper, finely diced

4 cloves garlic, minced

1 teaspoon dried thyme

2 teaspoons cayenne pepper, plus more to taste

4 bay leaves

1 teaspoon fine sea salt

1 teaspoon freshly ground black pepper

2 pounds jumbo (10/12) or colossal (8/10) shrimp, peeled and deveined

5 links fresh andouille sausage, boiled and cut into 1/4-inch rounds (see Notes)

2 (14 1/2-ounce) cans diced tomato

1 (14 1/2-ounce) can crushed tomato or 3 pounds Roma tomatoes, chopped

1 cup long-grain white rice

1 cup chopped scallions (optional)

Baguette for serving

Warm the oil in a large Dutch oven or stewpot set on medium heat. Sauté the celery, onion, peppers, and garlic until the vegetables soften, about 5 minutes. Add the thyme, cayenne pepper, bay leaves, salt, and black pepper, then stir with a wooden spoon.

Add the shrimp and stir. It's okay if the mixture turns a bit frothy as the moisture from the shrimp adds to the mix. When the shrimp turn pink and curl, after 3 to 4 minutes, take a large scoop or two out of the mix and set aside in a bowl (see Notes).

With the shrimp cooked, add the cooked andouille sausage. Then add the tomatoes and a bit more cayenne pepper to taste. Stir again.

Cover the pot, reduce the heat to low, and simmer for 30 minutes stirring occasionally. It should start to look "soupy" as the tomatoes render. If not, feel free to add a little water, or even half a bottle of beer.

Add the rice 45 minutes before serving as the jambalaya continues simmering. The rice will eventually "bloom" and absorb most of the liquid, but you don't want to leave the rice cooking in the mix so long that it turns mushy.

Garnish with some chopped scallions if you like, and serve in bowls along with a fresh baguette. (Leftover jambalaya, stored in an airtight, freezer-safe container, can keep, frozen, for up to 6 months.)

Notes: The andouille sausage has to be fresh, from a butcher, not the processed, packaged stuff, which will ruin the dish.

Let the scoop of trinity mix and shrimp cool, then store in an airtight container in the refrigerator. This is what you add to instant grits, along with a little shredded cheese, to make an easy, filling, and flavor-loaded shrimp 'n' grits breakfast.

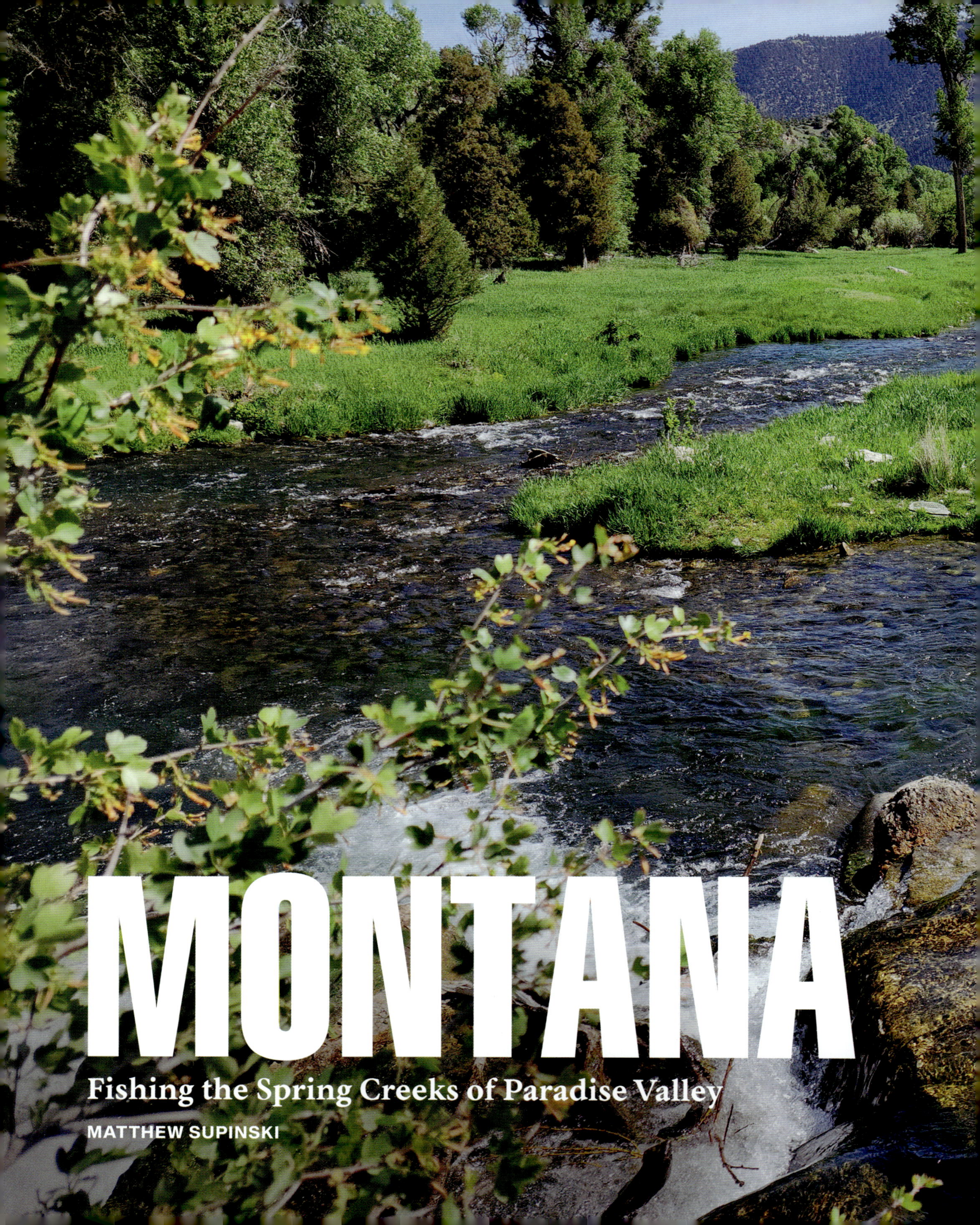

MONTANA

Fishing the Spring Creeks of Paradise Valley

MATTHEW SUPINSKI

"Next time you turn off a news cycle filled with shouting bobble heads convinced that America is devolving into a demonic inferno, questioning the greatness of your nation, maybe you should come here."
—ANTHONY BOURDAIN

It's those valleys with clean, cold-flowing, trout-filled rivers, and endless plains carved out by glaciers millennia ago, that give us mere mortals a vision of heaven. I assure you these heavenly places exist. This one is appropriately called Paradise Valley, in the Absaroka Range outside of Livingston.

The Big Sky karma is all about those cold, frosty mornings in wild wonderlands like Yellowstone or Glacier National Park—sacred natural treasures of our bold developing nation. Through the blowing geyser and morning fog, you see elk and bison graze as their nostrils snort steam in the subzero temperatures. Eagles and hawks soar above the rivers and valleys for a meal of crippled prey. Jim Harrison, author of *Legends of the Fall*, among many countless masterpieces, came to the Big Sky for its wild inspirational beauty. He was also a prolific fly fisher who loved big brown trout. Montana is a trout paradise you can only write superlatives about.

It is especially breathtaking in early summer, when everything comes alive as nature's big recharge and nourishment to all creatures begins. You can see and feel this natural Big Sky zen unfold as you stand on the Three Dollar Bridge over the iconic Madison River, or float the Big Hole near Melrose and watch the spring's brawling snowpack flows start to drop and clear nicely as the warmth of early summer begins. There you witness the first salmonfly emerge from the rocks like a tiny helicopter—then another . . . and another. It is just like they did for Brad Pitt in that movie that ran through it and elevated fly fishing forever. And as if someone threw a bowling ball into the river by the rocks, you see a trout come airborne as it engulfs a Plecoptera salmonfly—one that looks like an extraterrestrial species close-up. As you close your eyes, breathe in the fresh mountain air, and hear the gushing water, you are fully welcomed to Montana, where nature is a show-off everywhere you look.

On the Water

Each day began as the ranch roosters provided the alarm clocks. I poured a cup of tar called strong coffee and tied a few Pale Morning Dun emergers to replenish the boxes. One beast of a big-shouldered rainbow on Armstrong's, that fed by an undercut bank choked with watercress and a toppled old barbed wire fence post, kept culling out my fly arsenal. Many a cast fly landed on that post, since you had to get your fly tight just under it for a perfect, drag-free drift. After hooking that big bow and losing it twice (it was a jumper), I watched it rise on schedule and cue every day in its perfect lie—regardless of how much I harassed it. Dr. Trout himself, Bob Bachman, said the trout got big because they ate at the "prime seats in the river's restaurant." Eager to get on the water, I stuffed some artisan elk jerky, cashews, and bananas in my fishing vest, along with a celebratory flask.

Yet it was in those quiet, still moments that we were continually reminded how special this place was. As the sun set behind

PREVIOUS: The idyllic and iconic spring creeks of Paradise Valley, near Livingston. **OPPOSITE, CLOCKWISE FROM TOP:** The entry to legendary Armstrong Spring Creek, a.k.a. the graduate school of fly fishing; Pale Morning Dun (Jacklin); Doug Hatchimonji connects.

ARMSTRONG
SPRING CREEK
OFFICE

864
MADE IN USA

the Gallatin Range each evening, when we walked through the ranch on our way out, we knew that once you became a cowboy and a rancher you are one for life. Whether you are a gaucho in Argentina or on the open range in the American West, the pride and passion for what you do, and what you are part of, is the same. Your moxie is being tough enough to cut it by doing the hard ranch work, like taming a horse or lassoing a calf on the range. It is about being "all-hat-and-all-cowboy," and few can lay claim to that title. Posers need not apply. The same pride and passion goes for a true trout bum. Montana simply ordains that calling.

OPPOSITE: Rainbows become radiantly colored on very fertile spring creeks, with a year-round diet of crustaceans: shrimp and sow bugs, crayfish and sculpins; then all the mayfly, midge, caddis, and stone fly hatches. **TOP:** Paul Weamer, head of the Yellowstone Fly Fishing Volunteer Program, with a nice brownie. **BOTTOM:** A Yellowstone cutthroat.

The Spring Creeks and America's River

It's a mesmerizing place where you feel like you can reach out and touch the tops of the Absaroka Mountains, as gentle-flowing spring-fed waters create one of the most beautiful trout meccas on the planet.

My yearly healing waters were (and still are) the spring creeks outside of Livingston. They emanate from underground aquifers that feed into the big Yellowstone River. Historic names in fly fishing, like Joe Brooks, fished Armstrong's, Nelson's, and Depuy's spring creeks. They are held privately by the ranch families and sold in the manner of England's chalk stream beat system. It's a management tool where a limited number of anglers—anywhere from six on Nelson's to as many as sixteen on Depuy's—pay a daily fee, with reservations made well in advance. I've frequented all of them for decades and started to establish a relationship with the owners. It was interesting that the elderly mother or grandmother of the estate and ranch holds the reigns in Montana. Each year, the Nelson and Depuy matriarchs know I'll be the first to show up every morning and the last one to leave—often they scream for me at dusk that

"It's time to go!" I'm always tempted to do the dirty of fishing a mouse or sculpin at night, because I can't get enough. The matriarchs were kind enough, if requested, to leave me some stew in a thermos or some of their killer ranch-style meat loaf that I could eat at night. In the old days—and I mean the 1980s, before fly fishing in Montana became hugely popular—eatery places closed early.

An entire day fishing on the spring creeks starts with the spent spinner minutiae mania of the Trico hatch, if we rise early enough. Then, as consistent as a food truck pulling up at eleven a.m., the trout move into the cueing lanes and feeding niches for the Pale Morning Dun hatch—the yellow manna from heaven for a Paradise Valley trout. During very hot August afternoons, strong thunderstorms come over the mountain ranges almost daily. With the dark photoperiod conditions, the mayflies emerge and lay eggs in massive numbers, which the trout go crazy for. A Snowshoe Rabbit or CDC Emerger is serious dope. Spring-creek fly fishing is PhD stuff. You need perfect presentations, long leaders, and light tippets that can get you hooked up to big rainbows, cutthroats, and the always elusive and selective brownies. When those storms come in everybody goes running for cover, since a graphite fly rod sticking out of your arms in the middle of a cow pasture isn't exactly Darwin's idea of how the fittest survive.

One of these times, as the other anglers huddled in the ghillie huts or their vehicles, I decided to stick it out and risked my life for countless fourteen-to-eighteen-inch fat browns and rainbows stuffing their throats

The author fishes his PMD emergers as a big brown sips in a side slough on Nelson's Spring Creek. Some of the most selective sippers are in the back sloughs by old barbed wire fences and log jams, as the currents spin counterclockwise and make presentation a bear. A puddle or dump cast is necessary to get a good drag-free drift with long tippets.

ORVIS
864

with the Pale Morning Dun and sulfur-colored *Centroptilum* stillborn nymphs and cripple mayflies that couldn't hatch because of the heavy rain. It may have been the best emerger dry-fly fishing I ever experienced.

Once the sun and heat resumed after the storms, it was grasshopper time. Hopper fishing in Montana is probably the best you will find, as the winds that cut through the valley and the dry heat and leftover humidity from the storms combine to have hoppers jumping and flying everywhere in those cow pastures and plains. Today, Montana guides swear by the hopper-nymph–dropper setup on these streams as well as the big river tailwaters.

The fly-fishing cowboy chic trend that was created after everyone watched *A River Runs Through It*, and the allure of the big sky and an open, free-spirited ranching way of life, became the new buzz. It was a time when Ted Turner was buying up massive chunks of the state. Hell, he bought an entire side of the Gallatin Range. I know because he told me so when I bumped into him and his then-girlfriend Jane Fonda on Nelson's spring creek. They were both new to the fly-fishing gig and eager to learn. I told them how important the emerger was during the Pale Morning Dun hatch, before I even knew it was them. Back then you could bump into any movie star or celebrity just by going to a bar or walking down Park Street in Livingston.

OPPOSITE, CLOCKWISE FROM TOP LEFT: Grasshoppers, ants, beetles, crickets, oh my! . . . The terrestrial smorgasbord is on full display during a hot Montana afternoon; Tricos of Montana are slightly larger than their Eastern cousins, and here you can get away with #18—in the east it's #24s or nothing; caddis hatches, particularly grannom, can be heavy in Yellowstone Valley.

On the Table

Montana's Foodie Scene: Some Things Are Best Left Undone

Spring-creek trout are not usually early risers because the cold-water temperatures and nighttime cooling need the sun to stir up the food chain of aquatic hatches and terrestrials. And neither were big-city cowboys on vacation. Doing marathon walking, crawling on hands and knees to get near trout sipping by undercut banks, and sweating in cow pastures every day takes its toll. Each evening we rewarded ourselves graciously with a good number of cold Coors from the tap and bourbon by the firepit.

At the famous Chico Hot Springs near Emigrant, where we stay, the glitzy celebrity clientele evolved and Montana's cuisine had to adjust for its new diners. Up until the 1980s, steak house buffets loaded with chuck wagon stews, barbecue beef ribs, pork and beans, pan-fried fresh-caught trout, and damn good diner meat loaf were typical.

Montana is just another name for beef—high-end prime Angus beef that ends up in the finest steak houses. On each visit to this vast grazing mecca of bovine gastronomical sumptuousness, I proceeded to eat as much seared and rare prime Angus filet mignon and rib eyes as I could. No beef on the planet tastes as good as it does here. I was amazed at how good a simple New York strip could taste with just salt and pepper and chargrilled medium-rare. I found out that the Jordan Ranch near Livingston produced the finest beef in the area. All you can do is eat and keep eating it as long as you can afford it, because you won't taste anything that perfect again until you come back.

The Livingston Bar and Grill bartenders knew me and my fishing companions well. They knew the Stoli vodka martinis we liked, the

TOP: Warming hut on the spring creeks. **BOTTOM:** Flaming dessert at Chico Hot Springs. **OPPOSITE:** The Pacific coast *Oncorhynchus mykiss* rainbow has been introduced all over the world to the delight of anglers. The variations from one species to the next, along with mixing gene pools, have produced artistically beautiful creatures that even Monet's palette would have struggled to interpret.

bourbons after dinner, and our food orders. It was always the same: Cobb or Caesar salad, steak and fries, or the occasional cowboy-style loaded baked potato—fresh horseradish on the side, please.

At one point, the bison thing really kicked in. Grass-fed bison farms were all over. Ted Turner's chain, Ted's Montana Grill, was on a mission to teach the American palate the wonders of ranch-raised bison and their deliciousness. My first taste of it was in a ranch-style meat loaf, smothered with thick mushroom-cabernet gravy with bison drippings and mashed potatoes. It was insanely wonderful.

The hunter and forager eat well in Montana. Venison is supreme here, with elk being the king of meats right up with those prime Angus cuts. You grill elk tenderloin rare, with salt and pepper and a touch of Worcestershire, and possibly a wild berry sauce or demi-glace. Toss in mule deer, whitetail, and antelope, and you've got a grilled venison paradise. And while on the hunt, true epicurean hunters and anglers know how to pick morel mushrooms and look for wild berries that fuel dressings, sauces, jams, liqueurs, and pastries.

As for the king of the streams—trout—Montanans realized decades ago that their trout are national treasures. Thus, they practice catch and release like the anglers that come there. For the table they farm-raise all varieties of trout, especially rainbows and brook trout in spring-fed ponds and sectioned-off creeks. One boutique delectable in Montana is smoked trout, done with fruit woods, like cherry and apple, combined with hickory or mesquite.

Paradise Spring-Creek Salad
with Creamy Balsamic Vinaigrette

Watercress is a superfood. Low-lying valley springs are loaded with watercress. Combining these flavors is a form of food art that supplies the utmost nutritional excellence. Note: Please do not harvest watercress from designated trout streams. It is critical trout habitat.

Serves 4

5 to 8 ounces watercress

1 large Bartlett pear, julienned

8 ounces smoked rainbow trout or another smoked fish, sliced into ribbons

½ cup Gorgonzola cheese, crumbled

3 tablespoons extra-virgin olive oil

3 tablespoons balsamic vinegar

3 tablespoons mayonnaise

2 cloves garlic, minced

1 teaspoon Dijon mustard

1 teaspoon brown sugar

Coarse sea salt and freshly ground black pepper

Place the watercress, pear, trout, and cheese in a large bowl.

Blend the olive oil, vinegar, mayonnaise, garlic, mustard, sugar, and 2 tablespoons water until smooth. Season with salt and pepper. Drizzle over the salad and serve with any remaining dressing on the side.

Ranch Bison Meat Loaf
with Wild Mushroom Gravy

This meal embodies true ranch cooking for big, hard-working appetites. (Photo of dishes on following pages.)

Serves 4

MEAT LOAF

1 pound ground beef

1 pound ground bison

1 pound hot or sweet Italian sausage

1 large egg

3 tablespoons Worcestershire sauce

½ cup Italian-style seasoned breadcrumbs

1 cup grated Gruyère cheese, plus another ¼ cup to sprinkle on top

3 strips thick-cut bacon

WILD MUSHROOM GRAVY

2 tablespoons extra-virgin olive oil

8 ounces wild or button mushrooms, sliced

1 teaspoon dried thyme

¼ cup dry sherry

3 cups low-sodium beef broth

3 tablespoons unsalted butter

2 tablespoons all-purpose flour

Coarse sea salt and freshly ground black pepper

Make the meat loaf: Preheat the oven to 400°F.

In a large bowl, combine the beef, bison, sausage, egg, Worcestershire sauce, breadcrumbs, and 1 cup of the cheese. Shape into a loaf and place in a 9 x 5-inch loaf pan or a 9 x 13-inch baking dish.

Lay the bacon strips lengthwise down the loaf and sprinkle with the remaining ¼ cup cheese.

Bake for 45 minutes, until the meat in the center is cooked but still slightly pink.

Make the gravy: Heat the oil in a medium skillet over medium-high heat.

Add the mushrooms and thyme and sauté until the mushrooms are browned, about 8 minutes.

Add the sherry and cook until the liquid is almost completely evaporated, about 3 minutes.

Stir in the broth and bring to a boil. Reduce the heat to medium.

In a small saucepan, melt the butter and whisk in the flour to make a roux. Add the roux to the mushroom-broth mixture and fold in until smooth and the gravy begins to thicken, about 2 minutes.

Season with salt and pepper, then spoon over the meat loaf.

Sautéed Green Beans
with Red Peppers & Shallots

Serves 4

1 tablespoon extra-virgin olive oil

1 teaspoon unsalted butter

3 large shallots, diced

½ red bell pepper, seeded and diced

2 cloves garlic, minced

1 pound green beans, trimmed

¼ cup low-sodium chicken broth

Coarse sea salt and freshly ground black pepper

1 tablespoon low-sodium soy sauce

3 tablespoons Cointreau

In a large skillet over medium heat, warm the olive oil and melt the butter. Sauté the shallots and red pepper until softened, 2 to 3 minutes. Add the minced garlic and sauté until fragrant, 30 seconds. Add the green beans and sauté until they begin to brighten in color, 2 minutes.

Stir in the chicken broth and season with salt and pepper. Cover the skillet and simmer on medium-low heat until very little liquid remains, about 10 minutes.

Add the soy sauce and cook, uncovered, until the green beans are tender and the chicken broth has been absorbed, 5 minutes more.

Add the orange liqueur and cook until evaporated, about 1 minute. Season with salt and pepper and serve alongside the meat loaf.

Spring Creek
A year-round angling opportunity on limestone waters
by Matthew A. Supinski
Limestone Branch Distillery Co. · Lebanon, Kentucky
Since 1872
Yellowstone
Special Finishes Collection
Rum Cask
100
Lebanon, Kentucky

Chocolate Tart with Port Flathead Cherries

CHICO HOT SPRINGS RESORT, EMIGRANT, MONTANA
RECIPE FROM EXECUTIVE CHEF DAVID WELLS

Makes 1 (10-inch) tart or 6 (4-inch) tarts

PORT CHERRIES

1/2 cup sugar

1 1/2 cups port wine

3/4 cup Flathead cherries, pitted

DOUGH

1 1/2 cups all-purpose flour, plus more for work surface

1/4 cup sugar

1 teaspoon salt

1/2 cup (1 stick) unsalted butter, chilled

1 large egg, beaten

GANACHE

8 ounces semisweet chocolate

6 tablespoons unsalted butter

2 cups heavy cream

2 large egg yolks

Make the port cherries: Combine the sugar, port, and cherries in a small saucepan. Simmer until the sauce coats the back of a spoon. Cool and refrigerate, covered, until ready to use.

Make the dough: Sift the flour, sugar, and salt into the bowl of a food processor fitted with the metal blade. Cut the butter into small cubes and add to the flour mixture. Pulse until the mixture is sandy. Add the egg and pulse until just mixed. Turn out the dough and shape into a disk. Wrap with plastic and chill.

Preheat the oven to 350°F.

Roll out the chilled dough on a lightly floured surface to a 1/4-inch thickness and place in a 10-inch tart pan (or use a 4-inch-diameter cookie cutter to cut the dough into 6 circles for individual tarts). Place parchment paper on the dough. Weight with dried beans and bake until golden brown, 10 to 15 minutes. Remove from the oven and let cool.

Meanwhile, make the ganache: Place the chocolate and butter in a medium heatproof bowl. In a small saucepan, bring the cream to a boil. Pour the hot cream over the chocolate and butter. Let sit for 5 minutes. Add the egg yolks and whisk until all ingredients are combined.

When the tart shell has cooled, pour in the ganache and smooth the top with a silicone spatula. Refrigerate up to 8 hours to set. Remove from the tart pan and slice and serve with the port cherries or remove the individual tarts from the pans and serve with the port cherries.

NEW ZEALAND

Fishing the South Island for Brown Trout

KIRK DEETER

"Far away Tongariro! Green-white thundering Athabasca river of New Zealand! I vowed I would come again down across the Pacific to fish in the swift cold waters of this most beautiful and famous of trout streams. It is something to have striven. It is much to have kept your word."

—ZANE GREY

PREVIOUS: A rainbow caught near Wanaka. **ABOVE:** Landing a chunker brown trout on the Boyle River. **OPPOSITE:** A rainbow (*left*) and brown trout (*right*) in ultra-clear water.

In 1864 James Arndell Youl changed the fishing world forever. He organized the shipment of ninety thousand fertilized Atlantic salmon eggs aboard the clipper *Norfolk* from England to Australia. Unbeknownst to him, a few thousand stowaway brown trout ova from the River Itchen were snuck into some of the wooden crates that were packed with moss and stored in the ice hold of the ship. As the ice melted during the three-month journey, the moss stayed damp and cool enough for many of the eggs to survive. Soon after arrival, the ova were taken to a newly created hatchery on the River Plenty in Tasmania, and the first salmon and trout hatched within a month (the prime goal was to create a salmon fishery in the colony). After being released in the wild, the salmon were never seen again.

But the brown trout . . .

Oh, those brown trout, they not only survived, they proliferated. And brood stock produced more ova that were shipped to other parts of the British Empire—New Zealand being among the first places.

They also thrived there in the naturally cool, clear waters, particularly those on New Zealand's South Island. Rainbow trout from the McCloud River in California soon followed, and were planted in rivers on New Zealand's North Island. Today, the North Island is considered primarily the rainbow trout island and the South Island is the brown trout island, although both types of trout can be found in varying proportions throughout the entire country.

As such, New Zealand is considered one of the premier theaters for fly fishing—particularly sight fishing—in the entire world. If sight fishing is top of the fly-fishing game, the Kiwis are the uncontested masters.

On the Water

Trout fishing in New Zealand is an entirely artificial, human-influenced happening, decried by native-species purists who see the trout as invasive—yet celebrated as a renaissance in angling and a vital component of New Zealand's thriving outdoor adventure sports economy by many others. For what it's worth, Youl was knighted for his efforts, and now an average of twenty-five thousand American anglers visit far away New Zealand every year, just to experience this uniquely wonderful brand of fly fishing. This started nearly a century ago when writer Zane Grey first filed stories on the wonders of fly fishing here, and it shows no sign of dissipating anytime soon.

The number-one mistake many Yankee anglers make when they plan a trip to fly fish in New Zealand is to think that by traveling half a world away they'll find the fishing to be easy. After all, they've likely heard tales of the giant brown trout, the "mouse hatches," and all that. So, if you journey all that way, you're bound to find instant gratification, right?

Wrong.

New Zealand offers *the* most challenging sight fishing (especially dry-fly fishing) to be had anywhere in the world. It's brutally honest, technically demanding, yet ultimately rewarding. If you have a legitimate A game, you'll find nowhere more captivating. If, on the other hand, you're a mere dabbler with high expectations, while you'll no doubt end up mesmerized by the raw landscapes and the loving nature of most Kiwis, you will get schooled when you wade into these rivers to go fishing. That's why New Zealand is considered the graduate school of trout angling, and all fly fishers should respect it as such.

TOP: Scouting for the "alpha" fish in the currents.
BOTTOM: More brown trout, each with a unique spot pattern.

The Stealth Game

My experiences have all been on the South Island because I fancy brown trout most. Even before I ever made a first cast at a trout, I was given some lessons from local guides.

No cleats or studs on the bottom of your wading boots. The trout don't hear you grinding against the gravel on the river bottom as much as they feel it. But it spooks them nonetheless.

Those brightly colored fly lines and that wild Hawaiian shirt you wear? Put them back in the suitcase. Trout most definitely see colors, and in New Zealand, fly lines are muted tones like gray and brown, and the clothes you wear are drab and dull, if not full camouflage.

Most anglers won't insult the trout by attempting to throw a nine-foot leader their way. Kiwi fishing involves super-long, clear leaders, maybe fifteen feet or longer (which is not easy to cast straight with a small dry fly, but you figure it out with practice).

The guides don't even want you to land the fly directly in front of the fish, because even though they are clear and nearly invisible to the human eye, leaders make odd, tiny ripples on the water that these smart old fish will sense. Best to imagine casting toward the back of a car: if the fish is directly behind the license plate, you aim to hit the taillight that's closest to the main river current.

When you see a trout, watch it for a while to decipher not only what it's eating but the rhythm in which it feeds. Make every shot count, because there aren't many chances when fishing for wild New Zealand brown trout. Unlike many places where there might be multiple trout in a river's run, here it's usually a solitary player. If a couple are caught in a day that's a win. Catch several in a day and consider yourself extremely lucky (and good). But if you let the fish become aware of your presence, it will sulk off into the depths

TOP: Riding in a helicopter over the Southern Alps. **BOTTOM:** Spotting for fish in a glacial-fed river in the Fjordlands. **OPPOSITE:** Waterfall in Milford Sound.

and not show itself for quite a while. Mess up the run with an errant cast and it's game over. And then you walk . . . and walk . . . and walk, gazing into the river until you spot another player. That could be one hundred yards or it could be a mile.

This may seem nearly as intimidating as the Haka before an All Blacks rugby match, but the challenge of New Zealand trout fishing is overcome by the sheer kindness and resourcefulness of New Zealanders. It's the kind of place where you can still knock on a door and ask permission to fish the stream out back, and not only will they say yes, they might even bring you a cup of tea an hour or so later (this actually happened).

There are three different rivers named Hope River on the South Island, which I think is reflective of the optimistic nature of many Kiwis. And, after all, one of the greatest virtues of fly fishing is that it inspires hope. Think about it—with every cast you make, the first thing you feel is hope. Over the course of a day of peering into pools and making casts, that might add up to hundreds of mini-doses of hope, which is good for the spirit.

The South Island Is for Adventurers

The Hope River in the Canterbury area was the first I fished with guide Nic Robertson out of Riverview Lodge near Hanmer Springs, and I hooked a mighty brown on my third cast with a mayfly dry. This was during a "mouse year." In a mouse year, the beech trees produce especially large quantities of seeds. Mice climb the trees to reach the seeds and fall into the river where the trout eat them. They are an excellent source of protein, and the average fish might bulk up by a pound or more. When we got this one to the net, we weighed it . . . ten pounds.

I asked aloud if this was normal, and more specifically if I could expect to land

double-digit fish all day long. Nic reminded me of the name of another nearby river . . . Doubtful.

Another thing that's doubtful is that any person can fully absorb the vast array of fishing landscapes to be had on the South Island alone. But it's worth trying. Given the distance to reach New Zealand, it's worth hanging around for a couple weeks or more, if you can swing it, and tasting the different experiences.

Queenstown is the adventure center of the island in the heart of the Southern Alps region. This is where some twisted person first conjured up the concept of bungee jumping. North of Queenstown, through the lakeside town of Wanaka, is the Eleven Cedar Lodge on the Makarora River. The lodge flies guests by helicopter to remote rivers every day to fish, and you get to places that simply don't see people. I remember one day on a river so crystalline I could dip a tin cup into the water and drink it as I fished.

Less than an hour's drive south of Queenstown is the town of Athol. This area is more hilly than mountainous; here the Mataura River is legendary for big brown trout.

The Eleven Owen River Lodge in the Nelson Lakes/Murchison region is among the prettiest places to fish. They offer a wide range of options, including heli-fishing, and the lodge itself has a reputation for being one of the best epicurean destinations in New Zealand.

The "Top of the South" around the Marlborough District and the town of Nelson is known as one of the world's most prolific wine- and fruit-producing regions, and it's fun stalking giant brown trout in a river that flows through a vineyard. The Stonefly Lodge near Nelson on the Motueka River also offers the chance to helicopter into the Kahurangi National Park, which is an absolute must for anyone who wants a fishing experience that is truly unforgettable because of the lush, mountainous landscape, the enormous brown trout, clear water, and total isolation.

PREVIOUS: Malcolm Robertson tosses a nice loop over the Greenstone River. **OPPOSITE:** Fishing after being dropped off by Cedar Lodge's helicopter. **RIGHT:** Guide Stephen Greany with a brown caught in the Kahurangi National Park at the "top of the South."

ABOVE: In New Zealand, you might walk through a pasture filled with cows (or sheep) to find the river. **OPPOSITE (TOP):** After fishing, you can bask on the deck with some of the best wines in the world or (*bottom*) raise a toast to truly remarkable catches.

On the Table

New Zealand fishing lodges cater to a very selective clientele, so the food is typically innovative and hearty. Meals can feature an interesting mix of cultures, from Indigenous Polynesian Maori to classic British colonial, and much in between. The novelty of fishing—and eating—in New Zealand, of course, is that you find yourself in the Southern Hemisphere, where summer happens during our winter. Thus, you can leave places like Denver, Chicago, or Boston wearing long johns and a parka and fourteen to eighteen hours later, depending on flight connections and lay-overs, you're wearing shorts, flip-flops, and a T-shirt. Fruits and vegetables are largely in season, and there are numerous roadside markets and fruit stands with fresh berries, pears, plums, melons, grapes, and more.

The popular pavlova dessert, named in tribute to Russian ballerina Anna Pavlova, who toured Australia and New Zealand in the 1920s, is meringue-based, but the fresh fruit and cream topping steal the show.

New Zealanders are very proud of their farm-to-table culinary traditions with good reason. Maori tradition heavily involves root crops, while as with many places that were part of the British Empire, lamb is a staple meat. Throughout its history, the country has maintained a ratio of several sheep for every human, though that's becoming less pronounced as wool prices have bottomed out in recent years. As an island nation, New Zealand cuisine is also closely connected to the sea, with scallops, snapper, blue cod, and squid often featured prominently on menus. But it's the endemic green-lipped mussel that headlines New Zealand seafood. They are large, robust, and quite flavorful, even after having been flash frozen, which is how people from all around the world can and do order them.

EARLY TIMES
WOODFORD RESERVE

Grilled New Zealand Rack of Lamb

Nobody does rack of lamb with greater aplomb than the Kiwis (and I say that in deference to my many Aussie, English, and Colorado fishing friends). It's never complicated, other than the fact that you really need to land on the just-right rare to medium-rare meat temperature to bring forth the best flavors. Mind the fire and you're in business.

Serves 4

2 (8-rib) French-cut racks of lamb

4 tablespoons extra-virgin olive oil

8 cloves garlic, minced

1 tablespoon honey

2 tablespoons finely chopped rosemary leaves

Fine sea salt and freshly ground black pepper

Place the ribs on a platter. Mix the olive oil, garlic, honey, and rosemary leaves in a small bowl and season with salt and pepper. Brush all over the lamb. Cover with foil and refrigerate overnight to allow the flavors to fully absorb into the meat.

Preheat a charcoal grill to 400°F. Loosely wrap the bones in aluminum foil to prevent burning. Leave the meat exposed.

Once the grill has preheated, place the racks on the grates fat side down and grill for 4 minutes. Turn the racks and grill for another 4 minutes. Move the racks to the lower heat side, close the lid, and continue to cook over indirect heat until the meat is medium-rare, 15 to 20 minutes.

Let the meat rest for 10 minutes, then serve in two-bone portions or as single-bone "lollipops" with roasted potatoes on the side.

Roasted New Potatoes with Rosemary

1½ tablespoons extra-virgin olive oil

1 tablespoon dried rosemary

6 cloves garlic, minced

1 teaspoon fine sea salt

1 teaspoon freshly ground black pepper

1½ pounds new potatoes (medley, red, or Yukon gold), halved

Preheat the oven to 425°F . Line a baking sheet with parchment paper.

In a large bowl, combine the olive oil, rosemary, garlic, salt, and pepper. Add the potatoes and toss to coat thoroughly. Spread the potatoes in a single layer on the prepared baking sheet. Roast, flipping once, until golden brown and crispy on the outside and soft on the inside, 20 to 25 minutes.

Jo Midgley's Pavlova

OWEN RIVER LODGE, NEW ZEALAND

My Australian friends will bristle at the notion that I credit New Zealand for this dessert, since both countries claim to be its origin. Named after the famous Russian ballerina Anna Pavlova, who toured Australia and New Zealand a century ago, I had my first taste on New Zealand's South Island, so I'm sticking to that story. You can put your own spin on this sweet and refreshing treat by experimenting with fruit combinations, shapes, sizes, and more. This version comes from the famous Owen River Lodge courtesy of former owner (now world-class traveling angler) Felix Borenstein.

A scale is important for getting this recipe right! With a scale, the ingredients can be easily adjusted to the size of the pavlova required as you will need 1 part egg white to 2 parts sugar.

Serves 6

8 egg whites (weighed)

Granulated sugar (2 times the weight of the egg whites)

1 teaspoon vanilla extract

1 teaspoon white vinegar

1 tablespoon cornmeal

1 pint heavy cream

6 tablespoons confectioner's sugar

Fresh fruit or compote for topping

Preheat the oven to 260°F and line a baking sheet with parchment paper.

Zero a metal stand mixer bowl on a scale. Separate the eggs and place the egg whites into the bowl, then double the weight of the egg whites with sugar.

Fill the sink with 8 inches warm water. Place the bowl of egg whites and sugar into the warm water (this helps to melt the sugar crystals). When melted, whisk the egg whites and sugar together until the mix is thick enough that a spoon can stand up in it. Fold in the vanilla extract, white vinegar, and cornmeal.

Transfer the mixture to the prepared baking sheet and shape into a large round (or smaller, individual rounds). Bake until it barely starts to turn golden and starts to crisp (any longer and it will crack), about 30 minutes.

While the pavlova cools, make the whipped cream. In a chilled food processor bowl with whisk attachment, whip the heavy cream and confectioners' sugar to desired consistency.

Top the pavlova with whipped cream and fresh fruit or compote and serve.

POLAND

Fishing Pomerania and Carpathia for Brown Trout, Grayling & Atlantic Salmon/Sea Trout

MATTHEW SUPINSKI

"No invader has ever conquered the heart of Poland, that spirit which is the inheritance of sons and daughters, the private passion of families, and the ancient, unbreakable tie to all those who came before."
—JAMES A. MICHENER

PREVIOUS: Probing a Pomeranian wooded spring creek for trout, sea trout, and Atlantic salmon. **ABOVE:** The beauty of a true *pstrąg potokowy*, a Polish indigenous brown trout. They have survived warring invaders and overfishing, Nazi tanks, and the destruction of war. **RIGHT:** The dance of the large mayflies, *Ephemera danicas*, *simulans*, and *Hexagenias*, are the Holy Grail for the dry-fly fisher.

To say that I'm of Polish blood would be an understatement. A Polish compatriot is not hard to spot. There is something so inspiring and emotional about being Polish, being in the country, and letting everyone know you are Polish—I can't explain it. There is a spiritual bond, like you've known the person your whole life. There's pride and joy, sadness and regret. It's called *zal* in Polish and has no English translation other than deep remorse of what could have been—how people's lives and lost loved ones might have had different outcomes if Poland wasn't the moveable feast of Europe, sitting in between two bloodthirsty, venomous warrior nations.

Poland's valor and will to survive is perhaps due to the fact that no other country in Europe has seen more devastation by its conquerors and invaders. Several times in its sorrowful history, Poland completely lost its identity and its name was wiped off the map. Not to mention it lost millions more people during World War II than any other country. Its largest city, Warsaw, was totally leveled. Here, during its uprising, a nine-year-old boy with a few homemade Molotov cocktails held down an entire Nazi Panzer division for days through his cleverness and deception. Polish parents and grandparents teach their children to be proud of their heritage.

My northern dad fought the Nazis in the partisan underground after his Polish Army was obliterated. He was a colonel looking through his binoculars as the German blitzkrieg rained down a fiery hell and Armageddon on the Poles. My wonderful mother, from a farm family in Oświęcim, was taken away when she was young. She was placed in forced labor and worked as a nanny, housekeeper, and cook for one of the commandants of Auschwitz.

I hold some very powerful memories from my boyhood time in the old country. My passion for fly fishing was solidified there when I hooked my first Atlantic salmon on the river that ran through our family farm off the Baltic. It's also where I gained an appreciation for food and cooking.

My Enchanted Forest

As I wrote in *The Brown Trout–Atlantic Salmon Nexus*, "The summer of 1965 seemed like an enchanted fairy tale that I will forever enshrine for the rest of my life. To this day, my most vivid dreams take me to that surreal period when the vibrancy and magic of the natural world coexisted with how pure and simple life was, and still can be. It was also the time I learned to see and observe wild trout and salmon in their most feral and fascinating state of existence, just as they were millions of years ago."

Our taxi ride from the train station to the family farm went down narrow, densely forested gravel and dirt roads and past beautiful streams and rivers. All I could do was think of fishing. My dad had introduced me to the finer points of fly fishing by the time I was six. He taught me how to tie a crude Sawyer's pheasant tail nymph with copper wire in the field with my hands. He gave me his hand-me-down beat-up bamboo rod—one of several he acquired while learning to fly fish in England, after the war when he served as a displaced Polish officer in the British Army. Fishing and bird hunting where his passions—as well as making homemade sausages. As a result, I am a connoisseur of both to this day. He taught me how to tell a mayfly from a caddis fly, how to pick wild mushrooms, and how to pick ripe, juicy cherries without white worms in them.

The river of my dreams—the Wieprza—ran through the family farm. It looked like the forested rivers where I currently live in Michigan—much like the Pere Marquette—except it had more watercress, which mom made great salads out of with pears and rokpol, a Polish Roquefort. There were many icy-cold spring creeks that ran through the beautiful Pomorske forest by our farm. This Pomeranian land had traded hands with Germany and Sweden many times, which is obvious in the city of Gdańsk (called Danzig by the Germans) with its German and Scandinavian architecture and street names from its old Teutonic influence. The cuisine was a magnificent mix of old German and Slavic Polish, in a Prussian fusion. Here, pork was and is king, along with duck and fish.

The farm had houses and barns with thatched roofs. There were animals of all kinds running rampant, no running water or electricity. The deep starlit nights of the country kept us staring at the sky all night, as we often descended into sleep in the meadows with the sheep and cows.

On the Water

The true magic for me was in the *rzeka* (river). The waters were stunningly clear, wooded spring-creek jewels, with huge European red oak and birch trees lining the banks. These were faster waters, long meandering runs with beautiful vegetation, and several large deep crystal-clear pools. Here, my little architecturally minded cousins built a cool tree house over the pool with a swing rope to jump and swim from, and I soon found out how cold the water was even in the extreme heat of summer.

Migratory *Salmo* each have unique kypes. This beauty formed a "dolphin-nose" kype, cften genetic or because of jaw loss.

My Hero Arrives

My first day climbing up to the tree house I was called an *Amerykańska kura* (American chicken) because I was afraid of heights. But once up there, I was like a king on his throne. Always in search of fish, I noticed the big white mouth of a kype-jawed male brown trout finning close to the surface near the pool's overhanging banks. But I had no tackle.

The next day my knight in shining armor, my retired uncle Staszek, came to my rescue in a beat-up pickup truck. He was a local game warden who oversaw the "stave" (commercial fish ponds and lakes), the wildlife, the hunting, and, of course, the rivers and streams. After a warm embrace, he proceeded to show me his sporting cache—three bamboo fly rods: one from the now Czechia, one he built himself, and his personal treasured favorite English Hardy. He worked at the shipyards in Gdańsk after the war and claimed to have acquired those precious goods through the black market; I'm sure there were some stories behind their procurement.

The three reels were all German- or Dutch-made along with leather and wool fly wallets. In them were his favorites, like the Tup's Indispensable, Wickham's Fancy, Iron Blue, Pale Watery, and gorgeous Atlantic salmon flies. In Polish, he told me "Those trout in that big pool are downright impossible to catch in the summer. In the spring, they are a lot easier, when the water is higher and big *duże muchy* [mayflies like *Ephemera danica*] are on the water. That is when we get some big brown trout," he said. "But we can give it a go until the big fish come in." "Big fish?" I asked. Some of the browns I saw in the pool were up to twenty-plus-inches long. "The big *łosoś* [Atlantic salmon and sea trout] that come to

ORVIS

that pool after the strong rains of August and September. They are monsters!" he proclaimed excitedly.

The salmon used the smaller stream tributary of the main Wieprza near the tree house, since it had many runs full of very fine gravel for spawning. "Now when those first fish come in, you get a good crack at catching one of them," Uncle Staszek explained. "But once they settle into that pool, they have a nasty attitude and are downright impossible to catch—but they are fun to look at and watch swimming around—they are beautiful creatures." (To this day, the Wieprza still has Atlantic salmon, and colorful native resident and sea-run brown trout, despite the almost complete extirpation of indigenous salmon in Poland and its rivers being heavily polluted during the Communist occupation and the years of industrialization. The modern-day salmon-restoration stocking program has been slow and is now just starting to see some good runs coming back with wild reproduction.)

Three days of rain finally came, and, like clockwork, Uncle Staszek showed up with his bigger cane fly rod. "Let's go see if the monsters came in," he smiled. I could hardly contain myself as I ran down to the stream. "It's blown-out muddy and high!" I shouted. "Don't worry, this is what they need to come up. They'll be here, trust me!" my uncle replied. "You don't want the water to be too clear."

A couple days later, the fish gods smiled. I saw two humongous chrome fish leap. That was the first time I saw an Atlantic salmon up close—and it was beautiful. My uncle loaded up the bigger rod and put on a large, double-hooked English fly—a Green Highlander. "This should be the one they want," he said. "If not, I've got orange ones, and red and black ones. I'll go first and show you what to do if you get one on. They aren't little trout." After what seemed like an eternity of doing big roll single-spey casts, and swinging the wet

OPPOSITE: Stalking an ice-cold Wieprza River tributary. **TOP:** Art Merk, fly-wallet maker and deadly fly fisher, with a beast of a brown from the Dunajec River. **BOTTOM:** His beautiful fly wallet, pictured with Euro nymphs.

fly through the pool, he screamed *cholera* (a Polish swear word) as his rod bowed and a chrome silver missile was launched out of the pool. He asked me to hold on to the rod so I could say I caught it also. After three jumps, it was off—we both were extremely dejected. I didn't realize I was the one who screwed up—I had my hand on the reel knob and didn't let the fish run against the drag of the reel, thus breaking off. "Don't worry, there will be more," he calmly assured me. Just then another strong thunderstorm came upon us. At least I knew the fish were there.

After a riverbank lunch of rye bread and butter, Krakowska cold cuts, smoked trout, and pickled herring—with a shot or two of home-distilled vodka for my uncle—he left me one of his old hand-me-down big cane rods and some flies. "Give these flies a try. But remember, when they run, don't hold onto the line. Let the drag on the reel do its work. When the salmon is finally tired, beach it and bring it back." He left—and I now understood what I needed to do. That was the moment my passion for salmon began.

On the Table

Polish Comfort Fusion

Whereas the Italian kitchen has the potent scents of garlic, simmering tomato sauces, and basil, the Polish Carpathian and Pomeranian counterparts entice you with more earthy, peasant food scents, like the smells of dill, red cabbage, sauerkraut, smoked hams, and sausages that emanated from my grandmother's kitchen.

Today, Warsaw and other Polish cities and towns have become contemporary places. They have been restored by fusing modern design with renovations to the historic architecture damaged from the German and Russian invasions during the war. Warsaw is now an ultra-sophisticated city with chic dining and shopping establishments in its varied neighborhoods.

Top chefs there are driven for Michelin stars. Polish cuisine is a fusion of European influences from the French, Italians, and Scandinavians. These are blended with old-world dishes that come from distinct ecological regions of Poland.

But it is still those basic peasant dishes of the hard-working factory and craftsmen class that my parents were part of that brought us Polish comfort eats. The list is endless: pierogi, kielbasa, gołąbki, Kapusta hams, and duck blood soup called *czernina*, to name a few.

Yet a strong Polish culinary influence always comes from the forager and hunter (or angler). Wild mushrooms are prolific in Poland, along with green edibles from the forests and wetlands. Hunters procure fine venison like European stag, wild boar, bison, and, in medieval times, the aurochs, which might be coming back. Duck, grouse, pheasants, and geese are all delicacies. Such is this diversity that almost all of Europe seems to share and treasure from generation to generation.

Polish cuisine is hard to describe unless you've sunk your teeth into one of its dishes. It is so symbolically tied to emotions and the history of a desperate nation that time and time again struggled to avoid total collapse and decimation by its conquers. Everything here is done with love and passion for the family—both the living and the dead. And most important is the joy of having guests in the home to share the bounty.

After a day of fishing in Poland, it so wonderful to experience the local peasant cuisine of that area. In the north, it is the wild game dishes, smoked herring in wine sauce, and fresh fish from the Baltic. In the south, it is the duck, wild mushroom soups (like the one featured here), and pierogi stuffed with sauerkraut and cheese. So wonderful.

ABOVE: The Baltic Sea is the soul for fishery on the entire coastline of Polish Pomerania. **LEFT:** Polish Woven Nymph. **FOLLOWING:** The Polish Carpathian rivers of the San and Dunajec have become brown trout and grayling meccas for anglers from all over Europe.

12 PAS
240

Wild Mushroom Soup with Potatoes
(WHITE BORSCHT STYLE)

In Poland, wild mushrooms are the ultimate gastronomic passion. Everyone has their own version of a mushroom soup. This is my mother's recipe, which is more like a hearty stew and can be served as a meal in and of itself.

Serves 4

- 3 quarts low-sodium beef stock
- 3 pounds assorted wild mushrooms, such as shiitake, oyster, or traditional Polish cepes or borowik, sliced
- 1 pound button mushrooms, sliced
- 8 to 10 small new potatoes, quartered
- 5 carrots, finely chopped
- 5 ribs celery, finely chopped
- 2 large yellow onions, finely chopped
- 2 tablespoons unsalted butter
- 2 tablespoons all-purpose flour
- 1 cup sour cream
- ¼ cup apple cider vinegar
- 2 tablespoons finely chopped fresh parsley leaves
- 2 tablespoons finely chopped fresh dill leaves
- Coarse sea salt and freshly ground black pepper

In a large pot or Dutch oven, bring the stock to a simmer over medium-high heat. Add the mushrooms, potatoes, carrots, celery, and onions. Reduce the heat to medium and cover and cook until the vegetables are tender, about 1 hour. After 1 hour, bring to a boil over medium-high heat.

Meanwhile, in a small saucepan over medium heat, melt the butter, then add the flour and stir until smooth to make a roux. Remove 1 cup liquid from the soup and add it to the roux, whisking until thickened and no lumps remain. Add the thickened liquid to the soup, stir to combine, then let the soup cook a few minutes longer.

Add the sour cream and vinegar. Stir well and let simmer another 3 minutes. Add the chopped parsley and dill, then season with salt and pepper.

Ladle into individual bowls and serve.

Polonaise
Moderato

Gołąbki
(POMORSKIE STYLE)

If there was one food that sums up the culinary passion of Poland, gołąbki woud be it. It encompasses meat, vegetables, and starch—a complete meal.

Makes 12 rolls

1 medium head green cabbage

3 cups white vinegar

8 ounces ground beef

8 ounces hot or sweet Italian sausage

8 ounces bacon, cooked and crumbled

1 pound cremini, button, or shiitake mushrooms, finely chopped

1 large white onion, finely chopped

1 large egg

1 cup cooked rice (any type)

½ cup Italian breadcrumbs

Coarse sea salt and freshly ground black pepper

1 (23-ounce) plus 1 (10.75-ounce) can tomato soup

6 tablespoons tomato paste

Pinch sugar

Preheat the oven to 350°F.

Put the cabbage into a large pot, then add the vinegar and enough water to cover. The cabbage should be submerged in liquid.

Bring to a boil over medium-high heat. Cook until the cabbage leaves soften and become pliable (a fork will easily pull a leaf from the head), about 10 minutes. Drain in a colander and allow the cabbage to cool.

In a large bowl, combine the ground beef, sausage, bacon, mushrooms, onion, egg, rice, breadcrumbs, salt, and pepper. The meat mixture should be moist, like meat loaf.

Once the cabbage is cool enough to handle, peel off one leaf and lay it down flat on a work surface. Take about ¼ cup of the meat mixture and form it into a large, slightly elongated meatball. Place the meatball in the center of the cabbage leaf and fold the sides of the leaf over the meatball, then roll up the leaf. Place the roll in a 9 x 13-inch baking dish, seam side down. Repeat until you've used all of the meat mixture.

In a medium bowl, mix the tomato soup with the tomato paste and sugar. Pour this mixture over the stuffed cabbage. Cover the baking dish with foil and bake 1½ hours. Remove the foil and bake another 5 minutes, until the top is slightly browned.

QUEBEC
Fly Fishing Gaspé Rivers for Atlantic Salmon
MATTHEW SUPINSKI

"And so it went, up- and downriver. Charm and laughter and hawking the heavens. But the brilliant sun of a Gaspé Indian summer continued to beat down even as we swept our centerfold river with wets, caressed its smooth surface with dries. The salmon paid no heed to any pitch."

—ART LEE

When I develop a love for a place it's because of the fishing and the food. But in addition to possessing those attributes, Quebec's Gaspé Peninsula is a feral, deep-forest wonderland where some of the truly pristine rivers on the planet flow. Lurking in them are the most beautiful indigenous fish I have ever laid eyes on.

The Chic-Choc Mountains and woodlands, jutting up from the coastline of the Chaleur Bay, have a lush white and green canopy formed from a perfect mix of white spruce, birch, and pines, dotted with aspen and oaks. Crisp and rejuvenating pine tree aromas permeate through the limestone hollows, rocky ravines, and gorges along its rivers; they forever linger in your olfactory cache. The last stop of the Appalachian Trail meets the sea here, as the volcanic and sedimentary limestone bluffs formed six hundred million years ago peak to a majestic four thousand feet. Jagged rock formations form stunning waterfalls, like the one on the Dartmouth River. Here, the view from the walk bridge above its cascading waters sends me into reveries about the bounty of fish and shellfish in the sea, Atlantic salmon and trout in the rivers, and every wild game imaginable in the forests. It is the perfect ecological utopia for a hunter-gatherer.

PREVIOUS: A big part of the puzzle is finding the right pattern that will stir the pooled up salmon into the bite. Atlantic salmon want what they can't have. As curiosity killed the cat, same often goes with the fickle *Salmo salar*. **TOP LEFT:** The still, calcareous rock pools of the Grande Riviere insist on perfect presentations; a September fly box full of Doddi Orange and Orange Francis flies. **BOTTOM LEFT:** Probing the waters of the Grand Riviere of Gaspé. **OPPOSITE:** When a salmon takes off on a massive run down the York River and heads for the Bay de Chaleur, and you are into your backing, all you can do is pray that it eventually turns around and comes back to your pool.

ABOVE: Famous Gaspé guide Austin Clark brings the author to a hook-up on a pod of pooled-up salmon on the stunning Pabos River. **RIGHT:** The author battles a massive Atlantic on the famed elite White House Pool of the York.

My love for the Gaspé was born out of my true, relentless passion and obsession to chase its *saumon de l'Atlantique*. Its indigenous Atlantic salmon are some of the largest on the planet with beasts approaching fifty to sixty pounds. Norway may be the only other place that can also lay claim to such massive specimens. The Atlantic salmon, along with the indigenous brook trout, swim the Gaspé's lakes and rivers, including the Bonaventure River and Grande Rivière, with waters that have a bluish-green tint with zero sediment, since their oligotrophic nature comes from the calcium carbonate limestone bedrock and structure. This acts almost like an Icelandic volcanic-rock charcoal filter that purifies the water. Looking at a pool on these waters, you can see even the tiniest stone and gravel several feet down. Then there are the rivers like the Grand Cascapédia and York, which emanate from large spring-fed lakes and bogs with a tannic, tea-colored tint from its forests. In each of these waters, the salmon have run them to spawn for a million years, returning annually from their ocean hunting grounds off Greenland.

On the Water

Some of my best memories were made fishing on the north end of the peninsula near the city of Gaspé itself. Friend and Malbaie River Lodge owner Bill Greiner was my host for several of those visits, and as a lodge owner and fanatical salmon fly fisher he was a phenomenally creative guide. He was relentless in his pursuit to improvise new techniques for a fish so enshrined in tradition—yet one often not willing to bite. He guided out of an old van that looked like a trashed-up pawn shop, complete with fast food and snack wrappers, fly boxes, and soda and beer cans scattered everywhere. Surprisingly in the mess, he had everything he needed and every situation covered. Along with a never-give-up attitude, Bill always employed radical new concepts and fly designs—signs of a true compulsive salmon-bum sensei.

However, there is one important caveat that one can encounter on Gaspé rivers in the late summer or early fall: The fish may not bite! Unfortunately, this is perhaps the most familiar state a fly fisher has with Atlantic salmon. Therein lies the allure of the cheeky challenge—to fool a fish like the salmon that doesn't eat when it enters freshwater streams from the ocean. If you succeed in getting it to take your fly—especially one you tied yourself—it is the ultimate buzz.

Yet salmon are truly a fish of two seasons. Early June days with rivers running high from snow melt often make for amazing fishing in the Gaspé with lots of grabs and battles on aggressive fish fresh in from the ocean. Here, their strike instinct is still fully intact since weeks earlier they were hunting baitfish in the ocean. But as they get closer to spawning in the fall, the bite gets tough—at times impossible. Summers on Canadian Atlantic salmon rivers, now more than ever because of climate change, can be cruel to the fish and fishermen. The rivers can run warm or low from droughts, plus they can have ultra-clear waters that make for very difficult fly presentations. Couple all of this with stifling air temperatures and no rain and you have one very challenging conundrum. These are chief factors contributing to the salmon zip-jaw stalemate, not to mention *Salmo salar* being a fish of a thousand casts. When the bite is hot, the most often heard comment from an Atlantic salmon guide is, "I can't believe that fish took that bloody thing," pertaining to your god-awful fly choice, which you decided to use despite the frowns and headshaking of your more traditional fly-oriented guide. In these words of reflection, we begin to find the key to the paradoxical nature of the Atlantic salmon bite-trigger psyche. It's about cracking the enigmatic code: not so much when salmon are on the bite, but much more importantly, when they are not. There lies the rub.

Fishing and getting skunked is brutal with these fish. It stings even more since it often costs a small fortune to fish for them. It's especially frustrating when you can see them stacked by the hundreds in a perfect schooling formation in impeccably clear pool beats you are casting on. You watch them yawn at you, flip you the bird, move out of the way of your fly, or bump the fly aside with their snouts. It's totally demoralizing. Yet even changing flies and trying new patterns still leads to daily frustration. Days would go by without a hook-up in camp. Even when cold spells arrived and cooled things down, the *Salmo salar*'s dour attitude was impenetrable.

One splendid thing that unites salmon anglers and guides around the world is a strong camaraderie born out of love for the fish. You have plenty of time around whatever salmon lodge you're staying at to tell stories, share flies, solve riddles, and reminisce about when the salmon gods blessed you with a hook-up and the euphoria of that hard-fought catch. But mostly it's about the conundrum salmon leave you in when they refuse even the best of your flies and are off the beat.

A Ghillie's Touch

Gordie has been my wonderful guide for many recent visits. He is truly a charming guy, who has the most lovable, gentle personality—not a crusty, curmudgeonly salmon-fishing ghillie. His hobby was baking raspberry pies in the winter so he could deliver them and have a coffee talk with friends. Everyone looks out for one another in the bitterly harsh winters of Quebec. They also do a ton of chatting in the Gaspé—hours and hours, coffee pot after coffee pot of it. Just go to a Tim Hortons there, and it'll be filled with old-timers chatting on endlessly. Time means nothing.

But despite Gordie being a man for all seasons, he had a damn good knowledge of salmon behavior and fly selection. Gordie was exactly who I needed. We were a dynamic duo. I'll always remember the first time Gordie asked me what time we should meet for the next day's fishing and I replied noon. I thought he would keel over from shock. He liked this new schedule, and I also got to sleep in, after a few late-night drams of Scotch with the guests, which fueled theoretical discussions about *Salmo salar* selectivity. On occasion, most passionate salmon anglers find conversation just as fascinating as the fishing itself.

After many visits and skunked days, I was beginning to know the drill for cracking salmon lock-jaw syndrome. It was time to think like a salmon. The sun would stir up the protocol of the pooled-up salmon as it rose over the Atlantic Coast at around five a.m. The fish in the pool would move around for about an hour, line up in a pool pecking order,

LEFT: Nothing better than resting a pool, waiting for a rotation, and sipping a single malt Scotch on a Gaspé River. **OPPOSITE, CLOCKWISE FROM TOP:** To catch a salmon on a bomber is the highest echelon of the Atlantic salmon game; today's Gaspé dean, David Bishop, with a massive Grand Cascapédia beast of a salmon; one of the most beautiful fish on the planet doesn't need bling, but the author's reel and the topaz cheek of this gravid/September female takes the art to another level.

bump and nuzzle one another a little bit, and then settle into a long dormant sleep for the rest of the day. The regularity and regiment of this routine was uncanny. I had a plan. When Gordie picked me up at noon, I said, "Let's go grab a lobster sandwich at Pescheur," a seafood restaurant right on the boardwalk in the resort town of Perce. Then we would go down to the fishermen docks on the bay and watch them haul in super-large scallops, oysters, and lobsters (some of the finest come from Quebec).

For several days, the Zone Ecological Control (ZEC) assigned us to the Sardine Box beat of the Grande Rivière. It was an absolutely beautiful beat with crystal clear, aqua-blue sets of deep pools that held some very large salmon you could look in the eye. But they were extremely selective and sometimes almost impossible to catch. In this kind of water, you could watch the fish's reaction to your every cast and fly presentation. "Let's make sure we are at the Sardine Box at about five p.m.," I told Gordie. He was all in.

We arrived at the gazebo hut overlooking the pool at cocktail hour. The beasts—some approaching thirty pounds—were finning almost motionless several feet below the surface in one pool that had to be fourteen feet deep. They were comatose, totally dour. That was fine for me, since I knew things would change shortly. I poured a Scotch on the rocks and fired up a cigar, then kicked back. I rigged up one of my ugly Labatt's Blue Grizzly's—a rubber-legged concoction inspired by one of Bill Greiner's patterns. "As soon as the sun goes over that peak of the Chic-Choc, those fish will start stirring around. Trust me, they hate that blazing sun," I told Gordie.

CLOCKWISE FROM TOP: A perfect female Gaspé salmon dripping sea lice; Orange Francis Fly; clear, turquoise, volcanic-rock-filtered waters of the Gaspé. **FOLLOWING:** Carlota Bishop with a beautiful Grand Cascapédia salmon. The underwater world of the Gaspé, captured by world-renowned photographer Jean-Guy Beliveau.

At the top of the Sardine Box was a narrow, rocky ledge pool, fast-water shoot. It was well oxygenated and partially emanating from the river's many underground springs that kept the river cool all summer. The fish are drawn to these shallow areas, especially as the sun goes down. They are too big to lie in that shallow water during the day because of their paranoia of predation. Once I moved into position, I cast in an up-and-across downstream, fast-stripping presentation right below the surface. The fly pushed water and created a stir. The traditional salmon approach is to use a broadside down-and-across wet fly swing—so my calculated technique was going totally against the accepted grain. Perhaps that is why it is so deadly—the fish don't see anything like it. Remember: A salmon wants something it can't have.

After several presentations, and as the light was fading, my sweeping casts and strips yielded an explosion on the surface. The fish absolutely hammered the fly! I was grateful to be using a fifteen-pound Ultra Clear Maxima tippet. My heart shot up into my throat. Gordie was screaming in disbelief. After about a twenty-minute battle that went up and back downstream the pool several times, Gordie tailed the fish—he was still dumbfounded by its size. It was a large male with a kype jaw that would intimidate a crocodile. As I dripped in sweat from the long battle, we snapped tons of images on the Nikon of that stunning orange and black marble-spotted thirty-eight pounder before I released him to swim off into the darkness. The experience left us silent and in a state of shock as we packed up to leave.

On the drive back to Malbaie River Lodge, I smoked my cigar while grinning like a Cheshire cat that just ate a mouse. It was a quiet ride, with a must-stop at a roadside poutine and fries joint playing Quebecois country music. Gazing up at the stars, with the view of the Milky Way on that beautiful, clear Gaspé night on the high-forest hilltop road, it almost seemed like you could reach up and grab them.

Back at the lodge, I showed up well after dinner. Gordie warned me of my impending lecture, and he skedaddled fast. The wonderful yet stern chef was not happy with me and had left my plate of coq au vin covered with foil next to the microwave. As another lodge guest poured me a single-malt Scotch, I flashed around pictures of that huge Atlantic like a proud father. The other rods at the lodge went skunked. They fished all day and looked dejected and extremely sunburnt. I felt like a prophet of hope.

Their problem: They were leaving their beats too early so they would be on the chef's schedule—not on the salmon's.

The next day, everybody slept in, opting to go out later and have a lobster sandwich on the beach. They got to their designated river beats for the evening with a new attitude. That night everyone came back to the lodge late with salmon on their cameras. Big smiles and grateful thanks were bestowed upon me. But the chef was annoyed. I had changed her routine. I apologized, offering her a night off with a nice bottle of champagne, and told her I would cook. She accepted my apology, and she still cooked dinner.

Since salmon want what they can't have, using the same traditional flies, cast from the same rock and location, won't work after a while. Traditional patterns like the Blue Charm, Francis, and Undertaker are still killer patterns. But when salmon holding in the pools see the same patterns day after day, a certain malaise kicks in. That's why new patterns and techniques, like stripping Greiner's Rubber Legs, fishing more Riffle Hitches, and using mega-size Road Kill patterns, are deadly. Cracking the code involves challenging the protocol and being disruptive in your approach. Atlantic salmon fishing is like a mental chess game, and this is why we love it.

On the Table

Quebec's Comfort Eats

Aside from its never-ending stunning ecology and fishing, on a more intimate level the Gaspé experience is about its warm and friendly people and comfort foods. You get a very laid-back European vibe with French being spoken. Quebecers—a blend of Irish, Scottish, and mostly French Quebecois—all have their unique mannerisms. They came across the pond for the illustrious cod industry, logging, and fur trading of the past centuries. They each claim to have landed there first. You, as a stranger, are welcomed with sincere warmth.

One must embrace the gourmet comfort food of Quebec from several angles. No doubt the French influence is the strongest. But the English, Irish, and Scottish settlers have had an impact on its culinary history. The beauty of the combination is it relies on the practicality of the seasons, delicious taste, ease of preparation, and most importantly, the bounty of the land and sea.

The mackerel, halibut, salmon, and prawns, along with oysters, clams, scallops, and lobsters, are gifts from the sea. Grass-fed prime beef, pork, and chickens and geese are raised for foie gras and pâté. To add to this perfect surf and turf mix, the wilds of the forest bring elk and venison, moose and wild boar, and tremendous waterfowl migrations of duck and geese, not to mention a rich grouse and woodcock population.

But it is truly the local cuisine—hearty slow-cooked meat- and potato-filled shepherd's pies called tourtière; the cheesy, warm fondue and raclette dishes for the long winters; and excellent homemade soups like the traditional French onion—that offers such comfort. Along with the legendary poutine and tremendous bakery creations, they make you yearn for Quebecois food.

French Onion Soup

A traditional favorite in the comfort cuisine repertoire of all French cooking and Quebecois.

Serves 4

2 tablespoons extra-virgin olive oil

½ cup (1 stick) unsalted butter

3 to 4 medium yellow onions, sliced

5 cups low-sodium beef broth

2 tablespoons dry sherry

1 teaspoon dried thyme

Coarse sea salt and freshly ground black pepper

8 slices baguette

4 slices provolone cheese

2 slices Swiss cheese, diced

¼ cup grated Parmesan cheese

Heat the olive oil in a large pot or Dutch oven over medium heat, then melt the butter. Stir in the onions and sauté until tender and translucent but not browned, about 6 minutes.

Add the beef broth, sherry, and thyme, and season with salt and pepper. Simmer for 30 minutes.

Preheat the oven broiler.

Put individual crocks on a baking sheet. Ladle the soup into the crocks and place 2 slices of the bread on top of each. Layer the bread with provolone, diced Swiss, and Parmesan. Broil until the cheese bubbles and browns slightly, 2 to 3 minutes. Serve hot.

WRITING ON ATLANTIC SALMON
EDITORS: CHARLES
Published in association with the
Abel
Made in USA

Veal Marsala
with Wild Mushrooms & Pappardelle

When I returned on the train from one of my salmon trips, I had one of the most outstanding traditional dishes from a French-Italian chef in Gaspé, who also created the menu for VIA Canada Rail. He used local wild mushrooms, non-caged veal, and pappardelle noodles.

Serves 4

4 (4-ounce) veal cutlets

Coarse sea salt and freshly ground black pepper

½ cup all-purpose flour

2 tablespoons extra-virgin olive oil

4 tablespoons unsalted butter

1 pound wild, button, or cremini mushrooms, sliced

1 cup marsala

1 cup low-sodium beef broth, plus more as needed

2 teaspoons cornstarch

½ cup heavy cream

1 pound pappardelle noodles, cooked

Finely chopped fresh parsley leaves for serving

Season the veal on both sides with salt and pepper. Then put the flour in a shallow dish and dredge the veal, shaking off any excess.

In a large skillet over medium-high heat, warm the olive oil and melt 2 tablespoons of the butter.

Add the veal to the pan and cook until browned and cooked through, about 2 minutes per side. Use tongs to transfer the cutlets to a plate.

Add the mushrooms to the skillet and sauté until golden brown, about 5 minutes. Pour in the marsala and 1 cup beef broth and stir to deglaze pan, scraping up any browned bits. Lower the heat and simmer 5 to 6 minutes.

Whisk the cornstarch and heavy cream in a small bowl and add to the mushroom mixture and let it bubble and thicken for 1 minute.

Turn off the heat and stir in the remaining 2 tablespoons butter. Place noodles onto each of four plates and top each with a veal cutlet. Generously spoon sauce on top and sprinkle with parsley.

Gordie's Raspberry Pie

RECIPE FROM GORDIE DRODY

Gordie was my salmon ghillie on many of my trips to the magnificent Gaspé of Quebec. While he loved being a guide, his true passion was baking raspberry pies. A classic, rustic pie bursting with fresh raspberries and a flaky, buttery crust—his pies are simply the best on the planet.

Makes 1 (9-inch) pie

2½ cups all-purpose flour, plus 2½ tablespoons and more for dusting

½ teaspoon salt

½ cup shortening, chilled and cubed

½ cup (1 stick) unsalted butter, chilled and cut into pea-size pieces

⅓ cup cold water, plus more as needed

4 cups fresh raspberries

1 cup granulated sugar

1 large egg

Coarse sugar for sprinkling

Combine 2½ cups flour and the salt in a large bowl. Incorporate the shortening and butter into the flour with a fork. Then, use a pastry blender to blend until the mixture resembles coarse oatmeal. Add ⅓ cup cold water and blend again. Add more water, a tablespoon at a time, if the dough doesn't hold together. Divide the dough into two balls. Wrap and chill, if needed.

Gently stir together the raspberries and sugar in a medium bowl. Add the 2½ tablespoons flour and stir again until evenly coated. Set aside.

Preheat the oven to 425°F.

Lightly dust a work surface and rolling pin with flour. Roll out one dough ball 2 inches wider than a 9-inch pie plate. Transfer the dough to the pie plate and add the berry mixture. Roll out the second dough ball to 2 inches wider than the pie plate. Place over the filling and fold the edges of the top and bottom crusts together. Cut out a small rectangular piece in the center for venting.

In a small bowl, beat the egg with 1 tablespoon water and brush over the top crust. Sprinkle with the coarse sugar. Set on a baking sheet with parchment paper and bake for 20 minutes. Reduce the heat to 350°F and bake until the filling bubbles through the center vent and it starts to crack and overflow, 30 to 40 minutes more.

Let the pie cool at room temperature for several hours. For best texture, let it sit overnight and serve the next day.

Scottish Spey-, Dee-, and Akroyd-style tied flies are still the heart and soul of a salmon angler's fly box anywhere around the globe.

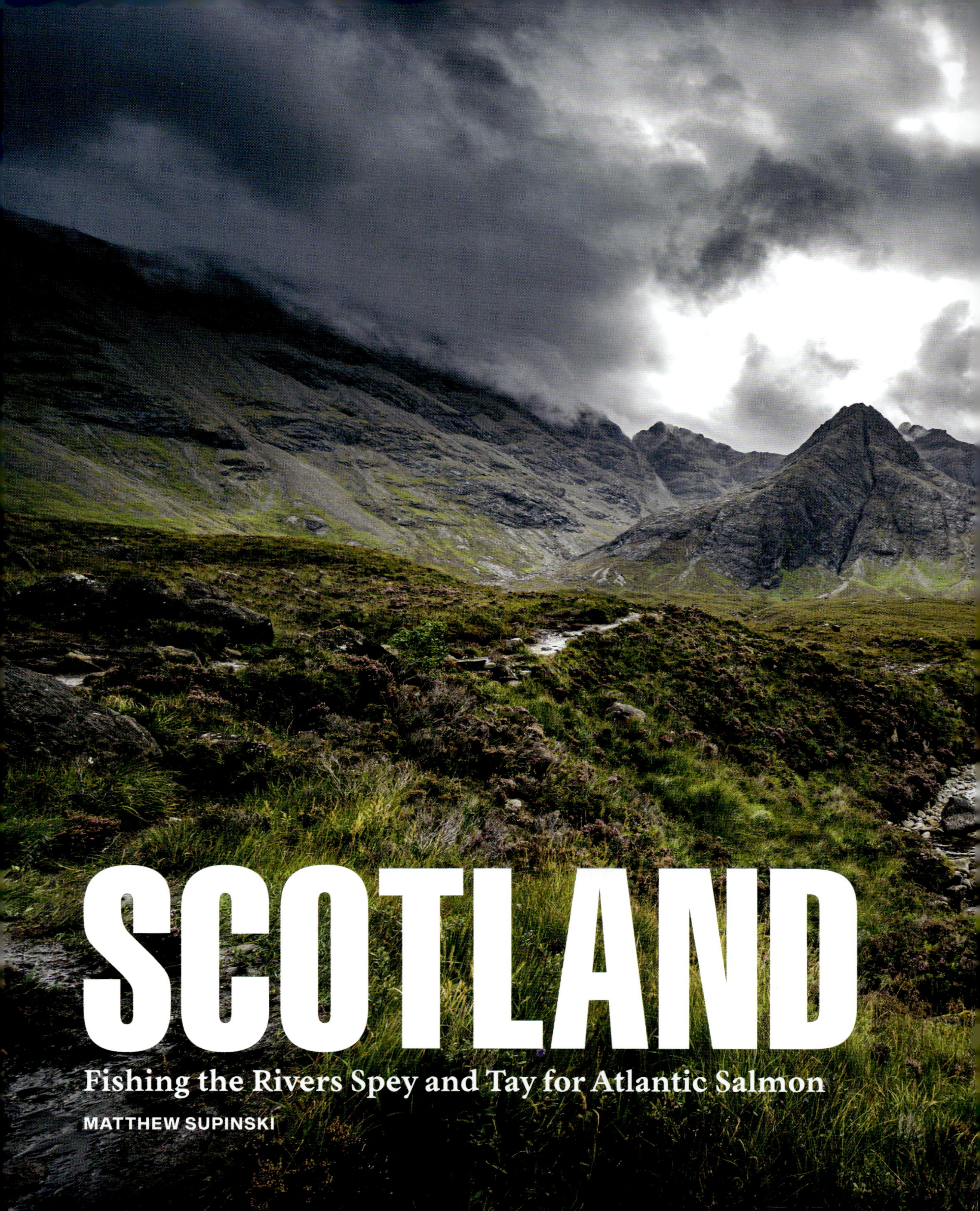
SCOTLAND
Fishing the Rivers Spey and Tay for Atlantic Salmon
MATTHEW SUPINSKI

"For once it was exactly as I'd pictured it, which is something a fisherman doesn't get to say very often. There were real castles and slate-roofed stone cottages scattered around a green river valley, ghillies in knee-high breeches and leather vests, a water bailiff in a deerstalker cap who slept days and ventured out only in the gloaming when poachers were about."
—JOHN GIERACH

Sometimes you come very close to envisioning a piece of heaven. Such was the case when I saw the stark yet breathtakingly stunning Scottish Highlands for the first time; my awestruck gasp hit me hard. The Highlands have an enchanting, eerie vibe—eliciting that goosebump sort of chill. This vast Viking and Celtic Valhalla is truly meant to be untamed—to be left alone to run full-bore wild. If England is about proper civility, Scotland is the savage free spirit we all want inside of us.

The Highlands are a postcard panorama of snow-capped mountains cropping up steeply from the lush green moors below. Here, the sapphire-blue lochs—one named Ness with a famous primordial leviathan resident—and gorgeous tea-stained rivers run down to the firths by the North Sea and ocean below them.

But it is in its storied rivers that swim the true sporting prize of Scotland—the majestic and revered Atlantic salmon. Along with its cousins, the brown trout and sea trout, they have fed the bellies of the Celts, Normans, and Vikings for centuries. At one time long ago, they returned to the rivers from their ocean feeding grounds by the hundreds of thousands annually. Today their runs are a mere flicker of their storied past. Yet Scottish salmon fishing is still a religion. Its rivers have a charismatic power to inspire the artistry of the meticulously tied salmon fly patterns, born out of tradition in this land of iconic waters lined with castles and estates from medieval times. The zen and beauty of the two-handed spey cast had its genesis. And for the soul and eyes, the stunning beauty of the fish transcends it all. We attest to their life force and power when we see them jumping the tallest waterfalls or traveling thousands of

PREVIOUS: The stark yet always breathtaking Scottish Highlands. **OPPOSITE:** The landing is often the most critical battle of the fight. **TOP:** Vala Arnadottir with a spey cast among the lush greenery of the Scottish Highlands. **BOTTOM:** A perfect *Salmo salar* specimen.

miles in the ocean to come back to the exact place where they were born. The saga of the salmon is one of the most incredible stories of nature. Despite a changing global climate and other human-induced obstacles that have wreaked havoc on their honed life strategies over the millennia, their will to survive is powerful. Scottish salmon are forever the true Caledonian royals.

On the Water

Scottish rivers are where spey-fly casting started several hundred years ago. Along with another two-handed passion they invented, golf, the Scot's have given us pastimes of fanatical devotion that require finesse and timing when using sticks: one to cast a fly, the other to hit a tiny ball.

We can't discuss the spey cast without mentioning the royal family. Though they couldn't conquer Scotland, the royal family made Scotland their summer destination. At Balmoral Castle, on the majestic salmon-rich River Dee, Queen Victoria, Queen Elizabeth, and now Queen Camilla have watched their families truly embrace this sporting tradition. Bird shooting and fly fishing are the true marks of a proper English gentleman and lady. They hunt grouse; go horseback riding; hike the highlands; play croquet, tennis, and badminton; and have proper British picnics. But it is the regal Atlantic salmon of the River Dee, which flows through the estate, that is the truly cherished prize of Balmoral.

TOP: The properness and tidiness of a Scottish Estate ghillie's outfitting room. **BOTTOM:** The magnificent River Dee, where the salmon for the Royal Family swim their way up to Balmoral Castle. **OPPOSITE:** The Scottish invented the salmon fly dynasty with their Spey- and Dee-style flies. An orange and black Akroyd-style tie took this beautiful fish.

SDS 11/12
Abel

The royals' love for salmon goes beyond an ordinary pastime. Queen Elizabeth was a fanatical spey caster. She had all her flies tied by the famous fly-tyer Megan Boyd. They are truly works of art capable of catching the Dee's salmon, which can be finicky and selective. The regal House of Hardy in London creates special spey rods for the royals. King Charles is on the water salmon fishing as often as he can. I saw Charles, then a prince, fly casting on the River Test when I fished the Orvis beat at the Broadlands. Back in the 1980s it was right next to his uncle's estate. King Charles has always been an active salmon conservationist and has been a vital force in the Atlantic Salmon Trust movement. Many images are circulated in the tabloids each summer of the royals spey fishing for salmon. And each year the royals host the Ghillies Ball at Balmoral.

Though the laws have been loosened and some public exceptions are unfolding today, Scotland still enshrines the king's land rights granted centuries ago. So, the rivers are owned by the land barons of that estate. They enforce the fishing beat and ghillie system, and you pay to fish a beat—you can't just go and fish like we can in North America.

When we visited our son at school in Edinburgh, I may have broken the law in the town of Dunkeld on the River Tay. Not knowing if it was illegal, I actually hooked a salmon under an old Romanesque bridge downtown on a Willie Gun tube fly. The locals gave me dirty looks as I suited up and waded out to the bridge abutment by the town park. I was standing on it when I caught the salmon. I couldn't imagine I was violating anyone's land rights to the water, since the bridge really belonged to the Romans! Occasionally, there are interpretive guidelines to age-old rules.

True spey lovers appreciate the fact that very often as we swing flies and spey cast for salmon, we know very well we might not catch a bloody thing. It is a pure stubborn devotion and passion to the art form that drives us. So, it isn't coincidental that a stubborn devotion such as spey swinging was founded in the land where stubbornness was refined. This whole swing mentality is born out of experiencing the savage take and battle that ensues when you hook a salmon or sea trout on the swing. We persist in doing it for the magic of the "tug is the drug," even under the most unfavorable conditions. Once you have experienced that remarkable, electrifying grab you are addicted for life.

Needless to say, spey casting, fly tying, and salmon are sacred to the Scottish. The River Tay, northwest of Edinburgh as you head up the sacred Scotch whiskey trail into the Highlands, is a magnificent river. Its broad country vistas and stunning pools and beats on the land-baron estates give you a semi-good chance at swinging a spey and catching the elusive and dwindling *Salmo salar*. Aside from salty-dog guide experiences with some Scottish ghillies, what impressed me the most was the tremendous pride and passion each estate and beat ghillie had for their profession. Though the runs continue to be drastically down, they still show up to work with a smile and ever-enthusiastic outlook despite the poor catch rates.

River Spey

I have been fly fishing in Scotland several times. One need only visit the Gordon Castle Estate on the River Spey to understand the majesty and time-honored tradition of the spey cast. It is said to be here and in the

CLOCKWISE FROM TOP: Fishing on Scottish rivers always brings a strong sense of history; this mature, pre-spawn Atlantic salmon has the beautiful orange, red, and black marbling of a brown trout—both species are closely related; Lucinda Ewin admires a beautiful brown that is an indigenous gem to all of England, Scotland, and Ireland.

ABOVE: A fat, chunky Scottish brown that fell for a March Brown. **OPPOSITE, CLOCKWISE FROM TOP:** Gordon Castle Estate on the River Spey where ghillies and anglers still dress in proper tweed suits; Willie Gunn Tube; a ghillie hut on the river's edge, where Scotch whiskey is enjoyed and tales of salmon that got away are spun.

surrounding beats on the Spey that "Welsh throw" or "greenheart sticks" casting had its birth. Fundamentally, the Spey passion and cast is not for everyone. It takes long hours of practice, physical coordination, and mental discipline. It will entail long hours of fishless days on the river learning to swing and present the fly properly, along with a firm dedication if you want to master it and maybe someday catch your dream salmon.

But unless you are on the Russian Kola or on an Icelandic river teaming with salmon near the Arctic Circle, you are going to earn and appreciate each beautiful salmon you are gifted on the swing. In all of fly fishing, this is one true secular passion that grips you and changes how you fish. Above all, it teaches patience, focus, discipline, and gratitude for when you finally catch a salmon on the means and terms you have chosen.

The Spey River Valley is everything you would imagine it to be, tucked comfortably in the Scottish Highlands. Driving through endless sheep and Angus cattle grazing in glens and picturesque moors, one picks up on a very unique smell, as single-malt distillers belch out aromas and evaporation steam as they burn the barley and malt necessary for their nectar of the whiskey gods.

Upon arrival, my host and whiskey master-distiller Willie Roy greeted me at my rental Opel. He looked at my luggage and my archaic (by today's standards) fifteen-foot, eleven-weight spey rod case, which weighed as much as my luggage. When we entered the manor, he immediately started to contact the estate's ghillie to come over for a whiskey and chat about our itinerary. I was pumped, but Willie was cautious and tried to immediately curb my enthusiasm. "Ya know, we haven't had a good run of salmon in a wee bit mate, so you will have to really work for them aye," he said. He then proceeded to settle me in my quarters and prepare me for three days of whiskey overindulgence. (At times I wondered if I might need to go into alcohol rehab when I returned home.)

Even though I was there for the salmon fishing, deep down I knew that I needed to have very low expectations. A salmon tug or even a glimpse of one would suffice. Enter in my ghillie, Iain. "Ya sure you don't want to still take the golf package lad?" he said sarcastically, as he waddled through the door of the manor's smoking parlor in muddied Wellington boots and smelling of pipe smoke. His gruff introduction was yet another sign of the reality, and I struggled to stay optimistic. When he asked about my favorite spey flies, I told him the Undertaker, a sparsely tied Willie Gunn tube, or a fishable Jock Scott variant. "Jock Scott was a bloody myth, lad, besides those flies won't work here," he said, smothering one of my last breaths of optimism. "Ya need a Kinermony Killer, me lad. I have a wallet of them, no worries!" A little optimism resurfaced. Meanwhile, I killed the stark pain of what might be on the river as I sipped on

SAGE X
KonneticHD Technology

BALMORAL

my first fifty-year-old cask reserve and deep down thought, I'm gonna like this guy; I have a soft spot for curmudgeons.

After my gloomy pregame fishing rehearsal with Iain, the entire evening became a *Fellini Satyricon*-esque Scottish food and grog binge. The finest smoked salmon, whiskey, stag tenderloin in demi-glace with local wild chanterelles, and estate-garden heirloom root vegetables and herbs were sinfully delicious. My love for Scotland grew by the mouthful.

Nevertheless, despite the runs of salmon being at an all-time low, swinging a true spey-style fly, on a two-handed spey stick, on the River Spey, was an almost spiritual experience—despite one hell of a hangover. The ten-inch brown trout I caught was a bonus. Fishing aside, the river is truly one of the most beautiful on the planet. You look up at stunning mountains and castles as stag and other wildlife graze. But in the end, its mostly about having the slightest of chances to catch one of the most regal and noble fish that have ever swum any river in the universe, especially on a rod and in a style that was invented there.

On the Table

Scottish Cuisine: Fusing Tradition with the Eclectic

They say you can define a culture and people by what they eat. So, if you want to call sheep's pluck (heart, liver, and lungs) ground up into a pudding and wrapped in the lining of a sheep's stomach cuisine, go for it! Haggis aside, Escoffier would applaud the Scots for their butchering talents. Boldness and subsistence have defined Caledonian dishes for centuries. But there are some truly galactic epicurean delights that Scotland produces.

Probably the finest is Scottish smoked salmon, with its light smoky-sweet flavor that matches perfectly with fresh dill.

Other highlights: delicious pot pies, blood pudding, Scottish breakfasts, scones, and butter cookies. And then there is fine Scottish whiskey, that amber-golden nectar that smells like the earth, and stings and comforts like the finest elixir. It is a true masterpiece of distillation. Whether in a complex chosen blend or single distillery malt style, these whiskeys have extreme complexity like the finest wines.

There are now Michelin-star haute cuisine stand-alone restaurants, and restaurants at lodges and castles throughout Scotland, serving up impressive farm-to-table fare with chefs who have honed their skills and developed their palates by venturing to France, Italy, Spain, and Asia.

Scottish culinary riches lie in what the land and sea provide. The fish and chips in Scotland, using fresh-caught pollack, cod, and haddock brought to the docks through the firths, can be euphoric. Lobsters, crabs, prawns, and all the flat fishes like Dover sole and turbot round out the fruits of the sea. The Angus beef is the finest and now exists on all continents. Smoking, grilling, and stuffing wild game have always been art forms in Scotland. Stag and deer, grouse and pheasant, rabbits, and ducks and geese have been used in every way in the modern Scottish chef's kitchen, always following the nose-to-tail approach, wasting nothing—from roasts and stews to pâtés, foie gras, and rillettes. A chef's imagination can run wild.

PREVIOUS: A beautiful male Atlantic salmon; keeping the fish wet and respected is essential. **OPPOSITE:** Scottish smoked salmon.

Scottish Eggs Benedict

There is nothing more divine than Scottish smoked salmon. A hearth/kiln cold-smoked piscatorial flesh of the Celtic gods, it is cured with a glaze of rum or Scotch whiskey. Serve with fresh dill, over a poached egg, delightful homemade hollandaise, capers, red onion, and fresh spring asparagus on an English muffin. Can be enjoyed as an appetizer, or for breakfast, brunch, or dinner.

Serves 2

½ cup (1 stick) unsalted butter

3 egg yolks

3 tablespoons Dijon mustard

Juice of ½ lemon

4 poached eggs

2 English muffins, toasted

4 slices cold-smoked Scottish-style salmon

¼ cup finely chopped red onion

¼ cup drained capers

Dill leaves for garnish

Paprika

Melt the butter in a small saucepan over very low heat. Once the butter has almost melted, add the egg yolks and stir constantly until thoroughly incorporated. Add the mustard and stir constantly until incorporated. Stirring constantly, add the lemon juice and incorporate. If the sauce starts to break, remove from the heat and add a little bit of water. Keep stirring until it comes together again.

Place one poached egg on each English muffin half. Ladle hollandaise sauce over the top, then place 1 slice of smoked salmon on each egg. Serve with some of the onion and capers, and garnish with dill and a sprinkle of paprika.

SHERRY OAK CASK
NATURAL COLOUR
PRODUCT OF SCOTLAND

Speyside Pot Pie

I had the most delightful shepherd's and pot pies in Scotland. When on the Spey, I had a chicken cordon bleu pot pie (called Gordon bleu for the castle estate). This dish is pure comfort food decadence.

Serves 4

2 sheets pie pastry dough

5 tablespoons unsalted butter

1 cup peeled, sliced carrot

1 cup coarsely chopped celery

1 cup thinly sliced leeks

1 tablespoon finely chopped fresh tarragon leaves

1/4 cup all-purpose flour

2 to 2 1/2 cups low-sodium chicken broth

1 cup heavy cream

Coarse sea salt and freshly ground black pepper

3 cups diced rotisserie chicken

1 cup diced smoked ham

1 cup frozen baby sweet peas

2 cups shredded sharp white cheddar cheese

1 egg, beaten

Preheat the oven to 400°F. Put 4 individual-serving-size crocks on a baking sheet and bring the pie dough to room temperature.

Melt 2 tablespoons of the butter in a medium saucepan over medium-high heat.

Add the carrot, celery, leeks, and tarragon, sautéing until slightly softened but not browned, about 3 minutes. Transfer to a small bowl.

Reduce the heat to medium and melt the remaining 3 tablespoons butter in the saucepan. Whisk in the flour, cooking until the mixture bubbles but doesn't brown, about 1 minute. Whisk in 2 cups of broth and cook for 1 minute.

Whisk in the cream and cook until the sauce has thickened, 2 to 3 minutes. Season with the salt and pepper. Add the remaining 1/2 cup broth if the sauce is too thick.

Add the cooked vegetables, chicken, ham, and peas to the sauce, mix gently, and taste for seasoning.

Halve the sheets of pastry. Pour the filling evenly into the crocks and top with the grated cheese. Cover each crock with pie dough and crimp the edges. Poke the tip of a knife or fork into the dough to make slits, then lightly brush the dough with egg.

Bake for 20 minutes, then reduce the temperature to 375°F and bake until the crust is golden brown and the filling is bubbling, another 25 to 30 minutes. Let rest 10 minutes before serving.

Acknowledgments

FROM KIRK DEETER

A Fishable Feast could not have happened without the steadfast support of my wife, Sarah, and son, Paul. Sarah has not only encouraged my fishing adventures for decades, she also jumped in and got elbows-deep making dishes in the kitchen, taking photos, and editing copy; she brought this one home. Paul is my fishing buddy and number one taste tester. I look forward to revisiting many of these places we have yet to fish together because I know he will appreciate them, even though I also know he'll probably outfish me. Thanks also to my parents, my brother, Drew, and his family, as well as my sisters-in-law, Susie and Katherine, and their families.

There are many friendships that have been cultivated over decades and thousands of river miles . . . which is really *why I fish.* Tim Romano has been a faithful business partner for nearly twenty-five years. I'm grateful for Terry Gunn, who gave me my first break when it came to writing stories about fly fishing, and Rodrigo Salles, my "jungle brother." Thanks to Felix Borenstein, who knows the best fishing spots in many places, especially New Zealand. Dave Karczynski is one of the best pure writers in the game now and Monte Burke is in his own league. Chris Elbow, master chocolatier, is consigliere on all things edible and an extraordinarily passionate angler. All you other friends—you know who you are—please accept this blanket thanks and know I appreciate you.

I must offer an extra-special nod of gratitude to my late friend, Chris Santella. Chris was the author of *Fifty Places to Fly Fish Before You Die* and a number of other great books. Chris and I traveled together and wrote stories in places like Alaska, Russia, and Ireland, so he was largely responsible for giving me the "travel bug." He knew he had terminal cancer when I first shared this book concept with him, yet he still coached us to give it some wings. When I got the news that he had passed away (a call from Romano), I was sitting on a bench along a chalk stream in England, and ironically (actually, I think not) that happened merely an hour or so after I got the e-mail from Rizzoli that said they wanted to publish this book. Not a coincidence in my mind.

Every day I appreciate the faith Chris Wood, the CEO of Trout Unlimited, placed in me to edit *TROUT* magazine. I believe, very much, in the work TU does to make most fly fishing possible in the first place, and I think TU fosters the conscience of trout and salmon fishing in America and beyond. Thanks to all the TU colleagues, members, and supporters.

Jim Muschett totally got it, and it was just a matter of time before we found some project to collaborate on. Tricia Levi is a fantastic editor who made this thing sing. Jan Derevjanik made it look better than I had dreamed it to be. It was an honor to work with the talent at Rizzoli.

How cool is it to have one of your fly-fishing heroes write a foreword for your book? Thanks Tom Rosenbauer, from your pal, "Coliguacho."

Lastly, I want to acknowledge my partner, Matt Supinski, and his wife, Laurie. I appreciate their patience, flexibility, and perseverance throughout the long journey of making this book. And now I just look forward to sharing more time together fishing—maybe cooking up a meal now and then—by the waters in Michigan where my fishing path started.

Acknowledgments

FROM MATTHEW SUPINSKI

When presented with the huge challenge of writing *A Fishable Feast* by my coauthor, first thoughts were . . . *Man! These stories are my life's memoirs flashing before my eyes . . . scary!* But it all flowed. This book was laid out before us through the natural beauty of this world, its diverse peoples, cultures, and bounty of the land and sea that creates soulful cuisines. All thanks and praise to God for his beautiful creation and the magnificent fish that swim its waters. We are only its humble stewards.

To the love and blessing of my life, my wife, Laurie, you are an amazing chef and mother. Thanks for enduring the kitchen intensity when I forget I'm not in the hotel business anymore. Thanks to my brilliant son, Peter, with such a bright future. I am so very proud of you. And to Joyce, my mother-in-law, thanks for always being there. Love you guys!

To my European-immigrant parents, Antoni and Natalia, who survived the most inhumane war this planet has ever witnessed. You taught me the value of a hard day's work while growing up in those ethnic, industrial neighborhoods. Thanks, Dad, for teaching me the love of trout, how to fly fish at an early age (plus setting those alarm clocks to be on the trout stream at dawn), and how to pick wild mushrooms. Thanks to my mom, whose kitchen was sacred, where she instilled the value of using every morsel of food, improvising on ingredients, and never wasting anything.

Thanks to our farm in Poland, where I was happily confined from school at an early age for being a mouthy, opinionated young boy who didn't fit into the Communist system with my Western capitalistic, entrepreneurial ideas. On that rustic homestead with no TV, running water, or phones, we learned to live off the land and watch nature unfold all around us. To the Wieprza River that ran through it, where I learned the ways of trout and salmon, and how to shoot pheasants with Uncle Staszek, and where I learned to butcher nose-to-tail and cook amazing soups with my grandmother. It was the ultimate farm-to-table tutelage.

To all the chefs, and food and beverage directors in my hotel career, who screamed at me, threw pots, and worked me to the bone, insisting on the perfection they knew I had in me.

Thanks to my fly-fishing mentors: Nick Lyons, for teaching me to write (still learning); Vince Marinaro, Ed Shenk, Carl Richards, and Dick Pobst; and to my guiding clients who have tolerated my intensity. And thanks to all those readers and supporters who have read all my books and articles, and listen to my *Hallowed Waters* podcast.

To Tom Rosenbauer, thank you for your friendship. I still owe you for writing the introduction for my *Nexus* book—and now for this one! It makes it all truly special (BTW, I have a new sandwich for you!).

Thanks to the amazing Jim Muschett, Tricia Levi, and Jan Derevjanik. Rizzoli's is the finest publishing team I have ever worked with. I'm truly honored.

To all those wonderful people who made my destinations possible: Austria: Albert Pesendorfer and Roman Moser; Catskills: Anthony Magardino and the Catskill Fly Fishing Museum, Johnny Miller, Joe Ceballos, and The Homestead; France: Guillaume and Claire Chauvelot, Nicolas de Toldi, Chef Rebekah Bowersox/Brooke, and Tommy Baltz; Great Lakes: Rick Kustich, Greg Senyo, and Mike Fiore; Italy: Luca Castellani and Sergio Mastriforti; Montana: Paul Weamer and Chef Dave Wells; Poland: Arek Kubala, Jacek Kaczynski, and Art Merk; Quebec: Gordie Drody, Bill Greiner, and David Bishop; Scotland: Gordon Castle Estate.

Tim Romano, you are amazing!

Finally, and most importantly, many thanks to Kirk and Sarah Deeter. It happened! Now, let's go fool a big brown trout!

DEYOUNG

KIRK DEETER is the editor-in-chief of *TROUT* magazine and the "vice president of angling" for Trout Unlimited. Really. He's also the editor of *Angling Trade* and a founding partner of Flylab.fish. A former editor-at-large for *Field & Stream*, Deeter has written stories on fishing from all fifty states and twenty-eight other countries around the world (and counting). He is the author of several other books, most notably *The Little Red Book of Fly Fishing*. He and his wife, Sarah, live in Steamboat Springs, Colorado.

MATTHEW SUPINSKI is a book author, fly-fishing guide and instructor, freelance writer and photographer, hospitality consultant, and former food & beverage director, chef, and hotelier. He is the host of the popular *Hallowed Waters* podcast. Among his acclaimed books are *The Brown Trout–Atlantic Salmon Nexus*, *Selectivity: The Theory and Method for Fly Fishing for Fussy Trout, Salmon, and Steelhead*, and *Steelhead Dreams*. He and his wife, Laurie—who was the recipe compiler/chef helper for this book—spend their time between homes in Michigan and their native New York. His website and fly recipes can be found at graydrake.com.

Laurie and Matthew Supinski at Aurora Lodge Hotel, Iceland

PHOTO CREDITS FOR KIRK DEETER'S CHAPTERS

Tim Romano: cover, pp. 2–3, 12–15, 20–35, 42–53, 76–87, 142–151, 178–187, 270–283, 289, 296, 306–319, 384, back cover

Terry Gunn: pp. 92–101

Rodrigo M. Salles, Danielle Bayer, Lucas de Zan, and Rafael Costa: pp. 4, 104–119, 378–379

Kirk and Sarah Deeter: pp. 9, 37, 38, 41, 55, 57, 88, 91, 103, 152–177, 188, 191, 285, 312, 316–317, 320, 323

PHOTO CREDITS FOR MATTHEW SUPINSKI'S CHAPTERS

All fishing and food images by the author, except:

Albert Pesendorfer: pp. 10–11, 58–59, 60, 62–63, 64 (top), 66–67, 69

Sjo/Austria/iStock Getty: p. 64 (bottom left)

John G Miller: pp. 63 (bottom right), 120–121, 125 (top and bottom right), 126 (bottom), 127

photographer3431/trout/iStock Getty: p. 123

The Catskill Fly Fishing Museum: pp. 124 (top), 130

John Clark: p. 131

Guillaume and Claire Chauvelot/Le Moucheron: pp. 192–193, 197 (top and bottom right), 203

LucThibault/France/iStock Getty: p. 194

Nicolas de Toldi/Gourmetfly.com: p. 195 (bottom)

Jack Perks/jackperksphotography.com: pp. 198–199

Terry Lawton: p. 200 (top and bottom right)

Thomas Baltz: p. 200 (bottom left)

Andrew Steele Nisbet: p. 201 (bottom)

Nick de Toldi/Gourmetfly.com: p. 204

Tom Rosenbauer: p. 205

Paul Moore/Andy Saunders: pp. 214–215

Rick Kustich/rickkustich.com: p. 216 (top)

Tommy Lynch/ thefishwhisperer.com: p. 222 (center)

Orchid Poet/Niagara/iStock Getty: p. 222 (bottom)

Tommy Lynch/Tom McGraw: p. 223

John Fabian/cbolodge.com: p. 224

Arni Baldursson/Lax-á Angling Club: pp. 232–233, p. 235 (top), p. 239, p. 241 (top), 362, 363, 366 (top and bottom right), 369 (bottom left)

Laurie Supinski: pp. 236–237, 244, 250–251

AlexRayes/seafood/iStock Getty: p. 245

Sergio Mastriforti: pp. 252–253, 256–257

Luca Castellani/lucacastellani.it: pp. 254-255 (all), 258, 259 (top), 261

Tom Walsh: p. 262

Glorez/butchershop/iStock Getty: p. 263

Paul Weamer/ volunteerflyfishing@yellowstone.org: pp. 286–287, 291

Tim Romano: p. 288 (top and bottom left), 296 (top and bottom)

Chris Laburtis: p. 297

Arek Kubala: pp. 324–325, 333, 334–335

Jacek Kaczynski: p. 326 (bottom)

Rafal Bartels: p. 330

Art Merk: p. 331 (top and bottom)

Donald Bourgouin: pp. 343, 346

Bill Greiner: p. 344

Dylan Bishop: p. 347

David Bishop: p. 351

Jean-Guy Beliveau: pp. 340–341, 352–353

ChunyipWono/Scotland/istockgetty: pp. 360–361, back cover

Gordon Castle Estate/ gordoncastle.co.uk: p. 364, 369 (top)

Adam Wilcox: p. 364 (bottom)

Gary Ewin: p. 366 (bottom left)

Trout Confetti/ Derek DeYoung Studios/derekdeyoung.com: p. 382

First published in the
United States of America in 2026 by
Rizzoli International Publications, Inc.
49 West 27th Street
New York, NY 10001
www.rizzoliusa.com

Quote sources:
p. 43: *The Gaucho Martín Fierro*
p. 105: *The River of Doubt: Theodore Roosevelt's Darkest Journey*
p. 121: "The Switzerland of America"
p. 163: *The Compleat Angler*
p. 193: *A Fly-Fisher's Life: The Art and Mechanics of Fly Fishing*
p. 215: *Wild Steelhead & Atlantic Salmon*
p. 233: *Fishing Atlantic Salmon*
p. 253: *The Italians*
p. 325: *Poland*
p. 341: *Wild Steelhead and Salmon*

Publisher: Charles Miers
Associate Publisher: James Muschett
Editor: Tricia Levi
Design: Jan Derevjanik
Copyeditors: Sarah Stump and Sarah Scheffel
Managing Editor: Lynn Scrabis

ISBN: 978-0-8478-7656-3
Library of Congress Control Number: 2025946099

Printed in China
2026 2027 2028 2029 / 10 9 8 7 6 5 4 3 2 1

The authorized representative in the EU for product safety and compliance is
Mondadori Libri S.p.A., via Gian Battista Vico 42,
Milan, Italy, 20123,
www.mondadori.it

Visit us online:
Instagram: @RizzoliBooks
Facebook.com/RizzoliNewYork
Youtube.com/user/RizzoliNY

MIX
Paper | Supporting responsible forestry
FSC® C104723

PAGES 378–379: Dining under the stars, near the water, somewhere deep in South America. **PAGE 382:** *Trout Confetti*, Derek DeYoung. **THIS PAGE:** Tierra del Fuego, Argentina